D0823689

Challenge of the Heart

LIBRARY OF
MARSHALL BLAKE HAY

Challenge of the Heart

Love, Sex, and Intimacy in Changing Times

EDITED BY JOHN WELWOOD

SHAMBHALA
Boston
1985

SHAMBHALA PUBLICATIONS, INC.
314 Dartmouth Street
Boston, Massachusetts 02116

© 1985 by John Welwood
All rights reserved
9 8 7 6 5 4 3
Printed in the United States of America
Distributed in the United States by Random House
and in Canada by Random House of Canada Ltd.

BOMC offers recordings and compact discs, cassettes
and records. For information and catalog write to
BOMR, Camp Hill, PA 17012.

Library of Congress Cataloging in Publication Data
Main entry under title:
Challenge of the heart.
   Bibliography: p.
   Includes index.
   1. Courtship—United States—Addresses, essays,
lectures.   2. Interpersonal relations—Addresses,
essays, lectures.   3. Intimacy (Psychology)—Addresses,
essays, lectures.   4. Sex—Addresses, essays, lectures.
I. Welwood, John, 1943–   .
HQ801.C434   1985   306.7'34   85-2461
ISBN 0-87773-331-7 (pbk.)
ISBN 0-394-74200-1 (Random House : pbk.)

This book is dedicated to all those couples and individuals who have accepted the challenge of the heart, by taking the risks involved in feeling the great tenderness and passion of being alive, and by being willing to *learn* how to love, despite everything.

Contents

Introduction

The difficulty of finding and maintaining a healthy, enduring relationship with a partner of the opposite sex has become a major life problem for increasing numbers of people today. Not only have the old ties holding couples together been rapidly dissolving, but the very notions of interdependence between men and women, and even heterosexuality itself, have come under increasing scrutiny, if not downright attack. It is hard to even think clearly about the nature of the problem without falling prey to stereotypes, clichés, myths, and fantasies of all kinds. This book springs partly from my sadness about the forces of disintegration that have overwhelmed so many couples today, and partly from a desire to provide some resources that can help and encourage people to keep moving forward in their search for a genuine and enlivening relationship.

Undoubtedly the best single way of describing the relations between men and women today is in terms of the *challenge* they pose. In order to meet this challenge, we need to understand why long-term relationships have become so difficult. If we can see how these difficulties are not simply the result of personal inadequacies and deficiencies, but are part of a universal problem, we can move beyond guilt and blame. We can begin to approach the man/woman question as a larger challenge of the heart, which calls on us to expand our sense of who we are and what we are doing here as human beings.

Understanding the present situation requires seeing where we have come from. Before the Industrial Revolution, marriage always existed within a network of wider social supports. The nuclear family was surrounded by a larger extended family of aunts, uncles, grandparents, cousins, and so on, which in turn had its place within a local community. These communities were part of larger tribes or nations that shared similar values and customs. Nations had religions that helped people understand their relation to the greater cosmos. In this way, couples found themselves firmly embedded in a larger context of society and the cosmos. They were never the kind of independent, autonomous units that they have become today, cut off from family, community, widely accepted values and social mores, and from spiritual teachings that helped them find a place in relation to the universe as a whole.

In traditional societies, arranged marriages were the norm—parents chose their children's mates, based on considerations of family, status, bloodlines, wealth, and, in the East, astrological compatibility. Marriage was an alliance of families, not individuals. It served to preserve family lineages and property and to socialize children into their place in the social fabric. No traditional society ever considered individuals' spontaneous feelings of love to be a valid basis for enduring relationships between men and women.

Moreover, no earlier society has ever tried, much less succeeded at, joining together romantic love, sex, and marriage in a single institution. Greek culture, for instance, joined sex and marriage but reserved the lofty sentiments of love for the relations between men and boys. In the courtly love of the twelfth century, from which all our romantic ideas spring, love between men and women was quite formally divided from marriage. One of the more famous rulings of the Courts of Love, which established the conventions of romantic love, left no doubt about this:

We declare and hold as firmly established that love cannot exert its powers between two people who are married to each other. For lovers give each other everything freely, under no compulsion or necessity, but married people are in duty bound to give in to each other's desires.[1]

Not until the nineteenth-century Victorians did a society envision marriage based on romantic ideals. But the casualty was sex—a woman was considered degraded or pathological if she had sexual feeling, desire, or pleasure. The enjoyment of sex was relegated to houses of prostitution, record numbers of which flourished in Victorian England.

It is only a very recent belief that love, sex, and marriage should blend together smoothly. We moderns are the first people to try to join romantic love, the free expression of sexual passion, and a monogamous marital commitment in a single arrangement. This attempt flies in the face of traditional views, leading observers such as Margaret Mead to conclude:

The American marriage ideal is one of the most conspicuous examples of hitching our wagon to a star. It is one of the most difficult marriage forms that the human race has ever attempted.[2]

Couples today are facing a unique combination of factors working against long-term commitment. All the old social and economic rationales for marriage have broken down or are in the process of doing so. Tight-knit families and communities no longer live and work together, serving as a support system for a couple. Even many of the old motivations for having children—carrying on the family name or trade, contributing to the family work and thus providing an economic asset—are gone. "Staying together for the kids" is no longer a compelling reason to maintain a marriage.

Furthermore, the emphasis on individualism in our society has led many couples to put their individual growth needs above the needs of the marriage as a whole. And with future shock—where everything in our culture is changing at geometrically faster rates each year—it is more difficult for two individuals to maintain parallel rates of growth and change so that they can continue to meet each other's needs in the same ways.

Another factor making relationships difficult is the pervasive confusion about sex roles. The roles used to be clearly distinct, with men focusing on work and women tending to the quality of relationships. Today, however, women who devote themselves to careers often have less time and energy to put into relationship-tending or into providing the nurturing that men so often count on from them. Similarly, many men have begun to question the benefits of working and slaving their whole lives to "bring home the bacon." So every couple has to work out for themselves what it means to be a man and a woman, both individually and in relation to each other, and this can often take quite a toll. As one feminist writer put it, "The hallmark of relations between the sexes these days [is] a crushing ambivalence. It is an ambivalence about whether or not the trade-offs now required of both men and women in relationships are, after all, worth the price and pain they extract."[3] There is also widespread confusion about what it really means to be a man or a woman; it seems that the masculine and feminine poles are undergoing a major period of realignment.

Moreover, growing up in an isolated nuclear family, separate from a larger kinship network, often does not provide children enough space from their parents. This means that they all too readily absorb the parents' neuroses, particularly through the inevitable psychic-erotic bonds that exist between parents and children. In other cultures, the extended family served to dilute the influence of the parents. In the Middle Ages, for instance, there was a custom called "fosterage," in which the child was taken away from the parents at an early age to be reared by other relatives. Traditional societies also had initiation rites at puberty that helped the child separate from the parent of the opposite sex. Without any such formal separation rituals, we have the unfortunate situation so common today in which a mother who is not feeling satisfied by her husband turns to the son for personal fulfillment, or a father unconsciously tries to keep his daughter's affections focused on himself. This results in a son's being tied to his mother, often trying to save her from her pain ("momma's boys"), and daughters trying to please their fathers ("daddy's little girls"). These secret pacts between parents and children directly affect later relationships, typically in the form of inexplicable fear and avoidance of commitment and intimacy.

Nor do we have much access to useful education about how to love another person, how to communicate genuinely and directly, or how to deal with the real difficulties that arise in every relationship. The myth of romantic love, as portrayed by Hollywood and the hype of a consumer society that uses sexual passion to sell goods and keep the economic wheels spinning, further complicates the task of discovering what real relationships require of us. We imagine, as the Beatles sing, that "Love is all you need—it's easy." No practice or guidance is necessary—just fall in love with Mr. or Ms. Right, and happiness is sure to follow. Not until recently did a society believe that happiness was either the goal or even a possible outcome of marriage. The problem is not that people in former times used to have happy marriages and we in the modern world have lost the knack. What is more true is that the history of marriage reveals a tremendous amount of strife, confusion, and even brutality between men and women throughout the ages. It has rarely been a harmonious or growth-enhancing institution in the Western world. What *is* different today is the widespread expectation that it should provide personal happiness, peace, and contentment. Measuring love purely in terms of feeling good leaves us unequipped to handle its hard, painful, or demanding aspects. When they inevitably appear, people can only imagine that there is something wrong—with themselves, with their partner, or with the relationship. We have little guidance about how to use the real difficulties of loving another person as a challenge to open the heart and become bigger human beings.

Finally, with the declining influence of traditional religion in our society, the modern couple is not only socially stranded, but also spiritually rootless. Many people try to fill the tremendous spiritual hunger they feel today through their romantic involvements. All our needs to relate to the larger powers of life beyond our isolated egos get funneled into our relationships. Our need to experience awe and devotion in the face of all that is greater than us often leads us to idolize and idealize the beloved—a sure-fire prescription for later disillusionment when we discover his or her real humanness.

Yet, despite all these difficulties, most people still seem to want the rooted sense of belonging that a committed relationship can provide. How then to proceed? We can't exactly fall back on the old prescriptions. Yet we have also found that the raging individualism of the past two decades (from "do your own thing" to "looking out for number one") only works against real commitment and engagement with others. The historic challenge couples are now facing is how to find a synthesis between the need for belonging or commitment and the need to be true to themselves as individuals, honest in relationships, and respectful of their different growth needs. Precisely because relationships no longer work very well when based primarily on social convention or personal pleasure, they are challenging us to become more conscious of the larger dimensions of our being as the sustaining ground for an enduring love. In this way, relationships can become an impetus for growth in consciousness, awareness, and inner strength.

We in the present generations are pioneers in territory that has never been fully and consciously explored. Men and women have never had to face each other with such honesty and awareness. We have to learn to become "warriors of the heart," approaching the challenges of intimacy in this time of uncertainty with bravery, gentleness, and, above all, a willingness to open to love's teachings by risking, and perhaps failing, again and again.

For the past six years I have been writing a book on love and man/woman relationships, which to my continuing surprise is still ripening into the final form it wants to take. As background research for that book, I read exhaustively in the literature of love. Although most of what I read proved disappointing, in that it failed to speak to my deepest questions, I did find some writings that provided useful directions. As part of that larger work-in-progress on relationships, I decided to gather together the writings I found most provocative or helpful along the way.[4]

This book is not intended to present an objective or evenly balanced survey of relationships. For instance, there are many issues it does not address, such as homosexuality, sexual politics, or raising a family. It is not just a collection of readings, but represents instead a very personal exploration of certain basic questions that have been with me for many years. I have chosen only material that spoke to me personally, that helped sharpen my own inquiry, that stated some key issue, or that, for some other reason I wanted to share with others who are seeking to find their way in this area.

The selections have been carefully arranged to build themes and explore issues from different, often complementary viewpoints. Although many of the contributors might not agree with each other, my intention was that their very differences would serve to provoke further inquiry on the part of the reader. The introductions discuss the main themes of the book and provide the threads which tie the various articles together.

The first section explores the contradictions as well as the possibilities inherent in erotic love. This leads into questions about the different natures of men and women and about the larger masculine/feminine polarity in the universe. The next section explores marriage, not as some final goal that a couple arrives at, but as an ongoing path of personal transformation. The fourth section looks at sexuality as an especially vivid meeting of two different worlds. And the final section considers relationships as a vehicle for developing power, wisdom, and inner truth.

It is all too easy to assume that the man/woman relationship is something with a fixed shape, handed down from time immemorial. But all that has really been handed down is a long history of love and warfare between men and women, stretching back to the beginnings of time. The present difficulties are challenging us to wake up and look more carefully at this relationship, which has been so unconscious for so long. If one of the functions of pain is to call our attention to what needs healing, then perhaps the pain of relationships today is calling on us to heal at last the wounds of the oldest ongoing war of all—between the sexes. Maybe we are only just beginning to realize this need to heal the thousands of years of fear, distrust, antagonism, and power struggles that have gone on between man and woman.

I hope that this book will inspire readers to reflect more deeply on what their own personal history with relationships is calling on them to discover. It is an expression of my wonder and awe in the face of the great mystery of the sexes, as well as my faith in the basic integrity of the man/woman bond. It is not meant to provide definitive answers, but rather to inspire the reader to appreciate the energy and the journey contained in the questions closest to his or her heart.

NOTES

[1] In Andreas (1941).
[2] Mead (1950), p. 342.

[3]Amanda Spake, "Women Going Solo," in *Ms.*, reprinted in *Utne Reader*, December 1984.

[4]Most of the readings in this book are excerpted from longer works. Readers interested in the original titles and works from which these selections have been drawn should refer to the Acknowledgments section at the end of the book.

I. Erotic Love:
The Puzzle and the Promise

Introduction

What is the nature of the love between men and women? Is the enchantment of falling in love an illusion, or does erotic love actually allow us to see another person more clearly? In the past, societies always had clear guidelines governing love relations between the sexes. What is unusual today is the lack of any social consensus or guidelines about the nature and purpose of the man/woman relationship—individuals and couples are left to work this out for themselves.

We have inherited a wide range of different views of love—from Christian temperance to romantic passion—which are reflected by the divergent perspectives of the authors in this section. At one extreme are those who see man/woman love primarily in terms of friendship. These writers, represented here by Scott Peck and Robert Johnson, often follow the argument of Denis de Rougemont in his classic, *Love in the Western World*, that passionate love is an adolescent search for continual transports of rapture and excitement. They do not consider falling in love to be real love. As Peck flatly states, "Love is not a feeling." For him, love is what is left after the initial excitement passes and one *chooses* to love, to be unselfish, to give of oneself when one does not necessarily "feel" like it. (Krishnamurti epitomized this approach when he wrote, "Love is not to do with pleasure and desire.")[1] These writers emphasize maturity, responsibility, and going beyond desire as the key to love. In traditional terms, they are referring to *agape*, willing the good of the other regardless of the consequences to oneself, as distinct from *eros*, the desire to find some larger fulfillment through union with the beloved.

A different point of view, expressed here chiefly by D. H. Lawrence, José Ortega y Gasset, Francesco Alberoni, Vladimir Solovyov, and Alan

Watts, is that falling in love actually opens up new perceptions of reality and allows us to touch the deepest springs of life. Not everyone can fall in love—it takes a certain openness, sensitivity, capacity for discernment and surrender, and willingness to risk. In Lawrence's perspective, desire, in its true nature as eros, is a source of power, the very same life energy that animates the trees, the grasses, and the whole natural world. The pure, dynamic nature of erotic passion should be distinguished from egocentric desire to have the beloved please us by conforming to our wishes.

In considering differing viewpoints on what "real" love consists of, perhaps the wisest approach is to recognize that each experience of love, at whatever level, depth, and intensity the individual discovers it, has its own validity. Surely there are as many experiences of love as there are different human types and temperaments, different levels of awareness and emotional sensitivity, different intensities and chemistries between particular couples. Each writer in this section expresses an important facet of the larger truth of love, although each of their perspectives is necessarily incomplete and one-sided. Yet if these divergences remind us of the blind men and the elephant, at least putting these different perspectives side by side helps us see why the truth of love cannot be captured within any single point of view. If love always seems to elude any final, authoritative definition, perhaps it is because its expanse is infinite. Insofar as we are lived by love, which encompasses us because it is so much larger than we are, we can never step completely outside of love and take an objective perspective on it. Love is not blind—we are the blind men, always discovering new facets, surfaces, and depths in this experience. Just when we think we finally have it figured out, a new surprise inevitably lies in wait just around the next bend.

If we can avoid trying to figure out which of the different perspectives presented here is right or wrong, we might see each of them as representing a particular local color on a *spectrum* of different experiences. Love visits us in many forms and colors. And though it may be true that the most refined form of love is agape—conscious love—who can say that the passion inspired by a graceful body and a delightful presence is to be appreciated any the less? Plato wisely understood that the most highly evolved forms of love grow from simpler forms. And if we think of the spectrum of love as a rainbow of different colors rather than a strictly hierarchical ladder, then we can appreciate how the deep crimsons of passion, the golden hues of friendliness and affection, and the sky blue of selfless love all have an equally essential place in human experience.

The Spanish philosopher Ortega y Gasset opens this section with an essay, written in 1940, in praise of romantic love. Genuine erotic love is marked by surrender, born out of enchantment with what is most lovable in another. Yet this enchantment is not possible without a well-developed capacity for curiosity and discernment, and a willingness to "migrate" outside our familiar self-boundaries to experience another person as wholly different. He distinguishes eros in its best sense—as discernment—from passionate obsession. Such love is not a blind instinct. It is a creative act only possible for individuals who are aware enough to truly "see" the other.

Scott Peck presents a different view of romantic love. For him, love is an act of choice, will, and effort that involves extending oneself for the sake of another, whether or not one *feels* loving at that moment. Peck's thought-provoking argument exposes the dangers of self-deception in romantic love. However, in reacting against the excesses of romantic nonsense in our culture, he tends to go to the other extreme, implying that any experience of love as effortless is not real. He regards falling in love as an illusion, nature's trick to get us married so that we can get on with propagating the species. Regarding love as a spectrum can help us appreciate the validity of Peck's viewpoint without necessarily accepting the either/or dichotomy he sets up.

Robert Johnson shares a similar perspective, praising the virtue of what he calls "stirring the oatmeal" love. He stresses how important it is for an ongoing relationship to be grounded in ordinary, earthy realities, rather than in romantic feelings, which he characterizes as "always directed at our own projections [and] fantasies." If two people in love treat each other less well than they treat their friends, he asks, how can this be called love? Certainly Johnson has a good point: it would be ideal if lovers treated each other as best friends. Yet if this does not always happen, is the validity of their love diminished? Perhaps men and women are working out more difficult issues than friends normally do, and thereby provoke and challenge each other in ways that are not always friendly.

Alan Watts would not agree that falling in love is simply projecting one's dreams of a fantasy savior/goddess onto another person. Instead, he sees falling in love as a moment of crazy wisdom that can provide an opportunity for a rare and precious glimpse of another person's real divinity. The only problem with falling in love, in Watts's view, is in expecting it to last, or in foreclosing such experiences with other people just because one is married.

Without condemning romantic love, Stanton Peele discusses the danger of its turning into an obsession. Where such addiction is full-blown, the fault does not belong to eros, but rather to the fragile, insecure sense of self that drives a person to take refuge in another person in the same way he or she might turn to drugs, alcohol, or even religion. Although erotic feelings are often expressed through the rhetoric of addiction ("I can't live without you," etc.), Peele's article helps us understand that erotic love does not have to be addictive. In the addictive relationship, the lovers build a private cocoon together and uncritically adapt to each other's fears and insecurities in order to create a new identity to replace their own sense of incompleteness.

Francesco Alberoni sees falling in love as a revolutionary act that breaks up habitual patterns of perception and changes one's whole relation to life. Like any revolution, this shift in perspective opens up a more expansive vision of what is possible. Unlike Peck, he does not consider the impermanence of falling in love as evidence that it is an illusion. If the flower is more short-lived than the fruit, does that make it any less real or valuable? Alberoni sees love in its deepest dimension as a refining fire. From his perspective, one must be careful lest "stirring the oatmeal" turn into a life of banal and habitual routine.

The nineteenth-century Russian theologian Vladimir Solovyov further examines the revolutionary impact of erotic love. For many people it is their most powerful experience of giving up the egocentric habit of assigning absolute value only to oneself, while denying it to others. Erotic love contains within it a special potential for liberating us from egoism because, unlike certain tamer forms of love, it "penetrates and possesses the whole of our being." The failures and illusions of erotic love over the centuries do not discourage Solovyov, for he sees the growth of love in humans as a long-term process. Like any revolutionary development, love must go through many centuries of trial and error before it is fully realized.

D. H. Lawrence's chapter celebrates desire as central to the love between man and woman. Lawrence starts with the interesting point that the opposite of eros is not hate, but individualism. In every relationship the desire to experience a larger connectedness beyond the confines of self is in dynamic tension with the opposite need to maintain one's individuality intact. Far from viewing the conflicting individual natures of man and woman as a problem, Lawrence rejoices in the inscrutability that characterizes the relationship between man and woman, for the very gap between the sexes energizes eros to leap across this gap. This chapter, with its humorous and provocative images, provides a cutting critique of current "new age" notions that couples should strive above all for harmony, balance, and freedom from strife. Lawrence sees conjugal strife as an inevitable result of a couple's desire to draw closer to each other.

The next chapter, by the Tibetan teacher Chögyam Trungpa, suggests a way of reconciling the divergent attitudes toward passionate love expressed so far in this section. He describes, on the one hand, a "free passion and warmth that flows effortlessly," allowing us to see "the whole way through" people's facades to the "pure gold" within. What is most genuine in falling in love is this generous, nonpossessive quality of passion. But when we then try to control or manipulate that passion or the person we feel passion toward, we become demonic. Like Midas, we can no longer appreciate the gold we see because we are trying so hard to possess it. From this possessiveness spring all the negative aspects of erotic love that Peck, Johnson, and Peele point out.

In the final chapter of this section, I explore certain problems that stem from confusing unconditional love—saying yes from the heart to another's basic being—and conditional love—saying yes to how another person pleases us and meets our needs. In its deepest essence, love is an experience of opening without conditions and surrendering to the larger sense of being we feel in the presence of the beloved. It can be confusing to say yes in such a big way to someone, while also having to say no to many of their actions, personality patterns, or ways of relating to us. This chapter discusses some of the differences between conditional and unconditional love, as well as ways of staying in touch with unconditional love beyond the first inspiration of falling in love.

Finally, I should mention that it was not an accident or an oversight that no women writers appear in this section. In searching through the literature, I found that women do not seem as interested as men in trying to define love in general, whereas they have quite a lot to say about more specific aspects of the experience, as we shall see in subsequent sections of the book.

NOTES

[1]Krishnamurti (1969).

Enchantment and Discernment

José Ortega y Gasset

Romantic Love—which is, in my view, the prototype and summit of all eroticism—is characterized by a feeling of being "enchanted" by another being, a feeling of being absorbed by him to the core of our being. Another way of saying this is that a person in love feels himself totally surrendered to the one he loves. The combination of these two elements, enchantment and surrender, is no accident. One is born out of and takes nourishment from the other. What exists in love is surrender due to enchantment.

A mother surrenders to her child, a friend to his friend, but not because of enchantment. The mother does so out of a deep-rooted instinct. The friend surrenders by a clear decision of his will. What is true of love, however, is that our soul escapes from our hand and is sucked in by the other. This suction which another person exercises upon our life uproots it and transplants it to the beloved, where the original roots seem to take root again, as in new soil. This absorption of the lover by the beloved is simply the effect of enchantment. Another being enchants us, and we feel this enchantment in the form of a continual, gently elastic pull from within.

Since love is the most delicate and total act of a soul, it will reflect the state and nature of the soul. If the individual is not sensitive, how can his love be sentient? If he is not profound, how can his love be deep? As one is, so is his love. For this reason, *we can find in love the most decisive indication of what a person is*. All other acts and appearances can deceive us with regard to his true nature, but his love affairs reveal to us the carefully concealed secret of his being. This is especially true in the choice of the beloved. In no other action do we reveal our innermost character as we do in erotic choice.

Frequently we hear that intelligent women fall in love with stupid men, and vice versa, foolish women with clever men. Although I have heard this many times, I have never believed it, and in every case in which I was able to draw closer and apply the psychological magnifying lens, I found either that those men and women were not actually intelligent or that their chosen ones were not stupid.

This interpretation of the amorous phenomenon is in direct opposition to the false mythology which makes of passion a primitive force engendered in the obscure bosom of human animality which brutally overpowers the person. I would say that love, rather than being an elemental force, almost resembles a literary genre. Certainly, if this claimed to be the final word, it would be excessive and unacceptable. All I wish to suggest, however, is that love is not an instinct, but rather a creation, and no primitive creation at that.

If one wishes to see clearly into the phenomenon of love, it is necessary, above all, to free oneself from the common idea which sees it as a universal sentiment. Love is an infrequent occurrence, a sentiment which only certain souls can hope to experience. Truly, falling in love is a marvelous talent which some creatures possess, like the gift of writing poetry, the spirit of sacrifice, melodic inspiration, or personal bravery. Not everyone falls in love, nor do those capable of falling in love fall in love with just anyone. The divine event occurs only when certain rigorous conditions are present. Very few can be lovers, and very few beloved.

All one has to do is to enumerate some of the conditions and assumptions of being in love to make its extreme infrequency obvious. We could say that these conditions form three classes, since there are three components of love: *perception*, in order to see the person who is going to be loved; *feeling*, with which we respond sentimentally to the vision of what is beloved; and the *constitution* of our being, the nature of the soul in its totality. Although perception and feeling may function properly, it is impossible for love to uproot, invade, or mold our character if the consitution of our soul is insubstantial and inflexible, dispersed or without vigorous resources.

In order to be enchanted we must be, above all, capable of *seeing* another person—simply opening our eyes will not do. We need a peculiar kind of initial curiosity which is much more integral, deep-rooted, and broad than mere curiosity about things (like scientific, technical, or tourist curiosity). We must be vitally curious about humanity, and more concretely, about the individual as a living totality. Without this curiosity, the most eminent creatures can pass before us and make no impression upon us.

Such curiosity, in truth, presupposes many other things. It is a vital richness which only organisms with a high level of vitality can possess. The weak individual is incapable of disinterested attention to what occurs outside of himself. He fears the unexpected, and he does not relate to others with total interest. The ability to interest oneself in a thing for what it is in itself and not for the profit which it will render us is the magnificent gift of generosity which flourishes only at the peaks of the greatest altitudes of vitality.

Most men and women live submerged in the sphere of their own interests and are incapable of feeling the migratory urge toward what is outside themselves. They live satisfied with the line of their horizon and do not miss other, vague possibilities which they might realize only at a cost. This limited range [of vision] is incompatible with deep-seated curiosity, which is, finally, an untiring instinct for migration, a wild urge to depart from onself to the other.

This curiosity, which is simultaneously an eagerness for life, can only be found in porous souls where free air—cosmic air charged with star-dust—circulates, unconfined by any limiting wall. But curiosity is not enough to make us "see" the delicate, complex structure of a person. Curiosity predisposes the eye, but the vision must be discerning. Such discernment is the prime talent and extraordinary endowment which acts as a component in love. It serves as a special intuition which permits us to gain an intimate, immediate knowledge of others, the nature of their souls in conjunction with the meaning expressed by their bodies. Thanks to this we can "discriminate" between people, appreciate their quality, their triviality or their excellence; in short, their degree of vital perfection.

Those who imagine love to be a half-magical, half-mechanical effect will oppose the claim that discernment is one of its essential attributes. According to them, love always blossoms "without reason." It is illogical, irrational and, in fact, excludes all discernment. This is one of the central points where I differ resolutely from commonly-accepted ideas.

Love does not spring up out of nowhere, but has its source in the qualities of the beloved. The presence of these engenders and nourishes love. To put it another way, no one loves without reason. Love loves because it sees that the object is lovable. In true love a moment of discernment is essential, revealing the character of the individual in which [romantic] sentiment has found "reason" to sprout and blossom.

This discernment may be great or small; it may be commonplace or inspired. And, like vision and intelligence, it is of course susceptible to error. Precisely because love makes mistakes at times—although much less frequently than is believed—we have to restore to it the attribute of vision, for as Pascal wished: "Poets have no right to picture love as blind; its blindfold must be removed so that it can have the use of its eyes."

Love Is Not a Feeling

M. Scott Peck

One result of the mysterious nature of love is that no one has ever, to my knowledge, arrived at a truly satisfactory definition of love. In an effort to explain it, therefore, love has been divided into various categories: eros, philia, agape; perfect love and imperfect love, and so on. I am presuming, however, to give a single definition of love, again with the awareness that it is likely to be in some way or ways inadequate. I define love thus: The will to extend one's self for the purpose of nurturing one's own or another's spiritual growth.

The act of extending one's limits implies effort. One extends one's limits only by exceeding them, and exceeding limits requires effort. When we love someone our love becomes demonstrable or real only through our exertion—through the fact that for that someone (or for ourself) we take an extra step or walk an extra mile. Love is not effortless. To the contrary, love is effortful.

By use of the word "will" I have attempted to transcend the distinction between desire and action. Desire is not necessarily translated into action. Will is desire of sufficient intensity that it *is* translated into action. The difference between the two is equal to the difference between saying "I would like to go swimming tonight" and "I will go swimming tonight." Everyone in our culture desires to some extent to be loving, yet many are not in fact loving. I therefore conclude that the desire to love is not itself love. Love is as love does. Love is an act of will—namely, both an intention and an action. Will also implies choice. We do not have to love.

We choose to love. No matter how much we may think we are loving, if we are in fact not loving, it is because we have chosen not to love and therefore do not love despite our good intentions. On the other hand, whenever we do actually exert ourselves in the cause of spiritual growth, it is because we have chosen to do so.

Of all the misconceptions about love the most powerful and pervasive is the belief that "falling in love" is love or at least one of the manifestations of love. It is a potent misconception, because falling in love is subjectively experienced in a very powerful fashion as an experience of love. When a person falls in love what he or she certainly feels is "I love him" or "I love her." But two problems are immediately apparent. The first is that the experience of falling in love is specifically a sex-linked erotic experience. We do not fall in love with our children even though we may love them very deeply. We do not fall in love with our friends of the same sex—unless we are homosexually oriented—even though we may care for them greatly. We fall in love only when we are consciously or unconsciously sexually motivated. The second problem is that the experience of falling in love is invariably temporary. No matter whom we fall in love with, we sooner or later fall out of love if the relationship continues long enough. This is not to say that we invariably cease loving the person with whom we fell in love. But it is to say that the feeling of ecstatic lovingness that characterizes the experience of falling in love always passes. The honeymoon always ends. The bloom of romance always fades.

The essence of the phenomenon of falling in love is a sudden collapse of a section of an individual's ego boundaries, permitting one to merge his or her identity with that of another person. The sudden release of oneself from oneself, the explosive pouring out of oneself into the beloved, and the dramatic surcease of loneliness accompanying this collapse of ego boundaries are experienced by most of us as ecstatic. We and our beloved are one! Loneliness is no more!

In some respects (but certainly not in all) the act of falling in love is an act of regression. The experience of merging with the loved one has in it echoes from that time when we were merged with our mothers in infancy. Along with the merging we also reexperience the sense of omnipotence which we had to give up in our journey out of childhood. All things seem possible! United with our beloved we feel we can conquer all obstacles. We believe that the strength of our love will cause the forces of opposition to bow down in submission and melt away into the darkness. All problems will be overcome. The unreality of these feelings when we have fallen in love is essentially the same as the unreality of the two-year-old who feels itself to be king of the family and the world with power unlimited.

Just as reality intrudes upon the two-year-old's fantasy of omnipotence so does reality intrude upon the fantastic unity of the couple who have fallen in love. Sooner or later, in response to the problems of daily living, individual will reasserts itself. He wants to have sex; she doesn't. She wants to go to the movies; he doesn't. He wants to put money in the bank; she wants a dishwasher. She wants to talk about her job; he wants to talk about his. She doesn't like his friends; he doesn't like hers. So both of them, in the privacy of their hearts, begin to come to the sickening realization that they are not one with the beloved, that the beloved has and will continue to have his or her own desires, tastes, prejudices, and timing different from the other's. One by one, gradually or suddenly, the ego boundaries snap back into place; gradually or suddenly, they fall out of love. Once again they are two separate individuals. At this point they begin either to dissolve the ties of their relationship or to initiate the work of real loving.

By my use of the word "real" I am implying that the perception that we are loving when we fall in love is a false perception—that our subjective sense of lovingness is an illusion. By stating that it is when a couple falls out of love they may begin to really love I am also implying that real love does not have its roots in a feeling of love. To the contrary, real love often occurs in a context in which the feeling of love is lacking, when we act lovingly despite the fact that we don't feel loving. Assuming the reality of the definition of love with which we started, the experience of "falling in love" is not real love for the several reasons that follow.

Falling in love is not an act of will. It is not a conscious choice. No matter how open to or eager for it we may be, the experience may still elude us. Contrarily, the experience may capture us at times when we are definitely not seeking it, when it is inconvenient and undesirable. We are as likely to fall in love with someone with whom we are obviously ill-matched as with someone more suitable. Indeed, we may not even like or admire the object of our passion, yet try as we might, we may not be able to fall in love with a person whom we deeply respect and with whom a deep relationship would be in all ways desirable. We can choose how to respond to the experience of falling in love, but we cannot choose the experience itself.

Falling in love is not an extension of one's limits or boundaries; it is a partial and temporary collapse of them. The extension of one's limits requires effort; falling in love is effortless. Lazy and undisciplined individuals are as likely to fall in love as energetic and dedicated ones. Once the precious moment of falling in love has passed and the boundaries have snapped back into place, the individual may be disillusioned, but is usually none the larger for the experience. When limits are extended or stretched, however, they tend to stay stretched. Real love is a permanently self-enlarging experience. Falling in love is not.

Falling in love has little to do with purposively nurturing one's spiritual development. If we have any purpose in mind when we fall in love it is to terminate our own loneliness and perhaps insure this result through marriage. Certainly we are not thinking of spiritual development. Indeed, after we have fallen in love and before we have fallen out of love again we feel that we have arrived, that the heights have been attained, that there is both no need and no possibility of going higher. We do not feel ourselves to be in any need of development; we are totally content to be where we are. Nor do we perceive our beloved as being in need of spiritual development. To the contrary, we perceive him or her as perfect, as having been perfected. If we see any faults in our beloved, we perceive them as insignificant—little quirks or darling eccentricities that only add color and charm.

If falling in love is not love, then what is it other than a temporary and partial collapse of ego boundaries? I do not know. But the sexual specificity of the phenomenon leads me to suspect that it is a genetically determined instinctual component of mating behavior. In other words, the temporary collapse of ego boundaries that constitutes falling in love is a stereotypic response of human beings to a configuration of internal sexual drives and external sexual stimuli, which serves to increase the probability of sexual pairing and bonding so as to enhance the survival of the species. Or to put it in another, rather crass way, falling in love is a trick that our genes pull on our otherwise perceptive mind to hoodwink or trap us into marriage. Without this trick, this illusory and inevitably temporary (it would not be practical if it were not temporary) regression to infantile merging and omnipotence, many of us who are happily or unhappily married today would have retreated in wholehearted terror from the realism of the marriage vows.

Love is an action, an activity. Love is not a feeling. Many, many people possessing a feeling of love and even acting in response to that feeling act in all manner of unloving and destructive ways. On the other hand, a genuinely loving individual will often take loving and constructive action toward a person he or she consciously dislikes, actually feeling no love toward the person at the time and perhaps even finding the person repugnant in some way.

The feeling of love is the emotion that accompanies the experience of cathecting. Cathecting is the process by which an object becomes important to us. Once cathected, the object, commonly referred to as a "love object," is invested with energy as if it were a part of ourselves, and this relationship between us and the invested object is called a cathexis. The misconception that love is a feeling exists because we confuse cathecting with loving. This confusion is understandable since they are similar processes, but there are also striking differences. First of all, we may cathect any object, animate or inanimate, with or without a spirit. Thus a person may cathect the stock market or a piece of jewelry and may feel love for these things. Second, the fact that we have cathected another human being does not mean that we care a whit for that person's spiritual development. The dependent person, in fact, usually fears the spiritual development of a cathected spouse. The mother who insisted upon driving her adolescent son to and from school clearly cathected the boy; he was important to her—but his spiritual growth was not. Third, the intensity of our cathexes frequently has nothing to do with wisdom or commitment. Two strangers may meet in a bar and cathect each other in such a way that nothing—not previously scheduled appointments, promises made, or family stability—is more important for the moment than their sexual consummation. Finally, our cathexes may be fleeting and momentary. Immediately following their sexual consummation the just-mentioned couple may find each other unattractive and undesirable.

Genuine love, on the other hand, implies commitment and the exercise of wisdom. When we are concerned for someone's spiritual growth, we know that a lack of commitment is likely to be harmful and that commitment to that person is probably necessary for us to manifest our concern effectively. In a constructive marriage, just as in constructive therapy, the partners must regularly, routinely and predictably, attend to each other and their relationship no matter how they feel. As has been mentioned, couples sooner or later always fall out of love, and it is at the moment when the mating instinct has run its course that the opportunity for genuine love begins. It is when the spouses no longer feel like being in each other's company always, when they would rather be elsewhere some of the time, that their love begins to be tested and will be found to be present or absent.

This is not to say that the partners in a stable, constructive relationship such as intensive psychotherapy or marriage do not cathect each other and the relationship itself in various ways; they do. What it does say is that genuine love transcends the matter of cathexes. When love exists it does so with or without cathexis and with or without a loving feeling. It is easier—indeed, it is fun—to love with cathexis and the feeling of love. But it is possible to love without cathexis and without loving feelings, and it is in the fulfillment of this possibility that genuine and transcendent love is distinguished from simple cathexis. The key word in this distinction is "will." I have defined love as the *will* to extend oneself for the purpose of nurturing one's own or another's spiritual growth. Genuine love is volitional rather than emotional. The person who truly loves does so because of a decision to love. This person has made a commitment to be loving whether or not the loving feeling is present. True love is not a feeling by which we are overwhelmed. It is a committed, thoughtful decision.

The common tendency to confuse love with the feeling of love allows people all manner of self-deception. An alcoholic man, whose wife and children are desperately in need of his attention at that very moment, may be sitting in a bar with tears in his eyes, telling the bartender, "I really love my family." People who neglect their children in the grossest of ways more often than not will consider themselves the most loving of parents. It is clear that there may be a self-serving quality in this tendency to confuse love with the feeling of love; it is easy and not at all unpleasant to find evidence of love in one's feelings. It may be difficult and painful to search for evidence of love in one's actions. But because true love is an act of will that often transcends ephemeral feelings of love or cathexis, it is correct to say, "Love is as love does."

Stirring the Oatmeal

Robert Johnson

Many years ago a wise friend gave me a name for human love. She called it "stirring-the-oatmeal" love. She was right: Within this phrase, if we will humble ourselves enough to look, is the very essence of what human love is, and it shows us the principal differences between human love and romance.

Stirring the oatmeal is a humble act—not exciting or thrilling. But it symbolizes a relatedness that brings love down to earth. It represents a willingness to share ordinary human life, to find meaning in the simple, unromantic tasks: earning a living, living within a budget, putting out the garbage, feeding the baby in the middle of the night. To "stir the oatmeal" means to find the relatedness, the value, even the beauty, in simple and ordinary things, not to eternally demand a cosmic drama, an entertainment, or an extraordinary intensity in everything. Like the rice hulling of the Zen monks, the spinning wheel of Gandhi, the tent making of Saint Paul, it represents the discovery of the sacred in the midst of the humble and ordinary.

Jung once said that feeling is a matter of the *small*. And in human love, we can see that it is true. The real relatedness between two people is experienced in the small tasks they do together: the quiet conversation when the day's upheavals are at rest, the soft word of understanding, the daily companionship, the encouragement offered in a difficult moment, the small gift when least expected, the spontaneous gesture of love.

When a couple are genuinely related to each other, they are willing to enter into the whole spectrum of human life together. They transform even the unexciting, difficult, and mundane things into a joyful and fulfilling component of life. By contrast, romantic love can only last so long as a couple are "high" on one another, so long as the money lasts and the entertainments are exciting. "Stirring the oatmeal" means that two people take their love off the airy level of exciting fantasy and convert it into earthy, practical immediacy.

Love is content to do many things that ego is bored with. Love is willing to work with the other person's moods and unreasonableness. Love is willing to fix breakfast and balance the checkbook. Love is willing to do these "oatmeal" things of life because it is related to a person, not a projection.

Human love sees another person as an individual and makes an individualized relationship to him or her. Romantic love sees the other person only as a role player in the drama.

A man's human love desires that a woman become a complete and independent person and encourages her to be herself. Romantic love only affirms what he would like her to be, so that she could be identical to anima. So long as romance rules a man, he affirms a woman only insofar as she is willing to change, so that she may reflect his projected ideal. Romance is never happy with the other person just as he or she is.

Human love necessarily includes friendship: friendship within relationship, within marriage, between husband and wife. When a man and a woman are truly friends, they know each other's difficult points and weaknesses, but they are not inclined to stand in judgment on them. They are more concerned with helping each other and enjoying each other than they are with finding fault.

Friends, genuine friends, want to affirm rather than to judge; they don't coddle, but neither do they dwell on our inadequacies. Friends back each other up in the tough times, help each other with the sordid and ordinary tasks of life. They don't impose impossible standards on each other, they don't ask for perfection, and they help each other rather than grind each other down with demands.

In romantic love there is no friendship. Romance and friendship are utterly opposed energies, natural enemies with completely opposing motives. Sometimes people say: "I don't want to be friends with my husband [or wife]; it would take all the romance out of our marriage." It is true: Friendship does take the artificial drama and intensity out of a relationship, but it also takes away the egocentricity and the impossibility and replaces the drama with something human and real.

If a man and woman are friends to each other, then they are "neighbors" as well as lovers; their relationship is suddenly subject to Christ's dictum: "Love thy neighbor as thyself." One of the glaring contradictions in romantic love is that so many couples treat their friends with so much more kindness, consideration, generosity, and forgiveness than they ever give to one another! When people are with their friends, they are charming, helpful, and courteous. But when they come home, they often vent all their anger, resentments, moods, and frustrations on each other. Strangely, they treat their friends better than they do each other.

When two people are "in love," people commonly say that they are "more than just friends." But in the long run, they seem to treat each other as *less* than friends. Most people think that being "in love" is a much more intimate, much more "meaningful" relationship than "mere" friendship. Why, then, do couples refuse each other the selfless love, the kindness and good will, that they readily give to their friends? People can't ask of their friends that they carry all their projections, be scapegoats for all their moods, keep them feeling happy, and make life complete for them. Why do couples impose these demands on each other? Because the cult of romance teaches us that we have the right to expect that all our projections will be borne—all our desires satisfied, and all our fantasies made to come true—in the person we are "in love" with. In one of the Hindu rites of marriage, the bride and groom make to each other a solemn statement: "You will be my *best friend*." Western couples need to learn to be friends, to live with each other in a spirit of friendship, to take the quality of friendship as a guide through the tangles we have made of love.

Divine Madness

Alan Watts

I would like to indulge in the discussion of a particularly virulent and dangerous form of divine madness called "falling in love;" which is, from a practical point of view, one of the most insane things you can do, or that can happen to you. In the eyes of a given woman or a given man, an opposite, who though to the eyes of everyone else is a perfectly plain and ordinary person, can appear to be a god or goddess incarnate; to be such an enchantment that one can say, in the words of an old song that probably dates me, "Every little breeze seems to whisper Louise." This can be seen as a strangely disruptive and subversive experience in the conduct of human affairs because you never know when it will strike, or for what reason. Once you get into it, it is something like contracting a chronic disease, and we sometimes try to resolve it by making it the basis for marriage, which is an extraordinarily dangerous thing to do.

When we go back to its origins in the Hebrew and Christian traditions, we find that the idea of marriage and the experience of falling in love are really rather separate things. In early agrarian cultures, no one ever chose their marriage partner. By and large marriage was an alliance of families. It was contracted not simply for the purpose of raising children, but also to create a social unit smaller than a village. The elders had an enormous voice in who their children were going to marry; and they would dicker amongst themselves and use go-betweens in considering not only whether this girl was suitable for their son, or vice versa, but also what kind of dowry she would bring, and whether it would be advantageous to the families to form such an alliance. Of course, until quite recent times, these things were always important in the marital affairs of royal families. Almost all royal families kept concubines and had outside arrangements when and if the king or queen should happen to fall in love, and this simply prevented monogamy from becoming monotony. To this day, marriage is a civil or religious ceremony, the basis of which is a legal contract where one signs on the dotted line.

Into the feudal conception of marriage there came what was called "The Cult of Courtly Love," which was largely a result of the poetic movement centered in Southern France during the Middle Ages—although its exact origin is something which scholars dispute. According to one theory,[1] the knight or courtly lover, who was also a poet, would select a lady to be his heart's desire—preferably a married lady—and he would yearn for her, sing songs under her window, and send her messages with little tokens of his devotion. But, according to this theory, he could never go to bed with her. Not only would that have been adultery, but it would have spoiled the state of being in love. The state of being in love was always to be an unfulfilled and unhappy state.

So then, as a result of the gradual fusion of these two approaches to the relationship of the sexes—the family alliance and the perpetual romance—we arrive at the idea of the romantic marriage in which the two trends are mis-allied, to say the very least. Herein, you are supposed to fall in love with someone of your own choice (and naturally it has to be that way if you are going to fall in love), and then you must enter into that relationship with a legal contract in which you stand before a magistrate or a priest and solemnly swear that you will be faithful to each other until death do you part—which sometimes leads to murder.

I would like to reflect a bit more on this particular form of madness, and to raise again a very disturbing question: Is it only when you are in love with another person that you see them as they really are? In the ordinary way, when you are not in love with a person, could it be that you see only a fragmented version of that being? When you are in love with someone, you do indeed see them as a divine being. Now, suppose that is what they truly are and that your eyes have by your beloved been opened, in which case your beloved is serving to you as a kind of guru. This is the reason why there is a form of sexual yoga which is based upon the idea that man and woman are to each other as a mutual guru and student. Through a tremendous outpouring of psychic energy in total devotion and worship for this other person, who is respectively god or goddess, you realize, by total fusion and contact, the divine center in them. At once it bounces back to you and you discover your own.

I do not regard falling in love as just a sexual infatuation because it is always more than that. When you fall in love it is a much more serious involvement. Falling in love is a thing that strikes like lightning and is, therefore, extremely analogous to the mystical vision. We do not really know how people obtain the mystical vision, and there is not as yet a very clear rationale as to why it happens. However, we do know that it happens to many people who never did anything to look for it. On the other hand, many people who have practiced yoga or zen disciplines for years and years have never seen it. The best approach seems to be to give up the whole idea of getting it because it is quite unpredictable, and like falling in love, it is capricious, and therefore crazy. If you should be so fortunate as to encounter either of these experiences, it seems to me to be a total denial of life to refuse it.

Interestingly, we say "falling" in love, and not "rising" into love. Love is an act of surrender to another person; it is total abandonment. In love you give yourself over, you let go, and you say, "I give myself to you." To many people this seems quite mad because it means letting things get out of control, and all sensible people keep things in control. Actually, the course of wisdom, what is really sensible, is to let go, to commit oneself, to give oneself up; and this is considered quite mad. It is thus that we are driven to the strange conclusion that in madness lies sanity.

NOTES

[1]De Rougemont (1956).

"Love" as an Addiction

Stanton Peele

There is an understandable resistance to the idea that a human relationship can be equivalent psychologically to a drug addiction. Yet it is not
unreasonable to look for addiction between lovers when psychologists
find the roots of drug addiction in childhood dependency needs and
stunted family relationships. Chein, Winick, and other observers interpret
drugs to be a kind of substitute for human ties. In this sense, addictive
love is even more directly linked to what are recognized to be the sources
of addiction than is drug dependency.

　　Almost everyone knows of people who replace romantic relationships
with other kinds of escapes, including drug escapes, at least until the next
relationship comes along. Immediately after or immediately before an
affair, such individuals are deeply immersed in psychiatry, religion, alcohol, marijuana, and the like. Just as some addicts shift between opiate,
alcohol, and barbituate addictions, so we find others using drugs inter-
changeably with all-consuming systems of belief or social involvements.
Consider this testimony by a member of a fanatical religious commune: "I
used to do acid, chug wine. I thought it was the answer. But it didn't
satisfy, just like everything else. I went to a head shrink . . . Nothing ever
did satisfy till I came to Jesus." He might have added, "I used to make it
with chicks," for other converts are spurned lovers who in an earlier era
would have entered a convent or monastery.

　　I know of a man who started drinking heavily after a long-time
woman friend left him. He couldn't sleep, and his heartbeat sometimes

sped up frighteningly when he wasn't doing anything. These are symptoms of acute withdrawal. We know they can occur—perhaps quite often
in certain groups and at certain ages—when one is deprived of a lover.
Popular music sings paeans to the experience as a hallmark of true love:
"When I lost my baby, I almost lost my mind . . . Since you left me baby,
my whole life is through." What is there about love that produces withdrawal in people we have all known, maybe even in ourselves? Can we
envision a kind of love that does *not* bring such devastation in its wake?
Let us look closely at how "love" can be an addiction, and how addictive
love differs from genuine love.

In a monograph entitled "Being in Love and Hypnosis," Freud noted
important parallels between love and another psychologically compelling
process—hypnotism. According to Freud, a person's self-love can be
transferred from the person's own ego to a loved object. When this occurs, the other person more and more gains "possession of the entire self-
love of the ego, whose self-sacrifice thus follows as a natural consequence.
The object has, so to speak, consumed the ego." The ultimate development of this sort of love is a state where the lover's ego "is impoverished,
it has surrendered itself to the object." Freud goes on to say:

*From being in love to hypnosis is evidently only a short step. There is the same
humble subjection, the same compliance, the same absence of criticism, toward
the hypnotist as toward the loved object. There is the same sapping of the
subject's own initiative . . . The hypnotist [as a model of a loved other] is the
sole object, and no attention is paid to any but him.*[1]

Love is an ideal vehicle for addiction because it can so exclusively
claim a person's consciousness. If, to serve as an addiction, something
must be both reassuring and consuming, then a sexual or love relationship
is perfectly suited for the task. When a person goes to another with the
aim of filling a void in himself, the relationship quickly becomes the
center of his or her life. It offers him a solace that contrasts sharply with
what he finds everywhere else, so he returns to it more and more, until he
needs it to get through each day of his otherwise stressful and unpleasant
existence. When a constant exposure to something is necessary in order
to make life bearable, an addiction has been brought about, however
romantic the trappings.

WHO IS THE INTERPERSONAL ADDICT?

Since the person who addicts himself to a lover has essentially the same
feelings of inadequacy as the drug addict, why should such an individual

choose another person, rather than a drug, for the object of his addiction? One characteristic which distinguishes the two groups of addicts is their social class. Opiate use is found primarily in people in lower social and economic positions, especially racial minorities. Lower-class whites more normally take to alcohol as their escape. Middle-class Americans, on the other hand, while not quite as prone to alcoholism and while certainly not interested in heroin, are no less subject to addictive tendencies; they just express them differently.

As a rule, other human beings play a role in the middle-class person's lifestyle that they do not for the lower-class person. To take an extreme case, Chein's analysis of New York City's heroin addicts shows that they are distrustful of people; drugs are the only things in their lives they feel they can rely on. Individuals in these settings more frequently suc- cumb to heroin addiction and debilitating alcoholism, while people (mainly lovers) serve the same purpose for those who are better off. In either case, the combination of dependency and manipulativeness that Chein observed in heroin addicts lies behind the addict's exploitativeness. Unsure of his own identity, the addict sees other people as objects to serve his needs. But for the drug addict, using people is only a means to other ends; for the middle-class addict, possessing people is the end.

When people are economically comfortable but still sense a large deficiency in their lives, their yearnings are bound to be more existential than material. That is, these yearnings are tied into their basic conception of and feelings about themselves. D. H. Lawrence describes such a case in his novel *Women in Love*. The character is Gerald Crich, the well-to-do son of an industrial magnate. When his father dies, Gerald's world begins to fall around him, and he experiences the spiritual catastrophe which leads him to a relationship of desperation with Gudrun Brangwen.

But as the fight went on, and all that he had been and was continued to be destroyed, so that life was a hollow shell around him, roaring and clattering like the sound of the sea, a noise in which he participated externally, and inside this hollow shell was all the darkness and fearful space of death, he knew he would have to find reinforcements, otherwise he would collapse inwards upon the great dark void which circled at the centre of his soul.[2]

The emotional state Lawrence depicts is very much like what R. D. Laing calls schizoid alienation, in which an individual is so detached from his or her experience that he cannot get from it a sense of himself as an inte- grated being. In *The Divided Self*, Laing suggests that schizoid alienation is not only a common contemporary form of madness, but also a prevalent feature of life in modern society. The "ontological anxiety"—uncertainty about our very existence—that Laing speaks of is what makes some of us compulsively seek relationships.

Gerald Crich is a fictional example of someone who lacks a well-developed core being, a secure sense of himself. A person feeling this inner emptiness must strive to fill it. In relationships, this can only be done by subsuming someone else's being inside yourself, or by allowing someone else to subsume you. Often, two people simultaneously engulf and are engulfed by each other. The result is a full-fledged addiction, where each partner draws the other back at any sign of a loosening of the bonds that hold them together.

ERICH FROMM: A POSITIVE CONCEPT OF LOVE

Love is the opposite of interpersonal addiction. A love relationship is based on a desire to grow and to expand oneself through living, and a desire for one's partner to do the same. Anything which contributes positively to a loved one's experience is welcome, partly because it enriches the loved one for his own sake, and partly because it makes him a more stimulating companion in life. If a person is self-completed, he can even accept experiences which cause a lover to grow away from him, if that is the direction in which the lover's fulfillment must take her. If two people hope to realize fully their potential as human beings—both together and apart—then they create an intimacy which includes, along with trust and sharing, independence, openness, adventurousness, and love.

When we speak of a desire for intimacy that respects the loved one's integrity, we naturally think of Erich Fromm's classic work, *The Art of Loving*. Fromm's theme is that man or woman can only achieve love when he has realized himself to the point where he can stand as a whole and secure person. "Mature *love*," Fromm states, "is *union under the condition of preserving one's integrity*, one's individuality." It requires "a state of intensity, awakeness, enhanced vitality, which can only be the result of a productive and active orientation in many other spheres of life." This permits us, as lovers, to manifest an *"active concern for the life and the growth of that which we love."*

Unless we have reached this state, "our feeling of identity is threatened and we become dependent on other people whose approval then becomes the basis for our feeling of identity." In that case, we are in danger of experiencing union *without* integrity. Such a union is a "full commitment in all aspects of life," but one which lacks an essential ingredient, a regard for the rest of the world:

If a person loves only one person and is indifferent to the rest of his fellow men, his love is not love but a symbiotic attachment, or an enlarged egotism.[3]

These comments, and much else that Fromm writes, reveal a sharp awareness of the potential for addiction inherent in the "powerful striving" man feels for "interpersonal fusion." Fromm notes that two passionately attracted people "take the intensity of the infatuation, this being 'crazy' about each other, for proof of the intensity of their love, while it may only prove the degree of their preceding loneliness."

CRITERIA FOR LOVE VS. ADDICTION

In Fromm's notion of integrity in love, we have the elements of a positive concept of love. By contrasting this model with that of addictive love, we can develop specific criteria for assessing the character of our relationships. These criteria are points at which a relationship either expresses health and the promise of growth, or leans toward addiction.

1. Does each lover have a secure belief in his or her own value?
2. Are the lovers improved by the relationship? By some measure outside of the relationship are they better, stronger, more attractive, more accomplished, or more sensitive individuals? Do they value the relationship for this very reason?
3. Do the lovers maintain serious interests outside the relationship, including other meaningful personal relationships?
4. Is the relationship integrated into, rather than being set off from, the totality of the lovers' lives?
5. Are the lovers beyond being possessive or jealous of each other's growth and expansion of interests?
6. Are the lovers also friends? Would they seek each other out if they should cease to be primary partners?

These standards represent an ideal, and as such they cannot be fulfilled completely even by the healthiest relationships. But given that every relationship is bound to contain some element of addiction, we can still tell what makes one predominantly addictive. This occurs, as in drug addiction, when a single overwhelming involvement with one thing serves to cut a person off from life, to close him or her off to experience, to debilitate him, to make him less open, free, and positive in dealing with the world.

D. H. Lawrence used the term *égoisme à deux* to describe the overgrown, quasi-permanent connection between two lovers. Like any form of addiction, an *égoisme à deux* involves people who have not received from life a self-completeness that would enable them to come to an experience whole in themselves. The result is that they are drawn to an object—the lover—which can secure their shallow or fragmented selves. But they become trapped by this object, because even as it stabilizes them, it prevents them from extending themselves outward to meet other people or events that they encounter. As their inadequacy and rigidity worsen, each must lean more heavily on the other. Thus they draw each other into an increasingly closed, isolated, and mutually protective relationship.

Because the partners in an addictive relationship are motivated more by their own needs for security than by an appreciation of each other's personal qualities, what they want most from each other is the reassurance of constancy. Thus they are likely to demand unchallenged acceptance of themselves as they are, including their blemishes and peculiarities. In exchange, they are willing to tolerate passively all similar quirks in each other's makeup. In fact, to justify their total involvement, the lovers may identify each other's idiosyncrasies as their standards for attractiveness. In this way they create a private world which others can't enter and would not want to enter.

Such lovers do, of course, require each other to change in certain ways. But the adaptations expected or demanded are entirely toward each other and do not entail an improved ability to deal with other people or the environment. As Germaine Greer's penetrating analysis puts it:

The hallmark of egotistical love, even when it masquerades as altruistic love, is the negative answer to the question "Do I want my love to be happy more than I want him to be with me?" As soon as we find ourselves working at being indispensable, rigging up a pattern of vulnerability in our loved ones, we ought to know that our love has taken the socially sanctioned form of egotism. Every wife who slaves to keep herself pretty, to cook her husband's favorite meals, to build up his pride and confidence in himself at the expense of his sense of reality, to be his closest and effectively his only friend, to encourage him to reject the consensus of opinion and find reassurance only in her arms is binding her mate to her with hoops of steel that will strangle them both. Every time a woman makes herself laugh at her husband's often-told jokes she betrays him. The man who looks at his woman and says, "What would I do without you?" is already destroyed. His woman's victory is complete, but it is Pyrrhic. Both of them have sacrificed so much of what initially made them lovable to promote the symbiosis of mutual dependence that they scarcely make up one human being between them.[4]

Paradoxically, at the stage where they have rejected the rest of the world—when they need each other most—the lovers have become least critical and aware of each other as unique individuals. The partner is just *there*, a completely necessary point of certainty in a bewildering and dangerous world. Under these conditions, acceptance of another is not a recognition of that person's integrity. Where need is so intense, there is no room in the lovers' minds for such a concept of dignity, either the other person's or one's own.

Then, too, the lovers' ultimate lack of interest in each other gives the lie to the romantic notion of addicted love as a kind of intense passion. The intensity that we see is that of desperation, not of a desire to know each other better. In healthy relationships the growing attachment to another person goes with a growing appreciation of that person; among these relationships are those inspiring love affairs where two people continually find new facets of each other to admire and delight in. In addiction what is apparent is not the intensity of passion, but its shallowness. There is no emotional risk in this sort of relationship, or, at least, the addict tries to eliminate that risk as much as possible. Because he is so vulnerable, what the addict is ideally striving for is perfect invulnerability. He only gives of himself in exchange for the promise of safety.

From this perspective, love at first sight becomes understandable in the sense that addiction to heroin on the first injection is understandable. A description by an addict in *The Road to H* of his first shot of heroin can apply equally well to the addicted lover's experience; "I felt I always wanted to feel the same way as I felt then." Both addicts have discovered something reassuring that they hope will never change. From the turmoil of their inner worlds, they recognize and latch on to the one sensation they have encountered which they feel can bring them peace.

Addicted lovers see each other more and more in order to maintain this secure state. They settle into each other, requiring over more frequent interactions, until they find themselves consistently together, unable to endure significant separations. When they are apart, they long for each other. The two people have grown together to such an extent that neither feels like a whole person when alone. The excitement that originally brought the lovers together has dissipated, yet the lovers are less able than before to be critical of their arrangement. Even if their contact degenerates into constant conflict, they cannot part.

As with heroin and its irrecoverable euphoria, or cigarettes smoked in routine excess, something initially sought for pleasure is held more tightly *after* it ceases to provide enjoyment. Now it is being maintained for negative rather than positive reasons. The love partner must be there in order to satisfy a deep, aching need, or else the addict begins to feel withdrawal pain. If the world he has built with the lover is destroyed, he desperately tries to find some other partner so as to reestablish his artificial equilibrium.

The addictive foundations of such a relationship are revealed when it ends in an abrupt, total, and vindictive breakup. Since the relationship has been the person's one essential contact point with life, its removal necessarily leaves him in a disoriented agony. Because the involvement has been so total, its ending must be violent. Thus it is possible for two people who have been the most intimate friends suddenly to turn around and hate each other, because they have been thinking more of themselves than each other all along.

When there is a willingness to examine one's motivations and behavior toward others, the idea of addiction can be treated not as a threatening diagnosis, but as a means for heightening the awareness of some dangers which are very common in relationships. By establishing the antithesis of addiction, we can delineate an ideal with which to oppose the tendencies toward self-suppression of others that can appear in love. Just as it is important to keep the addictive elements that are somewhere present in all human contact from becoming full-blown addictions, it is at least equally valuable to expand the positive, life-seeking potential that also exists within any relationship.

A loving relationship, as Erich Fromm makes clear, is predicated on the psychological wholeness and security of the individuals who come to it. Out of their own integrity, the lovers seek growth for each other and for the relationship. Respecting the people they are and have been, and the lives they have formed, they try to maintain the prior interests and affections they have known. Where possible, they want to incorporate these things into the relationship, in order to broaden the world they share. They also reserve the time—and the feeling—to keep up those activities or friendships which it would be impossible or inappropriate to offer each other.

Because they are well-composed individuals before the relationship is conceived, their approach to that relationship is not frantic. They may be passionately attracted and want very much to become better friends, but they also recognize there are points at which pressure and intensity are hurtful to what they desire. They accept the need for privacy and for different viewpoints and tastes, they realize that forcing certain commitments or declarations is unwise and ultimately self-defeating, and they appreciate that it takes time for two people to know each other and to discover the extent and depth of their compatibility. The fact that they are discriminating makes clear that their choice of each other has been made on both sides out of something other than desperation, and thus cannot be blown away by a chance wind. The lovers approach the relationship itself as an opportunity for growth. They want to understand more about it, about themselves, and about each other.

For these things to come about, a loving relationship must be a helping relationship. The lovers have to support each other in their areas of weakness and their areas of strength, though with a different attitude toward each. The first is understood as something undesirable which it may be hard to change. The second is welcomed, admired, utilized, and expanded. The aim is support for one's partner to become the best human being he or she is reasonably capable of being.

While it is impossible to overstate the role of nurturing and reassurance in love, it is also true that love itself is demanding and sometimes exhausting. The issue between addiction and love is whether the demands will be immediately self-serving, or whether they will be in the service of some larger sense of individual and mutual progress. Human emotion necessarily involves risk. The risk may stem from the chance that two people who do not allow their lives to be totally defined will evolve in different directions. There is always this danger in love; to deny it is to deny love. But where the people involved are genuine and self-sustaining, and where they have been in love, the parting—made with whatever pain and regret—will not be the end of them as individuals or as loving friends.

This feeling of existential confidence in oneself and one's relationships is hard to achieve, and may only very rarely be encountered. A host of social forces work against it, and, as a result, it is unfortunately easier to find examples of addiction than of self-fulfillment in love.

NOTES

[1]Freud (1965).
[2]Lawrence (1960c).
[3]Fromm (1956).
[4]Greer (1971).

Falling in Love

Francesco Alberoni

What is falling in love? It is the nascent state of a collective movement involving two individuals. There is a very close relationship between the great collective movements in history and falling in love. The forces they both liberate and put to work are of the same type; they involve many similar experiences of solidarity, joy in life, and renewal. We must dissociate ourselves from the current way of thinking which does not recognize falling in love as a state that is different from everyday life and sexuality. Falling in love—like every collective movement—belongs in the realm of the extraordinary. Falling in love challenges institutions on the level of their fundamental values. Its nature lies precisely in this, in not being a desire, a personal whim, but a movement that carries with it a plan for life and creates an institution.

Falling in love, when all goes well, ends in love; the movement, when it succeeds, produces an institution. But the relationship between falling in love and love itself, between nascent state and institution, is comparable to that between taking off or flying and landing, between being in the sky above the clouds and firmly setting foot on the ground again. Consider another image, that of the flower and the fruit. The fruit issues from the flower, but they are two different things. When there is fruit, there is no longer any flower. And there is really no point in asking if the flower is better than the fruit or vice versa. By the same token, there is no point in asking whether the nascent state is better than the institution. One does not exist without the other. Life is made up of both. Still, there is no point in confusing them, because they are distinct.

Every collective process divides something that was united by tradition, habit and institutions, and unites something that was divided by them. This is also true for falling in love. In feudal society, where the structure of kinship relations continued to exist even while a new bourgeoisie and a new intelligentsia were born, love struck like a spark between two individuals who belonged to two separate and noncommunicating systems. They sought out one another and united, transgressing the rules of the kinship and class systems. This was the case with Abelard and Heloise. Their love was a transgression that asserted itself as exemplary and right.

When Shakespeare, centuries later, represents Romeo and Juliet's love, he shows us an analogous situation: two hostile families between which marriage is prohibited. In this case, too, love presents itself as transgression. It separates what was united (Juliet from her family, Romeo from his) and unites what was divided (two enemies). No movement exists without a difference. These may be any difference and any transgression. It can be the simple fact that the boy is emotionally tied to his mother (or to his father), as in the modern world, and here the transgression is completely interior: the adolescent's rupture with the family of his childhood. For hundreds and hundreds of years, falling in love was presented as a rupture of the conjugal couple: adultery. But adultery is only a particular instance of a general rule: falling in love can occur only if it separates what was united and unites what needed to be divided.

The nascent state is the revelation of an affirmative state of being. There is no motive at all for saying "yes" to another person, no guarantee, but we say it anyway. When someone falls in love, he opens himself to a different existence without any guarantee that it can be realized. It is a lofty song that is never certain of finding an answer. Its greatness is desperately human, for it offers moments of happiness and eternity, creating a consuming desire for them, but cannot provide any certainties. And when a response comes from the other person, from the beloved, it appears as something undeserved, as a marvelous gift that the lover never thought he could have. This gift comes wholly from the other, from the beloved, by her own choice. Theologians have a term to indicate this gift: they call it *grace*. And when the beloved says that she loves him in return and makes love to him, when the lover feels the other's total abandon, then he is happy and time ceases to exist: that moment becomes eternal for him. He will never forget it, never be able to. If the lover feels he is loved in return, he has only to remember this to bear any pain or difficulty.

But if one day the beloved leaves him, then the memory, precisely because it remains immortal, will be the reason for his unhappiness, and everything else will seem like nothing in comparison to what he has lost. And that memory will endure until another nascent state remakes the past.

We are aware of this terrible risk, but when we fall in love, we face it. We have no guarantee that the road to a new life is not the road to desperation. Every meeting with the beloved could be the final one. The dimension of the love that finds its object is *the present*, that instant which is worth as much as the lover's entire past and everything in the world. As a result, the happiness we feel in love always contains a note of sadness, because when we "make time stop," we know that in doing so we sacrifice every certainty and every resource. "Stopping time" means happiness, but it also means giving up control over things.

This plunge into a life with no certainty of the future, this stopping of time, is represented in art as death. Only the love that ends in death can serve as a device for expressing every uncertainty, every doubt, every desire of the person in love as well as their dissolution beyond past and future in that eternal present which cancels out every question. Hence death is the artistic signifier of the end of time which the lover experiences. It is a fascinating fiction that has the power to evoke in us every pain of the search for love, and this makes us relive the tormenting desire for the absent beloved to such an extent that there is no longer any desire, only the peace of being absorbed in her. When Werther dies, he "stops time" for himself and for Lotte. In reality, love as an existential fact is made up of moments of eternity which it continually transcends.

Falling in love tends to result in a *fusion*, but it is a fusion of two different people. For love to occur, there must be a difference, and falling in love is a will, a drive to overcome this difference, which nonetheless exists and must exist. The beloved is interesting because she (or he) is different, because she bears her own unmistakable specificity. This specificity, this *uniqueness*, actually increases when we fall in love. We want to be loved insofar as we are unique, extraordinary, irreplaceable, absolutely ourselves. This cannot be achieved in organizations where all of us are replaceable, interchangeable. Nor can it be achieved in the everyday life of the family, because here we are unique and irreplaceable, but not extraordinary.

It is not enough to be adored by someone who has no value, by someone who is replaceable. We want to be experienced as unique, extraordinary, and indispensable by someone who is unique, extraordinary, and indispensable. For this reason, the experience of falling in love can only be monogamous; it is a claim of exclusivity and a recognition of the extraordinary made by someone who is so.

Each of us is different from every other person, as we know, but it is only when we fall in love that our irreducible individuality is grasped and appreciated completely. A sure and unmistakable sign of love is this appreciation of the other person's specificity and uniqueness. The appreciation we feel coming from her allows us to appreciate ourselves. This is the movement of individuation. But at the same time the experience of falling in love initiates a second movement, that of fusion, which is in a certain sense opposed to the first one. Fusion is directed toward producing a union of wills. A mutual love means that both lovers want what is important for each of them. Individuation differentiates, gives value to differences. Fusion occurs so that these differences merge to make up a single will. But precisely because these differences have become important, they tend to prevail and clash. Love is also a struggle. When we are in love, each of us tries to show off our best part, what we feel is most ours, most true, and we want this to be appreciated. But the other person appreciates something else more and reveals it to us.

So since love leads us to adopt the beloved's point of view, we must remake our self-image. The very desire to please the beloved leads us to change ourselves. In this way, each of us imposes his (or her) point of view on the other person and changes himself to give the other person pleasure. In all of this there is no imposition, but a continual deciphering, a continual discovery. Every aspect of the other person's behavior—every gesture, every glance—becomes a symbol to interpret. And we in turn are continual producers of symbols. In this process, which encompasses the present and the past, nature too is involved. Rain and sunshine, the shape of a cloud grow rich with values, come to signify something that is connected with the beloved and with our love for her; they have meaning, indicate a direction. Since there is an obstacle, since the other person is different, since her response is never absolutely certain or at least never perfectly suited to the question, the most casual incidents, things, combinations, become signals for interpretation, invitations, denials, omens. Every place where something significant happens becomes sacred.

Love produces a sacred geography of the world. That place, that house, that particular view of the sea or the mountains, that tree become sacred symbols of the beloved or of love. They become sacred zones, temples, because they hosted one of love's eternal moments or an omen. And as space is sanctified, so is time. If the period of happiness in the nascent state is the eternal present, the conjunction of these moments of eternity constitutes a liturgical year with its holy days. They are points of meaning and value, memories of exemplariness, of pain, of happiness, or even merely moments that are significant for the other person and become sacred for us. In this way, the experience of falling in love, as it unfolds, produces an objective sanctity. Space is composed of fixed points, while time is discontinous, composed of significant days, and both are sacred, as in religions. Falling in love reestablishes the division between the sacred and the profane and has a very strong sense of sacrilege. Even at a distance of years or decades, lovers who are now separated will not be able to get through certain days without being upset, will not be able to return to certain places without being flooded by nostalgia. This sacred space and time are immortal because they define the cirumstances under which the eternal present, the stopping of time, is made objective. Forgotten, they survive in the unconscious. Only another nascent state can erase them to create a new space and a new time.

Although falling in love is the arrival of the extraordinary, it can end in banality. The lover wants the other person's difference because this is actually what attracts him, insofar as it opens the way to a new life, but at the same time, he tries to limit this difference to reassure himself. This eruptive vitality frightens him; he wants it, but he would like it to be restrained.

Whenever we fall in love, the other person always appears rich with a superabundant life. The beloved is always a vital force—free, unforeseeable, polymorphous. She is like a marvelous wild animal, extraordinarily beautiful and extraordinarily alive, an animal whose nature is not to be docile, but rebellious, not weak, but strong. The "grace" we have discussed is the miracle that such a creature can become gentle toward us and love us. The one we love attracts and gives pleasure precisely because she possesses this force, which is free and liberating, but also unforeseeable and frightening. This is why the person who is more frightened imposes on the other a great many restrictions, a great many small sacrifices, all of which are basically intended to make her gentle, safe, and innocuous. And the other person gradually accepts them. She has friends, but she decides not to go out with them; she used to travel, but now she stays home; she used to love her profession, but now she neglects it in order to devote herself to her lover. To avoid upsetting her lover, she imperceptibly eradicates everything that may have that effect. She makes many small renunciations, none of which is serious. She gladly makes them, because she wants her lover to be happy, she tries to become what he wants her to be. Gradually, she becomes *domestic*, available, always ready, always grateful. In this way, the marvelous wild beast is reduced to a domestic pet; the tropical flower, plucked from its environment, droops in the little vase by the window. And the lover who asked her to become like this because he wanted to be reassured, because he was frightened by the new experience, winds up missing in her what he had previously sought and found. The person who stands before him is not the same one he had fallen in love with, precisely because at that time she was different and fully alive. He asked her to model herself on his fears, and now he faces the result of those fears—her nothingness—and he no longer loves her.

This often happens with men who fall in love with a young girl, with her youth, her possibilities. But they are afraid of her, so they ask her to give up her job and friends, to stop being flirtatious and witty, until she becomes pliable and dull. At which point they realize that they desire another young girl, that they have destroyed the one they are now with. I haven't chosen this example by chance: it is women in particular who suffer this violence and adapt themselves to this role. They are desired as long as they are free, because they express the vitality of freedom; then they are confined to domestic life, to harems, surrounded by endless restrictions, by a jealousy that is only their lover's fear of wanting what he originally wanted; finally, they are forced to become an everyday banality, the place where by definition not only falling in love, but even love itself inevitably ends.

Can the experience of falling in love be transformed into a love that preserves the freshness of that experience for years? Yes. For it to continue, however, the extraordinary experience must somehow continue in everyday life, must be realized as an extraordinary journey through existence which the lovers make together, side by side, after difficult tests, after discovery and confrontation, after constant reinterpretation of the world and constant reexamination of the past. For some, this may be a struggle, a kind of poetry; for others, simply the capacity to be constantly amazed by themselves and the world, as they constantly seek not what is reassuring or what has already been noted, but what is challenging, beautiful, creative. In this sense, the external journey is only the occasion, the vehicle for a continuous internal journey, just as the internal journey is continuously the stimulus for an external journey. In these situations, the experience of falling in love continues because the nascent state is reborn over and over, in a constant revision, rediscovery, renewal, self-renewal, a constant search for challenges and opportunities. Then we fall in love again with the same person.

I don't think there is any practical rule for how to behave—an art of staying in love—to be drawn from all this. Such rules are always instruments of self-deception, of falsification. Life creates the nascent state, it creates the encounter, the plans, the tests, and the opportunities, and it takes them away. We are afloat in this great sea like a small canoe in the middle of a storm. We don't make the waves, nor do we modify them. We can stay afloat, happily or with difficulty or in both ways, we may reach the shore or not reach it, and find joy in arriving or in not arriving.

What in fact is the banality of the everyday, if not the failure of the transforming and revolutionizing processes that the nascent state initiated? Falling in love is an exploration of the possible; the person we fall in love with offers us a way to modify our everyday experience radically.

Love Evolving

Vladimir Solovyov

The meaning of sexual love is generally supposed to consist in subserving the propagation of the species. I consider this view to be mistaken—not on the ground of any ideal considerations as such, but first and foremost on grounds of natural history. That the reproduction of living creatures does not need sexual love is clear if only from the fact that it does not even need the division into sexes. A considerable part both of vegetable and animal organisms multiply sexlessly: by division, budding, spores, grafting. Since it is the higher forms in both the organic kingdoms which reproduce themselves sexually, the conclusion to be drawn is that the sex factor is connected not with reproduction as such (which may take place without it) but with the reproduction of *higher* organisms. Hence the meaning of sexual differentiation (and, consequently, of sexual love) must be sought for not in the idea of generic life and its reproduction, but only in the idea of a higher organism.

A striking confirmation of this is provided by the following great fact. Among animals that reproduce themselves solely in the sexual way (the vertebrates), the higher we go in the organic scale, the less is the power of reproduction and the greater the force of sex attraction. In the lowest class of this section—the fishes—the rate of reproduction is enormous: the spawn yearly produced by every female are counted in millions; they are fertilized by the male outside the body of the female, and the way in which it is done does not suggest strong sexual attraction. Of all vertebrate creatures this cold-blooded class undoubtedly multiplies most and shows least trace of love-passion. At the next stage—among the amphibians and reptiles—the rate of reproduction is much lower than among the fishes; but, with a lower rate of reproduction, we find in those animals closer sexual relations. In birds the power of reproduction is much smaller than, for instance, in frogs, to say nothing of fishes, while sexual attraction and mutual affection between the male and the female are developed to a degree unexampled in the two lower classes. Among mammals (or the viviparous), reproduction is much slower than among the birds, and sexual attraction is much more intense, though for the most part less constant. Finally, in man the rate of reproduction is lower than in the rest of the animal kingdom, but sexual love attains the greatest force and significance, uniting in the highest degree the permanence of relations (as with birds) with the intensity of passion (as with the viviparous).

Thus sexual love and reproduction of the species are in *inverse ratio* to each other: the stronger the one, the weaker the other. Altogether, the animal kingdom as a whole develops in this respect in the following order: at the lowest level there is an enormous power of reproduction and a complete absence of anything like sexual love (since there is no division into sexes); further, in more perfect organisms there appear sexual differentiation and, corresponding to it, a certain sexual attraction, very weak at first; at the further stages of organic development it increases, while the power of reproduction diminishes (i.e., it increases in direct ratio to the perfection of the organism and in inverse ratio to the power of reproduction), until at last, at the top of the scale, in man, there may be intense sexual love without any reproduction whatever. If, then, at the two opposite poles of animal life we find, on the one hand, reproduction without any sexual love, and on the other, sexual love without any reproduction, it is perfectly clear that these two facts cannot be indissolubly interconnected; it is clear that each of them has an independent significance of its own, and that the meaning of one cannot consist in serving as a means for the other. The same conclusion follows if we consider sexual love exclusively in the human world, where it acquires, much more clearly than in the animal kingdom, an individual character, in virtue of which *precisely this* person of the opposite sex has an absolute significance for the lover as unique and irreplaceable, as an end in itself.

The meaning of love in general is *the justification and salvation of individuality through the sacrifice of egoism*. Starting with this general position can help us explain the meaning of sexual love. It is highly significant that sexual relations are not only called love, but are generally recognized as pre-eminently representative of love, being the type and the ideal of all other kinds of love (see The Song of Songs and the Revelation of St. John).

The evil and falsity of egoism certainly do not consist in the fact that man prizes himself too highly or ascribes absolute significance and infinite dignity to himself: he is right in this, for every human subject as an independent center of living power, as the potency of infinite perfection, as a being capable of embracing in his life and consciousness the absolute truth, has unconditional significance and dignity, is something absolutely irreplaceable and cannot prize himself too highly. Not to recognize one's absolute significance in this sense is tantamount to renouncing one's human dignity. The fundamental evil and falsity of egoism lie not in the recognition of the subject's own absolute significance and value, but in the fact that while he justly ascribes such significance to himself, he unjustly denies it to others; in recognizing himself as a center of life, which he is in reality, he refers others to the circumference of his being, setting upon them only an external and relative value.

Of course, theoretically and in the abstract every man who is in his right mind always admits that other people have exactly the same rights as he; but in his vital consciousness, in his inner feeling and in practice, he makes an infinite, incommensurable difference between himself and others: he, as such, is all, they, as such, are nothing. But it is precisely this exclusive self-affirmation that prevents man from being in fact what he claims to be. The unconditional significance and absoluteness which, speaking generally, he rightly recognizes in himself, but wrongly denies in others, is in itself merely potential. Only together with others can he realize his absolute significance and become an inseparable and irreplaceable part of the universal whole, an independent, unique and living organ of the absolute life. True individuality is a certain form of universal unity, a way of apprehending and assimilating the whole. In affirming himself outside of all else, man robs his own existence of its meaning, deprives himself of the true content of life and reduces his individuality to an empty form. Thus egoism is certainly not the self-affirmation and self-consciousness of individuality, but, on the contrary, its self-negation and destruction.

There is only one power which may and actually does undermine egoism at the root, from within, and that is love, and chiefly sexual love. The evil and falsity of egoism consist in ascribing absolute significance exclusively to oneself and denying it to others. Love compels us to recognize not in abstract thought, but in inner feeling and vital will the absolute significance of another person for us. Through love we come to know the truth of another not in abstraction but in reality, and actually transfer the center of our life beyond the confines of our separateness; and in doing so we manifest and realize our own truth, our own absolute significance, which consists precisely in the power of transcending our actual phenomenal existence and of living not in ourselves only but also in another.

All love is a manifestation of this power, but not every kind of love realizes it to the same extent or undermines egoism with the same thoroughness. Egoism is a real and fundamental force rooted in the deepest center of our being and spreading from there to the whole of our reality— a force that continually acts in every department and every detail of our existence. If egoism is to be thoroughly undermined, it must be counteracted by a love as concrete as it itself is, penetrating and possessing the whole of our being. The "other" which is to liberate our individuality from the fetters of egoism must be as real and concrete as we are, and at the same time must differ from us in every way, so as to be really "other." In other words, while having the same essential nature as we, it must have it in another way, in a different form, so that our every manifestation, our every vital act should meet in that "other" a corresponding but not an identical manifestation. The relation of the one to the other must thus be a complete and continual exchange, a complete and continual affirmation of oneself in the other, a perfect interaction and communion. Only then will egoism be undermined and abolished, not in principle only, but in all its concrete actuality. Only this, so to speak, chemical fusion of two beings of the same kind and significance, but throughout different in form, can render possible (both in the natural and the spiritual order) the creation of a new man, the actual realization of the true human individuality. Such fusion, or at any rate the nearest approximation to it, is to be found in sexual love, and that is the reason why it has an exceptional significance as a necessary and irreplaceable basis of all further growth in perfection, as the inevitable and constant condition which alone makes it possible for man to be actually in Truth.

Although we have to acknowledge the great importance and dignity of other kinds of love, nevertheless only sexual love satisfies two fundamental conditions without which there can be no final abolition of egoism through complete vital communion with another. Other kinds of love lack either the equality and interaction of lover and beloved, or the all-inclusive differences of complementary qualities.

In mystical love the object of love ultimately engulfs human individuality. If the object of love is there, there is no lover—he has disappeared, lost himself in the universal spirit. Parental love resembles sexual love in its intensity and concreteness, but here there can be no complete reciprocity and life-long communion, if only because the lover and beloved belong to different generations and that for the latter, life lies ahead in the future. A mother who puts her whole soul into her children certainly sacrifices her egoism, but she also loses her individuality. Besides, in maternal love there is really no recognition of the beloved's absolute significance and true individuality, for although a child is precious to its mother above all, this is precisely because it is *her* child. And friendship between persons of the same sex lacks the mutually complementary differences which are so important for overcoming egoism.

The meaning and value of love as a feeling consist in the fact that it makes us actually, with our whole being, recognize in *another* the absolute central significance which owing to egoism we feel in ourselves only. Love is important, not as one of our feelings, but as the transference of our whole vital interest from ourselves to another, as the transposition of the very center of our personal life. This is characteristic of every kind of love, but of sexual love pre-eminently; it differs from other kinds of love by greater intensity, greater absorption and the possibility of a more complete and comprehensive reciprocity.

The love-feeling demands fullness of union, but as a rule things go no further than striving and demand, and that too proves to be transitory. Instead of the poetry of union we have a more or less continuous, a more or less intimate, external and superficial nearness between two limited beings within the narrow framework of everyday prose. The object of love does not preserve in fact the absolute significance ascribed to it by the dream of love. To an outsider this is obvious from the first, and the involuntary tinge of irony that inevitably colors other people's attitude to lovers proves to be merely an anticipation of their own disillusionment. Sooner or later the ecstatic element of love disappears.

And so if we consider only that which generally happens and look only at love's actual outcome, love must be recognized to be a dream possessing us for a time and then disappearing without any practical result (since child-bearing is not the work of love as such). But if evidence compels us to admit that the ideal meaning of love is not realized in fact, must we admit that it is *unrealizable*? It would be quite unjust to deny that love is realizable simply because it has never yet been realized: the same was true in the past of many other things—all arts and sciences, civic society, control of the forces of nature, and so on. Rational consciousness itself before it became a fact in man was only a vague and fruitless striving in the animal world. A number of geological and biological epochs passed in unsuccessful attempts to create a brain capable of becoming an organ for the embodiment of rational thought. So far love is for man what reason was for the animal world: it exists in its rudiments or tokens, but not as yet in fact. The fact that love has not been realized

in the course of the comparatively few thousands of years lived by historical humanity gives us no right to conclude that it cannot be realized in
the future.

The task of love is to *actualize in fact* the meaning of love which is at
first given only as a feeling—to create a union of two limited beings. To
realize this unity or to create the true human being as the free unity of the
masculine and the feminine elements, which preserve their formal separateness but overcome their essential disparity and disruption, is the direct
task of love. If we consider the conditions required for carrying it out, we
shall see that it is only because those conditions are not observed that love
invariably comes to grief and has to be pronounced an illusion.

The first step towards successfully solving any problem is to state it
consciously and correctly; but the problem of love has never been consciously formulated and therefore has never been properly solved. People
have always regarded love solely as a given fact or as a state (normal for
some and painful for others) experienced by man, but not imposing any
obligations upon him. This love, left to itself from beginning to end,
disappears like a mirage. Of course, love is in the first place a fact of
nature (or a gift of God), a natural process arising independently of us;
but this does not imply that we cannot and must not stand in a conscious
relation to it and of our own will direct this natural process to higher
ends.

Everyone knows that in love there always is a special *idealization* of
the object of love which appears to the lover in quite a different light than
it does to other people. I am speaking of light not in a metaphorical sense
only, but of special sensuous perception as well: the lover actually *sees*,
visually apprehends, something different from what others do. True, for
him too this light of love soon disappears, but does that imply that it was
false, that it was merely a subjective illusion?

The power of love transforming itself into light, transfiguring and
spiritualizing the form of external appearances, reveals to us its objective
force, but it is for us to do the rest: we must understand this revelation
and make use of it so that it should not remain an enigmatic and fleeting
glimpse of some mystery.

The actual feeling of love is merely a stimulus suggesting to us that
we can and must recreate the wholeness of the human being. These hopes
will not be fulfilled until we decide fully to recognize and realize to the
end all that true love demands, all that is contained in the idea of it, with
a conscious attitude to love and real determination to accomplish the task
it sets us.

It is only together with all other beings that the individual can regen-
erate his individual life in true love. The individual never really separates

his own good from the true good of all that lives. The fact that the deepest and strongest manifestation of love is to be found in the relation between two beings complementary to each other by no means implies that this relation should be isolated and separated from all else as something self-sufficient; on the contrary, such isolation is the ruin of love. If the meaning of love requires the reunion of that which has been wrongly separated and demands the identification of one's own self with the other, it would be contrary to this to separate the attainment of our individual perfection from the process of universal unification, even if it were physically possible to do so.

If the root of false existence is impenetrability, i.e., mutual exclusion of one another's being, true life means living in another as in oneself or finding in another positive and absolute completion of one's own being. The foundation and pattern of this true life is and always shall be sexual or conjugal love. But that love cannot be realized without a corresponding transformation of the whole external environment; the integration of the individual life necessarily requires the same integration in the domains of social and of cosmic life.

The Stream of Desire

D. H. Lawrence

Love is a relationship between things that live, holding them together in a sort of unison. There are other vital relationships. But love is this special one.

In every living thing there is the desire, for love, or for the relationship of unison with the rest of things. That a tree should desire to develop itself between the power of the sun, and the opposite pull of the earth's centre, and to balance itself between the four winds of heaven, and to unfold itself between the rain and the shine, to have roots and feelers in blue heaven and innermost earth, both, this is a manifestation of love: a knitting together of the diverse cosmos into a oneness, a tree.

At the same time, the tree must most powerfully exert itself and defend itself, to maintain its own integrity against the rest of things.

So that love, as a desire, is balanced against the opposite desire, to maintain the integrity of the individual self.

Hate is not the opposite of love. The real opposite of love is individuality.

We live in the age of individuality, we call ourselves the servants of love. That is to say, we enact a perpetual paradox.

Take the love of a man and a woman, today. As sure as you start with a case of "true love" between them, you end with a terrific struggle and conflict of the two opposing egos or individualities. It is nobody's fault; it is the inevitable result of trying to snatch an intensified individuality out of the mutual flame.

Love, as a relationship of unison, means and must mean, *to some extent*, the sinking of the individuality. Woman for centuries was expected to sink her individuality into that of her husband and family. Nowadays the tendency is to insist that a man shall sink his individuality into his job, or his business, primarily, and secondarily into his wife and family.

At the same time, education and the public voice urge man and woman into intenser individualism. A certain amount of time, labour, money, emotion are sacrificed on the altar of love, by man and woman: especially emotion. But each calculates the sacrifice. And man and woman alike, each saves his individual ego, intact, as far as possible, in the scrimmage of love. Most of our talk about love is cant, and bunk. The treasure of treasures to man and woman today is his own, or her own ego. And this ego, each hopes it will flourish like a salamander in the flame of love and passion. Which it well may: but for the fact that there are two salamanders in the same flame, and they fight till the flame goes out. Then they become grey cold lizards of the vulgar ego.

It is much easier, of course, when there *is* no flame. Then there is no serious fight.

You can't worship love and individuality in the same breath. Love is a mutual relationship, like a flame between wax and air. If either wax or air insists on getting its own way, or getting its own back too much, the flame goes out and the unison disappears. At the same time, if one yields itself up to the other entirely, there is a guttering mess. You have to balance love and individuality, and actually sacrifice a portion of each.

You have to have some sort of balance.

The Greeks said equilibrium. But whereas you can quite nicely balance a pound of butter against a pound of cheese, it is quite another matter to balance a rose and a ruby. Still more difficult is it to put male man in one scale and female woman in the other, and equilibrate that little pair of opposites.

Unless, of course, you abstract them. It's easy enough to balance a citizen against a citizeness, a Christian against a Christian, a spirit against a spirit, or a soul against a soul. There's a formula for each case. Liberty, Equality, Fraternity, etc., etc.

But the moment you put young Tom in one scale, and young Kate in the other: why, not God Himself has succeeded as yet in striking a nice level balance. Probably doesn't intend to, ever.

Probably it's one of the things that are most fascinating because they are *nearly* possible, yet absolutely impossible.

How can I equilibrate myself with my black cow Susan? I call her daily at six o'clock. And sometimes she comes. But sometimes, again, she doesn't, and I have to hunt her away among the timber. Possibly she is lying peacefully in cowy inertia, like a black Hindu statue, among the oak-scrub. Then she rises with a sighing heave. My calling was a mere nothing against the black stillness of her cowy passivity.

Or possibly she is away down in the bottom corner, lowing *sotto voce* and blindly to some far-off, inaccessible bull. Then when I call at her, and approach, she screws round her tail and flings her sharp, elastic haunch in the air with a kick and a flick, and plunges off like a buck rabbit, or like a black demon among the pine trees, her udder swinging like a chime of bells. Or possibly the coyotes have been howling in the night along the top fence. And then I call in vain. It's a question of saddling a horse and sifting the bottom timber. And there at last the horse suddenly winces, starts: and with a certain pang of fear I too catch sight of something black and motionless and alive, and terribly silent, among the tree-trunks. It is Susan, her ears apart, standing like some spider suspended motionless by a thread, from the web of the eternal silence. The strange faculty she has, cow-given, of becoming a suspended ghost, hidden in the very crevices of the atmosphere! It is something in her *will*. And then, she doesn't know me. If I am afoot, she knows my voice, but not the advancing me, in a blue shirt and cord trousers. She waits, suspended by the thread, till I come close. Then she reaches forward her nose, to smell. She smells my hand: gives a little snort, exhaling her breath, with a kind of contempt, turns, and ambles up towards the homestead, perfectly assured. If I am on horse-back, although she knows the grey horse perfectly well, at the same time she *doesn't* know what it is. She waits till the wicked Azul, who is a born cow-punching pony, advances mischievously at her. Then round she swings, as if on the blast of some sudden wind, and with her ears back, her head rather down, her black back curved, up she goes, through the timber, with surprising, swimming swiftness. And the Azul, snorting with jolly mischief, dashes after her, and when she is safely in her milking place, still she watches with her great black eyes as I dismount. And she has to smell my hand before the cowy peace of being milked enters her blood. Till then, there is something *roaring* in the chaos of her universe. When her cowy peace comes, then her universe is silent, and like the sea with an even tide, without sail or smoke: nothing.

That is Susan, my black cow.

And how am I going to equilibrate myself with her? Or even, if you prefer the word, to get in harmony with her?

Equilibrium? Harmony? with that black blossom? Try it!

She doesn't even know me. If I put on a pair of white trousers, she wheels away as if the devil was on her back. I have to go behind her, talk to her, stroke her, and let her smell my hand; and smell the white trousers. She doesn't know that I am a gentleman on two feet. Not she. Something mysterious happens in her blood and her being, when she smells me and my nice white trousers.

Yet she knows me, too. She likes to linger, while one talks to her. She knows quite well she makes me mad when she swings her tail in my face. So sometimes she swings it, just on purpose: and looks at me out of the black corner of her great, pure-black eye, when I yell at her. And when I find her, away down the timber, when she is a ghost, and lost to the world, like a spider dangling in the void of chaos, then she is relieved. She comes to, out of a sort of trance, and is relieved, trotting up home with a queer, jerky cowy gladness. But she is never *really* glad, as the horses are. There is always a certain untouched chaos in her.

Where she is when she's *in* the trance, heaven only knows.

That's Susan! I have a certain relationship to her. But that she and I are in equilibrium or in harmony, I would never guarantee while the word stands. As for her individuality being in balance with mine, one can only feel the great blank of the gulf.

Yet a relationship there is. She knows my touch and she goes very still and peaceful, being milked. I, too, I know her smell and her warmth and her feel. And I share some of her cowy silence, when I milk her. There *is* a sort of relation between us. And this relation is part of the mystery of love: the individuality on each side, mine and Susan's, suspended in the relationship.

> *Oh gentlemen, hark to my hymn!*
> *To be a primrose is my whim*
> *Upon the floor,*
> *And nothing more.*

One understands Wordsworth and the primrose. Wordsworth gathered it into his own bosom and made it part of his own nature. "I, William, am also a yellow primrose blossoming on a bank." This, we must assert, is an impertinence on William's part. He ousts the primrose from its own individuality. He doesn't allow it to call its soul its own. It must be identical with *his* soul. Because, of course, by begging the question, there is but One Soul in the universe.

This is bunk. A primrose has its own peculiar primrosy identity, and all the overselling in the world won't melt it into a Williamish oneness. Neither will the yokel's remarking: "Nay, boy, that's nothing. It's only a primrose!"—turn the primrose into nothing. The primrose will neither be assimilated nor annihilated, and Boundless Love breaks on the rock of one more flower. It has its own individuality, which it opens with lovely naïveté to sky and wind and William and yokel, bee and beetle alike. It *is* itself. But its very floweriness is a kind of communion with all things: the love unison.

You see it is not so easy even for a poet to equilibrate himself even with a mere primrose. He didn't leave it with a soul of its own. It had to have his soul. And nature had to be sweet and pure, Williamish. Sweet-Williamish at that!

And we must always beware of romance: of people who love nature, or flowers, or dogs, or babies, or pure adventure. It means they are getting into a love-swing where everything is easy and nothing opposes their egoism. Nature, babies, dogs are *so* lovable, because they can't answer back.

A man isn't going to spread his own ego over a woman, as he has done over nature and primroses, and dogs, or horses, or babies, or "the people," or the proletariat or the poor-and-needy.

Man is an individual, and woman is an individual. Which sounds easy.

But it's not as easy as it seems. These two individuals are as different as chalk and cheese.

As subjects, men and women may be equal.

But as objects, it's another pair of shoes. Where, I ask you, is the equality between an arrow and a horseshoe? or a serpent and a squash-blossom? Find me the equation that equates the cock and the hen.

You can't.

As inhabitants of my backyard, as loyal subjects of my *rancho*, they, the cock and the hen, are equal. When he gets wheat, she gets wheat. When sour milk is put out, it is as much for him as for her. She is just as free to go where she likes as he is. And if she likes to crow at sunrise, she may. There is no law against it. And he can lay an egg, if the fit takes him. Absolutely nothing forbids.

Isn't that equality? If it isn't, what is?

Even then, they're two very different objects.

As equals, they are just a couple of barnyard fowls, clucking! generalized!

But dear me, when he comes prancing up with his red beard shaking, and his eye gleaming, and she comes slowly pottering after, with her nose to the ground, they're two very different objects. You never think of equality: or of inequality, for that matter. They're a cock and a hen, and you accept them as such.

You don't think of them as equals, or as unequals. But you think of them *together.*

Wherein, then, lies the togetherness?

Would you call it love?

I wouldn't.

Their two egos are absolutely separate. He's a cock, she's a hen. He never thinks for a moment that he is a hen like herself. I never hear anything in her squawk which would seem to say: *"Aren't I a fowl as much as you are, brute!"*

There's a cock and there's the hen, and their two egos, or individualities, seem to stay apart without friction. They never coo at one another, nor hold each other's hand. I never see her sitting on his lap and being petted. True, sometimes he calls for her to come and eat a titbit. And sometimes he dashes at her and walks over her for a moment. She doesn't seem to mind. I never hear her squawking: *"Don't you think you can walk over me!"*

Yet she's by no means downtrodden. She's just herself, and seems to have a good time: and she doesn't like it if he's missing.

So there is this peculiar togetherness about them. You can't call it love. It would be too ridiculous.

What then?

As far as I can see, it is desire. And the desire has a fluctuating intensity, but it is always there. His desire is always towards her, even when he has absolutely forgotten her. And by the way she puts her feet down, I can see she always walks in her plumes of desirableness, even when she's going broody.

The mystery about her, is her strange undying desirableness. You can see it in every step she takes. She is desirable. And this is the breath of her life.

It is the same with Susan. The queer cowy mystery of her is her changeless cowy desirableness. She is far, alas, from any bull. She never even remotely dreams of a bull, save at rare and brief periods. Yet her whole being and motion is that of being desirable: or else fractious. It seems to unite her with the very air, and the plants and trees. Even to the sky and the trees and the grass and the running stream, she is subtly, delicately and *purely* desirable, in cowy desirability. It is her cowy mystery. Then her fractiousness is the fireworks of her desirableness.

To me she is fractious and tiresome. Yet the subtle desirableness is in her, for me. As it is in a brown hen, or even a sow. It is her sex, no doubt: but so subtle as to have nothing to do with function. It is a mystery, like a delicate flame. It would be false to call it love, because love complicates the ego. The ego is always concerned in love. But in the frail, subtle desirousness of the true male, towards everything female, and the equally frail, indescribable desirability of every female for every male, lies the real clue to the equating, or the *relating*, of things which otherwise are incommensurable.

And this, this desire, is the reality which is inside love. The ego itself plays a false part in it. The individual is like a deep pool, or tarn, in the mountains, fed from beneath by unseen springs, and having no obvious inlet or outlet. The springs which feed the individual at the depths are sources of power, power from the unknown. But it is not until the stream of desire overflows and goes running downhill into the open world, that the individual has his further, secondary existence.

Now we have imagined love to be something absolute and personal. It is neither. In its essence, love is no more than the stream of clear and unmuddied, subtle desire which flows from person to person, creature to creature, thing to thing. The moment this stream of delicate but potent desire dries up, the love has dried up, and the joy of life has dried up. It's no good trying to turn on the tap. Desire is either flowing, or gone, and the love with it, and the life too.

This subtle streaming of desire is beyond the control of the ego. The ego says: "This is *my* love, to do as I like with! This is *my* desire, given me for my own pleasure."

But the ego deceives itself. The individual cannot possess the love which he himself feels. Neither should he be entirely possessed by it. Neither man nor woman should sacrifice individuality to love, nor love to individuality.

If we lose desire out of our life, we become empty vessels. But if we break our own integrity, we become a squalid mess, like a jar of honey dropped and smashed.

The individual has nothing, really, to do with love. That is, his individuality hasn't. Out of the deep silence of his individuality runs the stream of desire, into the open squash-blossom of the world. And the stream of desire may meet and mingle with the stream from a woman. But it is never *himself* that meets and mingles with *herself*: any more than two lakes, whose waters meet to make one river, in the distance, meet in themselves.

The two individuals stay apart, for ever and ever. But the two streams of desire, like the Blue Nile and the White Nile, from the mountains one and from the low hot lake the other, meet and at length mix their strange and alien waters, to make a Nilus Flux.

See then the childish mistake we have made, about love. We have *insisted* that the two individualities should "fit." We have insisted that the "love" between man and woman must be "perfect." What on earth that means, is a mystery. What would a perfect Nilus Flux be?—one that never overflowed its banks? or one that always overflowed its banks? or one that has exactly the same overflow every year, to a hair's-breadth?

My dear, it is absurd. Perfect love is an absurdity.

Perfect love, I suppose, means that a married man and woman never contradict one another, and that they both of them always feel the same thing at the same moment, and kiss one another on the strength of it. What blarney! It means, I suppose, that they are absolutely intimate: this precious intimacy that lovers insist on. They tell each other *everything*: and if she puts on chiffon knickers, he ties the strings for her: and if he blows his nose, she holds the hanky.

Pfui! Is anything so loathsome as intimacy, especially the married sort, or the sort that lovers indulge in!

It's a mistake and ends in disaster. Why? Because the individualities of men and women are incommensurable, and they will no more meet than the mountains of Abyssinia will meet with Lake Victoria Nyanza. It is far more important to keep them distinct than to join them. If they are to join, they will join in the third land where the two streams of desire meet.

Of course, as citizen and citizeness, as two persons, even as two spirits, man and woman can be equal and intimate. But this is their outer, more general or common selves. The individual man himself, and the individual woman herself, this is another pair of shoes.

By turning ourselves into integers: every man to himself and every woman to herself a Number One; an infinite number of Number Ones; we have destroyed ourselves as desirous or desirable individuals, and broken the inward sources of our power, and flooded all mankind into one dreary marsh where the rivers of desire lie dead with everything else, except a stagnant unity.

It is a pity of pities women have learned to think like men. Our education goes on and on, on and on, making the sexes alike, destroying the original individuality of the blood, to substitute for it this dreary individuality of the ego, the Number One. Out of the ego streams neither Blue Nile nor White Nile. The infinite number of little human egos makes a mosquito marsh, where nothing happens except buzzing and biting, ooze and degeneration.

And they call this marsh, with its poisonous will-o'-the-wisps, and its clouds of mosquitoes, *democracy*, and the reign of love!

You can have it.

I am a man, and the Mountains of Abyssinia, and my Blue Nile flows towards the desert. There should be a woman somewhere far South, like a great lake, sending forth her White Nile towards the desert, too; and the rivers will meet among the Slopes of the World, somewhere.

But alas, every woman I've ever met spends her time saying she's as good as any man, if not better, and she can beat him at his own game. So

Lake Victoria Nyanza gets up on end, and declares it's the Mountains of Abyssinia, and the Mountains of Abyssinia fall flat and cry: *"You're all that and more, my dear!"*—and between them, you're bogged.

I give it up.

But at any rate it's nice to know *what's* wrong, since wrong it is.

If we were men, if we were women, our individualities would be lone and a bit mysterious, like tarns, and fed with power, male power, female power, from underneath, invisibly. And from us the streams of desire would flow out in the eternal glimmering adventure, to meet in some unknown desert.

But don't, dear, darling reader, when I say "desire," immediately conclude that I mean a jungleful of rampaging Don Juans. When I say that a woman should be eternally desirable, *don't* say that I mean every man should want to sleep with her, the instant he sets eyes on her.

On the contrary, Don Juan was only Don Juan because he *had* no real desire. He had broken his own integrity, and was a mess to start with. No stream of desire, with a course of its own, flowed from him. He was a marsh in himself. He mashed and trampled everything up, and desired no woman, so he ran after every one of them, with an itch instead of a steady flame. And tortured by his own *itch*, he inflamed his itch more and more. That's Don Juan, the man who *couldn't* desire a woman. He shouldn't have tried. He should have gone into a monastery at fifteen.

Desire is a living stream. If we gave free rein, or a free course, to our living flow of desire, we shouldn't go far wrong. It's quite different from giving a free rein to an itching, prurient imagination.

The living stream of sexual desire itself does not often, in any man, find its object, its confluent, the stream of desire in a woman into which it can flow. The two streams flow together, spontaneously, not often, in the life of any man or woman. Mostly, men and women alike rush into a sort of prostitution, because our idiotic civilization has never learned to hold in reverence the true desire-stream. We force our desire from our ego: and this is deadly.

Desire itself is a pure thing, like sunshine, or fire, or rain. It is desire that makes the whole world living to me, keeps me in the flow connected. It is my flow of desire that makes me move as the birds and animals move through the sunshine and the night, in a kind of accomplished innocence, not shut outside of the natural paradise. For life is a kind of Paradise, even to my horse Azul, though he doesn't get his own way in it, by any means, and is sometimes in a real temper about it. Sometimes he even gets a bellyache, with wet alfalfa. But even the bellyache is part of the natural paradise. Not like human *ennui*.

So a man can go forth in desire, even to the primroses. But let him refrain from falling all over the poor blossom, as William did. Or trying to incorporate it in his own ego, which is a sort of lust.

Everything that exists, even a stone, has two sides to its nature. It fiercely maintains its own individuality, its own solidity. And it reaches forth from itself in the subtlest flow of desire.

It fiercely resists all inroads. At the same time it sinks down in the curious weight, or flow, of that desire which we call gravitation. And imperceptibly, through the course of the ages, it flows into delicate combination with the air and sun and rain.

At one time, men worshipped stones: symbolically, no doubt, because of their mysterious durability, their power of hardness, resistance, their strength of remaining unchanged. Yet even then, worshipping man did not rest till he had erected the stone into a pillar, a menhir, symbol of the eternal desire, as the phallus itself is but a symbol.

And we, men and women, are the same as stones: the powerful resistance and cohesiveness of our individuality is countered by the mysterious flow of desire, from us and towards us.

It is the same with the worlds, the stars, the suns. All is alive, in its own degree. And the centripetal force of spinning earth is the force of earth's individuality: and the centrifugal force is the force of desire. Earth's immense centripetal energy, almost passion, balanced against her furious centrifugal force, holds her suspended between her moon and her sun, in a dynamic equilibrium.

So instead of the Greek: *Know thyself!* we shall have to say to every man: *"Be Thyself! Be Desirous!"*—and to every woman: *"Be Thyself! Be Desirable!"*

Be Thyself! does not mean *Assert thy ego!* It means, be true to your own integrity, as man, as woman: let your heart stay open, to receive the mysterious inflow of power from the unknown: know that the power comes to you from beyond, it is not generated by your own will: therefore all the time, be watchful, and reverential towards the mysterious coming of power into you.

Be Thyself! is the grand cry of individualism. But individualism makes the mistake of considering an individual as a fixed entity: a little windmill that spins without shifting ground or changing its own nature. And this is nonsense. When power enters us, it does not just move us mechanically. It changes us. When the unseen wind blows, it blows upon us, and through us. It carries us like a ship on a sea. And it roars to flame in us, like a draught in a fierce fire. Or like a dandelion in flower.

I am myself, and I remain myself only by the grace of the powers that enter me, from the unseen, and make me forever newly myself.

And I am myself, also, by the grace of the desire that flows from me and consummates me with the other unknown, the invisible, tangible creation.

The powers that enter me fluctuate and ebb. And the desire that goes forth from me waxes and wanes. Sometimes it is weak, and I am almost isolated. Sometimes it is strong, and I am almost carried away.

But supposing the cult of Individualism, Liberty, Freedom, and so forth, has landed me in the state of egoism, the state so prettily and nauseously described by Henley in his *Invictus*:

> *It matters not how strait the gate,*
> *How charged with punishment the scroll:*
> *I am the master of my fate!*
> *I am the captain of my soul!*

As a matter of fact, it is the slave's bravado! The modern slave is he who does not receive his powers from the unseen, and give reverence, but who thinks he is his own little boss. Only a slave would take the trouble to shout: *"I am free!"* That is to say, to shout it in the face of the open heavens. In the face of men, and their institutions and prisons, Yes-yes! But in the face of the open heavens I would be ashamed to talk about freedom. I have no life, no real power, unless it will come to me. And I accomplish nothing, not even my own fulfilled existence, unless I go forth, delicately, desirous, and find the mating of my desire; even if it be only the sky itself, and trees, and the cow Susan, and the inexpressible consolation of a statue of an Egyptian Pharaoh, or the Old Testament, or even three rubies. These answer my desire with fulfillment. What bunk then to talk about being master of my fate! when my fate depends upon these things:—not to mention the unseen reality that sends strength, or life, into me, without which I am a gourd rattle.

Love and Grasping

Chögyam Trungpa

There is a vast store of energy which is not centered, which is not ego's
energy at all. It is this energy which is the centerless dance of phenomena,
the universe interpenetrating and making love to itself. It has two characteristics: a fire quality of warmth and a tendency to flow in a particular
pattern, in the same way in which fire contains a spark as well as the air
which directs the spark. And this energy is always on-going, whether or
not it is seen through the confused filter of ego. It cannot be destroyed or
interrupted at all. It is like the ever-burning sun.

But when the heat is filtered through ego, it becomes stagnant,
because we ignore the basic ground, refuse to see the vast space in which
this energy occurs. Then the energy cannot flow freely in the open space
shared with the object of passion. Instead it is solidified, narrowed and
directed by the central headquarters of ego to move outward in order to
draw the object of passion into its territory. We extend our tentacles
and try to fix our relationship. This attempt to cling to the situation makes
the communication process superficial. We just touch another person's
surface and get stuck there, never experiencing his whole being. We are
blinded by our clinging. The object of passion, instead of being bathed in
the intense warmth of free passion, feels oppressed by the stifling heat of
neurotic passion.

Free passion is radiation without a radiator, a fluid, pervasive warmth
that flows effortlessly. It is not destructive because it is a balanced state of
being and highly intelligent. By opening, by dropping our self-conscious

grasping, we see not only the surface of an object, but we see the whole way through. We appreciate not in terms of sensational qualities alone, but we see in terms of whole qualities, which are pure gold. We are not overwhelmed by the exterior, but seeing the exterior simultaneously puts us through to the interior. So we reach the heart of the situation and, if this is a meeting of two people, the relationship is very inspiring because we do not see the other person purely in terms of physical attraction or habitual patterns. We see the inside as well as the outside.

This whole-way-through communication might produce a problem. Suppose you see right through someone and that person does not want you to see right through and becomes horrified with you and runs away. Then what to do? You have made your communication completely and thoroughly. If that person runs away from you, that is his way of communicating with you. You would not investigate further. If you did pursue and chase him, then sooner or later you would become a demon from that person's point of view. You see right through his body and he has juicy fat and meat that you would like to eat up, so you seem like a vampire to him. And the more you try to pursue the other person, the more you fail. Perhaps you looked through too sharply with your desire, perhaps you were too penetrating. Possessing beautiful keen eyes, penetrating passion and intelligence, you abused your talent, played with it. It is quite natural with people, if they possess some particular power or gifted energy, to abuse this quality, to misuse it by trying to penetrate every corner. Something quite obviously is lacking in such an approach—a sense of humor. If you try to push things too far, it means you do not feel the area properly; you only feel your relationship to the area. What is wrong is that you do not see all sides of the situation and therefore miss the humorous and ironical aspect.

Sometimes people run away from you because they want to play a game with you. They do not want a straight, honest involvement with you, they want to play. But if they have a sense of humor and you do not, you become demonic. This is where *lalita*, the dance, comes in. You dance with reality, dance with apparent phenomena. When you want something very badly you do not extend your eye and hand automatically; you just admire. Instead of impulsively making a move from your side, you allow a move from the other side, which is learning to dance with the situation. You do not have to create the whole situation; you just watch it, work with it and learn to dance with it. So then it does not become your creation, but rather a mutual dance.

On Love: Conditional and Unconditional*

John Welwood

At the very heart of our experience of being human, each of us has an intuitive sense of the value of unconditional love. We discover the greatest joy in loving when we can suspend judgments and open fully to the vivid reality of another's being. And we usually feel most loved when others recognize and respond to us wholeheartedly. Unconditional love has tremendous power, activating a larger energy which connects us with the vastness and profundity of what it is to be human. This is the energy of the heart.

We often experience glimpses of unconditional love most vividly in beginnings and endings—at birth, at death, or when first opening to another being, in love. At these times we feel moved and inspired by the very presence of another person's existence. Tough, frozen places inside us begin to melt and soften as the circulation of love warms us like spring sun. Yet soon enough, especially in intimate relationships, we come up against inner fears, restraints, or cautions about letting our love flow so freely. Will we get swept away? Can we let ourselves feel this open? Will we get hurt? Can we trust this person? Will we be able to get our needs met in this relationship? Can we live with those things that irritate us in the other? These cautions lead us to place conditions on our openness: "I can only be this open and vulnerable with you *if*. . . I get my needs met; you love me as much as I love you; you don't hurt me; etc."

*Adapted from a talk presented in San Francisco, September 1983.

This pull between loving unconditionally and loving with conditions heightens the tension between two different sides of our nature—the personal wants and needs of our conditioned self and the unconditional openness of the heart. Yet this very tension between conditional and unconditional love, if clearly seen and worked with, can actually help us learn to love more fully. The friction between these two sides of our nature can ignite a refining fire that awakens the heart to the real challenge, the outrageous risk, and the tremendous gift of human love.

UNCONDITIONAL LOVE

The expression of unconditional love follows the movements of the heart, which is its source. We could define "heart" as that "part" of us where we are most tender and open to the world around us, where we can let others in and feel moved by them, as well as reach outside ourselves to contact them more fully. The unconditional love that springs from the heart has both a receptive side—appreciating others as they are and letting them touch us—and an active side—going out to meet, touch, and make contact, what the existentialists call "being-with."

It is the heart's nature to want to circulate love freely back and forth, without putting limiting conditions on that exchange. The heart looks right past things that may offend our personal tastes, often rejoicing in another's being despite all our reasonable intentions to maintain a safe distance, play it cool, or break off contact if a relationship has become too painful. Love in its deepest essence knows nothing of conditions and is quite unreasonable. Once the heart has opened and we have been deeply touched by another person, we will most likely feel affected by that person for the rest of our lives, no matter what form the relationship may take. Unconditional love has its reasons which reason cannot know.

CONDITIONAL LOVE

Yet, insofar as we are not just pure heart, but also have conditioned likes and dislikes, certain conditions always determine the extent of our involvement with another person. This is inevitable. As soon as we consider the *form* of relationship we want with someone, we are in the realm of conditions. Because we are of this earth, we exist within certain forms and structures (body, temperament, personality characteristics, emotional needs, likes and dislikes, sexual preferences, styles of communication, life-styles, beliefs and values) that fit more or less well with someone else's structures.

Conditional love is a feeling of pleasure and attraction based on how fully someone matches our needs, desires, and personal considerations. It is a response to a person's looks, style, personal presence, emotional support—what he or she does for us. It is not something bad, but it is a lesser form of love, in that it can be negated by a reversal of the conditions under which it formed. If someone we love starts acting in ways we don't like, we may not like him as much anymore. Conditional liking inevitably gives way to opposite feelings of fear, rage, resistance, or hatred when our structures rub up against another person's structures. Yet beyond both conditional yes and conditional no lies the larger unconditional yes of the heart.

CONFUSING THE TWO ORDERS OF LOVE

Attraction to another person is often most intense when the two orders of love are in accord: this person not only touches our heart, but also fulfills certain conditions for what we want from an intimate partner. On the other hand, it is quite confusing when these two orders do not mesh. Perhaps this person meets our conditions, yet somehow does not move us very deeply. Or else he or she touches our heart, so that we want to say yes, while our personal considerations and criteria lead us to say no to a committed relationship. To clear up some of the confusions in relationships, we need to distinguish between these two orders of love.

One common mistake is to try to impose our conditional no on the larger yes of the heart. For instance, perhaps we decide to end a relationship because it is impossible to get certain essential needs met. Our heart, nonetheless, whose nature is to say yes, may want to keep right on loving the other person just the same. Trying to cut off the love that is still flowing toward the other person can do damage to us by constricting the very source of joy and aliveness inside us.

Every time we try to close our heart to someone we love, even in times of separation, we only create greater pain for ourselves and make it harder to open up again the next time we fall in love. In fact, it may not actually be possible to close the heart. What we *can* do is to *close off* the heart, by building a solid wall around it. The danger here lies in closing ourselves off from people in general and closing ourselves *in*. Damming up the natural outflow of the heart leaves us with a pool of stagnant energy that may breed psychological dis-ease. I am by no means suggesting that we should stay in a relationship that doesn't work just because we may feel unconditional love toward the other person. We may even have to break off contact and communication with someone in order to recover from the pain of a relationship. But this does not mean that we have to close off the heart. Even if we feel hatred toward an ex-lover, it is helpful to acknowledge that we can only feel this way because of the heart's openness, because we feel so vulnerable to this person. Then our feelings of hatred do not have to become solid, frozen into our character, but can eventually pass without turning into a weapon or doing real harm.

Another common way of confusing the two orders of love is to try to impose the yes of the heart on the no of our personal considerations. A common misconception of unconditional love is that it requires putting up with everything someone does. A recent article in a scientific bulletin illustrated this misconception when it stated, "Unconditional love and support can be damaging to the development of a child's self-esteem. . . . Most parents are too concerned with making life easy for their children."[1] The confusion here lies in equating unconditional love with uncritical praise, permissiveness, or indulgence of another's actions.

Imagining that we should tolerate unconditionally that which is conditioned—another's personality, actions, or life-style—is a confusion that often has painful consequences. Unconditional love does not mean having to like something we in fact dislike or saying yes when we need to say no. Unconditional love arises from an entirely different place in us than conditional like and dislike, attraction and resistance. It is a being-to-being acknowledgment. And it responds to that which is itself unconditional—the intrinsic goodness of other people's tender, open hearts, beneath all their defenses and pretenses. Arising from our own basic goodness,[2] unconditional love resonates with and reveals unconditional goodness in others as well. The goodness of the human heart, which is born tender, responsive, and eager to reach out and touch the life around us, is unconditional in that it is not something we have to achieve. It simply *is*.

The parent-child relationship provides our first experience of the harmful ways in which conditional and unconditional love get mixed up. Although most parents originally feel a vast, choiceless love for their newborn child, they eventually manage to place conditions on their love, using it as a way of controlling the child, turning it into a reward for desired behaviors. The result is that as children we rarely grow up feeling loved for ourselves, just as we are. We internalize the conditions our parents put on their love, and this internalized parent (the "superego" or "inner critic") often rules our lives. We keep trying to please it, while it in turn continually judges us as never good enough. So we start to love ourselves conditionally as well. We think we have to earn love, as a reward for being good. We only like ourselves *if*—if we live up to some standard, if we prove ourselves, if we are a good boy or girl, a good achiever, a good lover, etc. We come to distrust that our basic nature is intrinsically good or that we could simply be lovable just for being ourselves. Internalizing the restrictions placed on love in our family, we create an elaborate system of dams, checks and blockages, armoring and tensions in the body that constrict the free flow of love. And so we perpetuate the pain and confusion that springs from putting conditions on the love that wants to flow freely from the heart.

Nonetheless, underneath these distortions of love, and all the disappointment, anger, rebellion, or hatred that may arise between parents and children, most of us can find deep down in this connection a larger, choiceless love that has no why or wherefore—it simply is, and it never entirely disappears, no matter what happens. No matter how their love gets distorted, parents and children remain vulnerable to each other. Despite themselves, they can never entirely cut off the unconditional openness of their hearts toward each other.

TRUSTING IN THE GOODNESS OF THE HEART

As a spontaneous expression of the heart, unconditional love is naturally available to everyone, especially in the early stages of a relationship. Yet it often becomes obscured by a couple's struggles to see if they can fit, communicate, meet each other's needs, or create a working partnership. It may also get buried beneath preoccupation with hassles of everyday life, family responsibilities, and work demands. How can we stay in touch with the revitalizing presence of unconditional love in an ongoing relationship?

The most obvious answer is to learn to trust in the heart. Yet how do we do this? We need an actual way to develop this trust, not as an article of belief or hope, but as a living experience.

The best training I have found for developing this trust is mindfulness meditation, which comes from the Buddhist tradition. The Buddhist term for unconditional love is *maitri*, which means all-encompassing warmth and friendliness toward one's own experience. *Maitri* develops gradually but very concretely through the practice of mindfulness and awareness. Mindfulness involves just sitting and being in the moment, without doing anything, without trying to concentrate on anything, think good thoughts, or even get rid of thoughts. While letting thoughts and feelings arise and pass away, the practice is to keep returning attention to the breath, which is a literal expression of well-being and presence even in the midst of the most unsettling states of mind. Through this practice, we can gradually realize that, underneath all our confusions, we are basically good, simply because we are present, awake, responsive to life, and facing the world with a tender heart. In glimpsing this basic goodness, we can begin to let ourselves be because we do not have to try to *prove* that we are good.

The process of discovering basic goodness can be likened to clarifying muddy water—an ancient metaphor from the Taoist and Buddhist traditions. The basic nature of water is essentially pure and clear, though its turbulence often stirs up mud. Our minds are also like this, essentially clear and open, but muddied with the turbulence of conflicting thoughts and feelings. If we want to clarify the water, what should we do? What else but let the water sit? Not trusting our own basic goodness is like not trusting that water is essentially pure and that mud settles out by itself. In trying to prove that we are good, we struggle against the dirt, but that only stirs up more mud. Taking up self-improvement programs out of self-doubt is like adding bleach to the water. By contrast, relaxing into the basic goodness we begin to feel when we just let ourselves be awakens the natural warmth of the heart.

As this warmth of the heart radiates outward, it soon meets its first challenge: the tight, constricted, closed-off parts of ourselves and others. Although we may be tempted to fight against these tight places in a struggle to get rid of them, this only stirs up more mud. Even if we could get rid of the mud, we would lose many of the essential minerals and nutrients it contains. What allows the dirt to settle, so that the basic goodness hidden within neurotic patterns can emerge, is the attitude of *maitri*—unconditionally opening to and "being-with" those parts of ourselves that seem most unlovable (our fear, anger, self-doubt, etc.).

These parts of us that give us the most trouble are like children in need of our attention, whom we have cut off from our unconditional love. We say to ourselves, in effect, "I can only love me *if* I don't have this fear, etc." However, any part of us that is cut off from our love eventually becomes sick, for it is the circulation of the heart's energy that keeps us healthy. Circulation is an essential principle of health throughout the natural world, as we can see in the constant cycling and flow of water, which is the cradle of life and the predominant element in the human body. To remain clean and life-giving, it must circulate, rising to the heavens from the ocean, then falling on the mountains and rushing in clear streams back to the sea. The sea itself circulates around the globe, its ebb and flow renewing the shores of the earth it touches. The circulation of blood in the body removes toxins and brings new life in the form of oxygen to the cells. Eastern medicine emphasizes a subtle stream of life energy—sometimes called *ch'i* or *prana*—whose circulation throughout the body and between body and world maintains physical health.

Psychologically, it is the circulation of unconditional love that keeps us healthy. Every child intuitively knows this. As children internalize the conditions placed on love by their parents and the world around them, withholding love from certain parts of themselves, these parts get cut off from the stream of life-enhancing awareness and caring. In mythological terms, the parts that are cut off turn into dragons and demons. As Rilke writes, "Perhaps all the dragons in our lives are princesses who are only waiting to see us act, just once, with beauty and courage. Perhaps everything terrible is, in its deepest essence, something helpless that needs our love."[3] In certain spiritual traditions, the alchemy of turning dragons into princesses is called *transmutation*. The Tantric Buddhist tradition, for instance, considers every neurotic pattern to have an enlightened energy—some quality of basic goodness—locked up in it, just as muddy water already contains pure water within it.

Experiences in psychotherapy continually provide examples of this. For example, one client who suppressed her anger and took it out on herself found that when she could befriend this energy, it no longer had a nasty edge. It was more like a radiant fire or a sharp sword of discrimination which allowed her to penetrate through deception, hypocrisy, and muddled states of mind. Another client who always played the victim discovered that feeling sorry for himself was an indirect way of trying to care for himself and acknowledge his basic goodness. A third client discovered in her pattern of always trying to please people one of her greatest strengths: a tremendous sensitivity to others and a real devotion and concern for their well-being. Every neurotic pattern seems to have enlightened potential in it. That is why we do not have to throw out the dirt. Insofar as a therapist can bring caring attention to those places in their clients that are hurt or cut off, helping to awaken the basic goodness lying dormant within them, psychotherapy can be a genuine healing relationship.[4]

BREAKING OPEN THE HEART

Intimate relationships also offer a promise of healing, for they have potential to free up the flow of unconditional love to those parts of us that are wounded, cut off, or deprived of caring. However, the very promise of exchanging unconditional love often stirs up unrealistic hopes of realizing perfect love and union. Insofar as we are creatures of this earth, with all the limitations and imperfections that entails, human relationships can never completely or perfectly manifest the unconditional love we may know and feel in our heart. Because two people live in space and time, with different experiences, temperaments, timing and rhythms, likes and dislikes, they can never fully actualize absolute unconditional union in any conclusive, uninterrupted way.

In fact, the very vulnerability and openness lovers feel with each other also seems to intensify their conditioned needs, fears, and inner obstacles to free-flowing love. So, although intimacy awakens an old, deep longing to share unconditional love and perfect union, the conditions of our earthly natures conspire to frustrate its perfect expression and realization. We may experience moments, glimpses, waves of union with another, but they soon pass and leave us inescapably alone. We can never expect another person to provide all the love we might need.

The pain of this contradiction between the perfect love in our hearts and the obstacles to its realization in ongoing relationships often breaks the heart—open. As the Sufi master Hazrat Inayat Khan wrote, "The pain of love is the dynamite that breaks open the heart, even if it be as hard as a rock."[5] More precisely, the heart itself cannot break, or break open, in that its essential nature is already soft and receptive. What *can* actually break open is the wall around the heart, the defensive shield we have constructed to try to protect our soft spot. It seems that the only way to move through the disappointments of relationships without harming ourselves and others is actually to open up the heart *more* at the very moments we would most like to close it off. Just as dams in a stream accentuate the force of the water rushing against them, so the obstacles to perfect expression of love, both in ourselves and others, can actually help us feel the force of our love more strongly. By opening up the floodgates of the heart at this point, we prevent the resistances in the stream of love from blocking its flow and forming a stagnant swamp.

Seeing the obstacles to love, in ourselves and others, hurts, angers, and disappoints us. How can we open up the heart further at this point, when the pain we feel makes us want to close off behind an even more protected wall? In order to find an opening in the midst of this pain, it is important not to deny it or to be artificially "loving." This only pushes the hurt and anger deeper inside, where it often has harmful consequences. Instead, we have to start with where we are—which involves *being-with* our hurt or opening to our anger about not getting all our needs met and *letting that be*, without having to do something about it. This is *maitri*—warmth and caring for ourselves—in action. In opening to the pain of loving, we bleed, yet this bleeding itself can help awaken the heart, allowing energies in us to circulate that may have been coagulated.

So, in contacting what is most alive in us when we feel the obstacles to love—the rawness and tenderness of the "broken" heart—we actually open the heart wider. By opening our heart to our real feelings, without denial or manipulation, we are manifesting gentleness and caring toward ourselves. In this experience of *maitri*, we discover that we can in fact give to ourselves the unconditional love we most hunger for. The painful truth is that no one else can ever give us all that we need in just the way we want. When we use that pain to help us touch what is most tender and alive in us, we begin to wake up from the poverty of depending on others to the majesty and richness we carry inside.

Touching the depth of feeling in our heart also helps us see through others' imperfections, allowing us to touch their hearts more readily. Breaking open the heart awakens us to the mystery of love—that we can't help loving others, in spite of and including all the things we don't like about them, for no other reason than that they move and touch us. What we love, it seems, is not just their heart, but also their heart's struggle with all the obstacles in the way of its full, radiant expression. It's as though our heart wants to ally itself with their heart and lend them strength in their struggle to realize their unconditional goodness, beyond all their perceived shortcomings. In fact, if those we love were perfect embodiments of what we desire, they might not touch us so deeply. Their imperfection seems to give our love a purchase, a foothold, something to work on. The obstacles to love are what force our heart to break open, to stretch and expand to embrace all of what we are in our humanness. In this way, unconditional love becomes a deepening realization and an ongoing practice, beyond its initial spontaneous appearance in the first flash of falling in love.

This breaking open of the heart is the transmuting force in the alchemy of love that allows us to see the unconditional goodness of people in and through all the limitations of their conditioned self. It helps us to recover the beauty in the dragon and to realize how the unconditioned and conditioned sides of human nature are always intertwined, making up one whole cloth. The overflow of the broken-open heart starts as *maitri*, then radiates outward as compassion toward all other beings who have a tender heart, who hide their tenderness out of fear of being hurt, and who need our unconditional love to help awaken their hearts as well.

DISCUSSION

Q: Isn't what you are saying about unconditional love creating another set of expectations and ideals? Isn't this a trap?

A: That's a good point. Any time we have an image of what love should look like, we are in the realm of conditional love. Unconditional love means being in the present, being-with and letting be. Who knows what that will actually mean in practice, from moment to moment? We have to be willing to *not know* beforehand what form our love will take. If we make unconditional love into another ideal, we are striving to live up to an image in the mind. Then we cannot really be with another person freshly in the moment or let ourselves be. This is where meditation can be particularly helpful in relationships—in teaching us to drop our ideas about who we are and what we should be. Every idea we have about love is conditioned. Unconditional love arises from our unconditioned nature. Sometimes we can only contact this unconditional quality through the pain of giving up our expectations about how love should be. It's what we're left with when all our ideal images fall away: just being here and being real.

Q: How can you love someone unconditionally and still get angry with him? I don't understand this.

A: Anger is a way of saying no to something we don't like, just as conditional love is a way of saying yes to what we do like. Conditional love is a response to the pleasure others give us, whereas anger is a response to the pain we feel with them. Most of this pain comes from two people's differences rubbing up against each other. We feel hurt by the ways the other person's individuality or separateness excludes, ignores, intrudes upon, or negates us in various ways. Anger usually contains some intelligence, and is an integral part of being in relationship with someone who is different from us. It may point to those places where the other person is shutting us out, and where we would like to be able to communicate more fully.

Although anger is the opposite of conditional love, it does not negate or contradict unconditional love. It is a reminder of our openness and tender heart. We could not get so enraged with those we love unless we felt this larger vulnerability with them. To let ourselves be touched also involves letting ourselves be scraped, rubbed raw, and wounded. If we can allow the pain of anger to remind us of this tenderness, then it need not turn into a harmful weapon. If you can feel your rawness when your partner says, "Go to Hell," and keep your heart open even to your own angry feelings, then it's possible to make genuine contact through an angry exchange instead of just walking away or suppressing your rage. Even if you both wind up exploding at each other, this too can deepen your connection if it blasts open the shell around the heart as well as the frozen identities in which you're both stuck. In this way, the pain of anger calls up the larger power of the heart to reconcile the clash between two individuals' differences. If you can't fight with those you love, you may not be able to touch the full depths of love that are possible with them either. You may be holding on to a safe identity and be unwilling to risk yourself by acknowledging how much they really affect you.

The unconditional yes of the heart has plenty of room to accommodate both conditional yes and conditional no. The heart's yes in no way means that we should always be sweet and "loving." In fact, unless we feel free to say no in anger, we cannot say yes wholeheartedly because our suppressed nos will lurk in the background. They will cause us to close off in subtle, indirect ways that actually create much more distance between two people than honest anger would. When you keep your heart open in the midst of your anger, then anger can be a vehicle for communication.

Q: Your analogy of the purity of water reminded me of being struck as a new parent by the radiance of my daughter when she first came into the world. And even though a lot of mud got mixed in with that radiance over the years, I can still see that pure quality in her. When I first began doing therapy, I was working with severely disturbed patients from the back wards of mental hospitals. And the times I was most successful with them was when I could see a spark of that radiance still glowing in them, which had often been buried underneath the traumas in their lives. Sometimes it was just the tiniest glimmer. I learned to see that in my patients by first being a parent and seeing it in my child. Of course, there are plenty of times when I really hate what my daughter does.

A: And that's fine. That doesn't have to undermine your unconditional love for her at all. If you can let her feel your anger and let her get angry at you as well, you are teaching her about what it means to be a real person. Letting your child or any person have the whole range of his or her experience—that's perhaps the greatest gift you can give to others.

NOTES

[1] *Brain/Mind Bulletin*, vol. 9, no. 10, May 1984.
[2] For a fuller discussion of "basic goodness," see Trungpa (1983).
[3] Rilke (1984), p. 92.
[4] See Welwood (1983).
[5] Khan (1962), p. 164.

II. What Do Men and Women Really Want?

Introduction

It is difficult to talk about male and female today without getting involved in discussions of sexual politics, the history of centuries of male dominance, and the endless debate about whether the differences between the sexes are primarily cultural or biological. To say what it means to be a man or a woman is to risk attack from one or another sexual "constituency." Even the claim that men and women differ at all is a call to arms in certain camps.

Little is being written today that explores how men and women can be mutually helpful to each other in these times of difficult transitions. All too much of the recent writing on the sexes consists of diatribes by men and women against each other—which only perpetuates the age-old war. In putting together this section of the book, I have tried to sidestep issues of sexual politics to focus instead on the psychological and cosmic dimensions of masculine and feminine. These chapters explore basic life issues people face in being men or women as well as the interrelatedness of masculine and feminine both within and between individuals.

The Roszaks begin this section with a brief portrayal of the modern man/woman game, where both sexes, by trying to live up to an image of what they think they should be, reach a standoff inside themselves and with each other.

John Sanford's chapter is a concise exposition of the Jungian view of how the feminine side of a man (the anima) and the masculine side of a woman (the animus) are mutually projected on each other in a relationship. This kind of projection certainly plays a part in most experiences of falling in love, and the Jungian perspective helps us understand the illusions and perplexities that often arise between men and women. Yet the appealing simplicity of this explanation is also perhaps its potential problem, if it lulls us into thinking there is a simple explanation for the mysterious magnetism between the sexes.

In the next chapter, Sukie Colegrave summarizes one of the most comprehensive views of the cosmic interaction of masculine and feminine—the theory of yin and yang, which pervades every aspect of Chinese thought and culture. In viewing masculine and feminine as expressions of two larger principles that operate throughout all phenomena, this perspective immediately takes us out of the realm of sexual politics and twentieth-century chauvinisms. The differences between men and women are accounted for in terms of their varying proportions of yin and yang. Both sexes have access to both masculine and feminine principles operating inside them, although men generally have a larger proportion of yang energy, and women a larger proportion of yin. As an ancient Chinese medical text states, "As a male, man belongs to yang; as a female, woman belongs to yin. Yet both, male and female, are products of two primary elements, hence both qualities are contained in both sexes."[1] Notice that this text does not say, "Yang belongs to man," but rather, "Man belongs to yang." In other words, neither sex exclusively owns masculine or feminine energies; rather, each sex is primarily guided by one of these larger cosmic principles.

Colegrave describes the feminine principle in terms of relatedness, the masculine in terms of separateness and differentiation. The feminine is the principle of *connecting* with the larger, encompassing energies of life, while the masculine is the principle of *executing* focused activity. Masculine consciousness (whether in a man or a woman) enjoys studying discrete phenomena and ideas in their own right, while feminine consciousness (in a man or a woman) works with ideas in the context of personal experience, understanding the universal in and through the personal.

Colegrave also emphasizes the importance of distinguishing matriarchal consciousness—that diffuse awareness *preceding* careful distinctions and a clear sense of individuality—from a more highly developed feminine consciousness that *sees beyond* individual differences to larger patterns of connectedness. This distinction allows us to trace a certain dialectical interplay of masculine and feminine principles in history. Prehistoric societies, according to certain cultural anthropologists, were under strict matriarchal rule, symbolized by the Great Earth Mother, ancient goddess of fertility. Colegrave suggests that one of the functions of masculine consciousness is to break away from the enveloping grip of the Great Mother and to establish distinctions, boundaries, and self-consciousness. Once these distinctions have been made, feminine consciousness finds its voice in pointing out the larger relationships between the things that masculine consciousness has divided.

No doubt to ensure that they would not be dominated again by the matriarchal consciousness they broke away from, men institutionalized male dominance through a patriarchal system. Male privilege, analytical thinking, technology, and the exploitation of nature are manifestations of patriarchal consciousness still very much with us. Yet, in true dialectical form, this patriarchal consciousness has also led to the rise of a more refined feminine consciousness, especially in the last hundred years, when women have begun to step out of men's shadows and articulate their own perceptions of the world. This new feminine consciousness has also been calling forth a new consciousness from men, different from the old patriarchal mentality. (One instance is the new appreciation by many scientists of larger patterns of relatedness in the cosmos beyond the old Newtonian world-view.) While women were finding new strength in the sixties, men were beginning to soften their hard, macho facades to explore inner awareness, tenderness, and more colorful outer forms of expression than grey flannel and crewcuts. The word *androgyny* became current in the seventies to describe a more balanced development of yin and yang in both sexes.

In the eighties another shift in this dialectical interplay of masculine and feminine consciousness seems to be occurring. Feminism has become less militant, while men have begun to take a new look at what it means to be a man, beyond both the old machismo and the new androgyny. This is the issue that Robert Bly addresses in the next chapter. Bly resurrects an ancient image that has appeared in the art and mythology of many cultures: the wildman. "Wildness" here does not mean savagery (although Bly obscures this point by describing it as "primitive" and "instinctive"— terms which usually imply a backward direction). Rather, the wildman symbolizes a certain natural male intelligence, connected to the energies of the earth and the cosmos, deep within the consciousness of every man. Bly urges men to get back in touch with this wild man inside themselves, whose vigorous spirit has too often been broken by dreary social role-playing and meaningless work, or by mothers' injunctions to be a "nice boy."

In the next chapter, D. H. Lawrence describes a certain quality of the pure male spirit when it dares to express itself fully. It is an expression of man's essence to venture into the unknown and be willing above all to risk—primarily to risk his known self, his polished, secure self-image— in order to meet the challenge of uncharted reality, both inside himself and in the world around him. From Lawrence's perspective, the fundamental work of the man/woman relationship is not to get to "know" each other so much as to explore together the great unknown that their inter-action brings into view. In his view, "The sexual act is not for the deposit-ing of the seed. It is for leaping off into the unknown, as from a cliff's edge, like Sappho into the sea."[2]

To be able to take these risks and bring their full maleness and fe-maleness into their relations, Robert Stein stresses, men and women have to be initiated into adult manhood and womanhood. This involves sepa-rating from inner and outer parents. The uninitiated child within us makes demands on our partner that are left over from childhood. (And in our culture, where initiation rites are practically nonexistent, most couples get caught in some form of this parent-child dynamic.) If this situation goes unchecked, it eventually destroys the vital sexual balance between a man and a woman. Stein's article reinforces Bly's emphasis on the importance of the father-son connection, for it is often up to the father in our culture to help the son separate from his mother and become "his own man." The wild man is the opposite of the "momma's boy," just as the wild woman is the opposite of "daddy's little girl." One of the most valuable functions of psychotherapy is to help people make the necessary psychic separation from their parents and the compulsions of the inner child, so that they can realize genuine intimacy with others.

Lillian Rubin presents an extremely clear and intelligent portrait of the different struggles men and women face in making this separation, especially from their mothers. The difficulty men have with separating from their mothers, particularly in a society where the father-son bond has been weakened, sheds light on many of their fears of intimacy and female power in later life. Women's natural identification with their mothers helps explain their greater empathy and affinity for intimate communication, as well as their need to establish clear boundaries as separate individuals in relationships. Rubin's article adds to the case made by Bly, Stein, and Lawrence for the importance of initiation to help guide individuals through the crucial task of separation from parents. And in ascribing major differences between men and women to their different ways of dealing with separation and unity in childhood, she also provides an alternative to the insoluble "culture-versus-biology" debate.

In the next chapter Ruth Hoebel discusses certain painful conse-quences of the denial of the feminine. When a man denies his feminine qualities, he consequently needs women in order to feel whole in himself. But that arrangement gives a man his sense of individuality at the expense of the woman's individuality. Hoebel envisions a dawning of feminine genius as women increasingly discover and value their nature.

Eleanor Bertine has a somewhat subtler and more complex vision of the issue of individuality and relationship. She sees the development of

a woman's consciousness in three main stages. In the first stage she unconsciously acts from the "archetypal matrix of yin." Insofar as a woman
contains a large proportion of yin, the centripetal energy that holds things
together, she often keeps a relationship together through her ability to
serve, to complement and harmonize, and to tend the needs of the couple
as a whole. If a woman expresses her yin nature unconsciously and automatically, however, she often winds up playing the role of a man's anima,
finding her own identity primarily through her relation to him. Her yin
talents may be used to lure and bind a man to her, in the form of the
proverbial "feminine wiles."

In the next stage, she rebels against this secondary position and
discovers her power as a woman and her independence as an individual in
her own right. Having discovered her individuality and independence,
she can then explore the deep, archetypal qualities of femininity again,
this time without being enslaved by them. This third stage is that of the
"true eros woman," as distinct from the "anima woman" who serves as
a symbol and an object for man's ends. Whereas Hoebel sees women's
growth as a straight line proceeding from the archetypal feminine toward
greater independence and individuality, Bertine sees it as a more dialectical
process. In her view, the fully developed woman can accept and express
both her yin qualities of yielding and devotion, and the yang qualities of
clarity and independence garnered from her revolt against the role of
always pleasing men.

Bertine sees masculine consciousness as more attuned to the impersonal flow of energy between two people, and the feminine as more concerned with personal relationship, with the cohesion between the poles
that allows the current to flow. The alchemy that can happen between
men and women depends on their remaining two clearly distinct poles. If
women can stand clear and independent of men, while still preserving
their connection with their primal feminine roots, the integrity of the
poles can be maintained. Bertine's perspective is helpful because she
points out a pathway through the "theoretically irreconcilable conflict" so
many women experience today between their yielding yin qualities and
their often fierce desire for independence. What this path requires is
greater consciousness, often arrived at through the transformative heat of
the man/woman alchemical ferment. This article, originally presented as
a talk in 1947 and clearly ahead of its time, presents a remarkably balanced
view, not often expressed, of the challenges women face in relationships.

Finally, Anne Morrow Lindbergh beautifully describes the essential
role of solitude in helping a woman reconnect with the cosmic currents
that keep her wild female spirit alive. She sees solitude as an especially
powerful means of renewal for women, who often spend so much energy

nurturing others. Of course, just being alone in itself is not enough; a woman must use that time to reconnect with her own wild spirit, which can often go dry when she is too caught up in the world of relationships, work, and duty.

In the wake of the feminist revolt, both men and women are being challenged to discover what is most authentic in their different natures. We are in a time of great ferment, with men and women struggling hard with their own natures and with one another. These struggles are part of a larger journey we are making, which we can better appreciate by understanding its stages, not only for each individual, but also for human consciousness as a whole.

The three stages in a woman's development, as Bertine outlines them, strongly parallel certain stages that men today are going through as well. The unconscious anima woman seems to match the unconscious macho man. In the second stage, women's search for independence and strength is paralleled by men's exploration of their softer, gentler side. And finally, the fully developed woman who lives with "freedom, vision, and gay humorousness" because she is neither enslaved by nor fighting her feminine nature, would be matched by the fully developed male who neither apologizes for his power nor fears his own tenderness. As Bertine points out, very few women have reached this third stage where they can embrace and express both their power and their soft, yielding side. Many women today are still struggling to attain or prove their individuality and independence. In that stage, they often experience a great deal of anger and competitiveness with men and become suspicious of their softer feminine qualities. Women's attempts to reevaluate the old male/ female roles and realign the power between the sexes has led to much confusion and turmoil, yet it has been an important step. Perhaps at last we are moving toward the next step, in which men and women can come together again in love and mutual respect, from positions of equal power, without having to blame each other or apologize for who they are.

We are suffering from a lack of positive images of the genuine, powerful male and the genuine, powerful female, and of ways in which the two can mutually help each other. Among women, neither the seductress, the man-hater, nor the man-imitator is fully in touch with her real power. Among men, the same can be said for the Don Juan, the "hard-driver," and Bly's "soft male." Very few men today have progressed beyond macho attitudes, fully integrated their feminine side, and found a place of true power, where they are confident in their strength, and have no need to dominate or defend themselves against women.

Perhaps the images of the wild man and the wild woman can serve as a starting point for helping us recognize the real differences between the sexes, as well as the real strengths within each. It is important to realize that our deep male or female nature—the wild man and the wild woman inside us—is not a regression to something "primitive." Mythological prototypes of wild maleness and femaleness—such as Dionysus, Artemis, Siva, and Kali—are portrayed as highly conscious beings. Tibetan (Tantric) Buddhism has a tradition of what is called "crazy wisdom," which literally means "wisdom gone wild." In this tradition, wisdom must develop first, before it can "go wild," returning to a natural, primordial state of simplicity and freedom. In the Tantric tradition, wild feminine energy is symbolized by the wrathful/playful dakini, whose energetic dance has the liberating effect of cutting through all projections, fantasies, and intellectualized views of life. As one woman Buddhist describes this wild female energy:

Being a dynamic principle, the dakini is energy itself; a positive contact with her brings about a sense of freshness and magic. She becomes a guide and a consort who activates intuitive understanding and profound awareness. Rather than relating to her mate from a stance of poverty, Sleeping Beauty to be awakened by the prince, she is already awake and dancing and does not need to sap the energy of her consort to feel balanced. She can give and receive from the stance of wholeness and richness.[3]

This dynamic, awakening quality of wild feminine energy is rarely portrayed in our culture, especially as being at all friendly to men. We are more familiar with images of Artemis, the witch, or the Amazon, which portray a stage of women's independence that is unfriendly to men. Yet in the Tibetan tradition, the dakini is often one of man's or woman's greatest helpers on the path of enlightenment. She may be fierce or challenging, but her basic purpose is to awaken and inspire. The energizing dance of the dakini reminds us to beware of overly facile distinctions such as identifying the masculine simply as active and creative and the feminine simply as passive and receptive. Although images of the wild man and wild woman may point the way, we still do not know what fully developed, powerful men and women will look like. The potential to make this discovery for ourselves is one of the main opportunities hidden within the often painful struggle between men and women today.

NOTES

[1]*The Yellow Emperor's Classic of Internal Medicine*, translated by Ilza Veith, p. 9.
[2]Lawrence (1936), p. 441.
[3]Allione (1984), pp. 36, 41.

The Man/Woman Game

Theodore and Betty Roszak

He is playing masculine. She is playing feminine.

He is playing masculine *because* she is playing feminine. She is playing feminine *because* he is playing masculine.

He is playing the kind of man that she thinks the kind of woman she is playing ought to admire. She is playing the kind of woman that he thinks the kind of man he is playing ought to desire.

If he were not playing masculine, he might well be more feminine than she is—except when she is playing very feminine. If she were not playing feminine, she might well be more masculine than he is—except when he is playing very masculine.

So he plays harder. And she plays . . . softer.

He wants to make sure that she could never be more masculine than he. She wants to make sure that he could never be more feminine than she. He therefore seeks to destroy the femininity in himself. She therefore seeks to destroy the masculinity in herself.

She is supposed to admire him for the masculinity in him that she fears in herself. He is supposed to desire her for the femininity in her that he despises in himself.

He desires her for her femininity which is *his* femininity, but which he can never lay claim to. She admires him for his masculinity which is *her* masculinity, but which she can never lay claim to. Since he may only love his own femininity in her, he envies her her femininity. Since she may only love her own masculinity in him, she envies him his masculinity.

The envy poisons their love.

He, coveting her unattainable femininity, decides to punish her. She, coveting his unattainable masculinity, decides to punish him. He denigrates her femininity—which he is supposed to desire and which he really envies—and becomes more aggressively masculine. She feigns disgust at his masculinity—which she is supposed to admire and which she really envies—and becomes more fastidiously feminine. He is becoming less and less what he wants to be. She is becoming less and less what she wants to be. But now he is more manly than ever, and she is more womanly than ever.

Her femininity, growing more dependently supine, becomes contemptible. His masculinity, growing more oppressively domineering, becomes intolerable. At last she loathes what she has helped his masculinity to become. At last he loathes what he has helped her femininity to become.

So far, it has all been very symmetrical. But we have left one thing out.

The world belongs to what his masculinity has become.

The reward for what his masculinity has become is power. The reward for what her femininity has become is only the security which his power can bestow upon her. If he were to yield to what her femininity has become, he would be yielding to contemptible incompetence. If she were to acquire what his masculinity has become, she would participate in intolerable coerciveness.

She is stifling under the triviality of her femininity. The world is groaning beneath the terrors of his masculinity.

He is playing masculine. She is playing feminine.

How do we call off the game?

Projecting Our Other Half

John Sanford

Men are used to thinking of themselves only as men, and women think of
themselves as women, but the psychological facts indicate that every
human being is androgynous.[1] "Within every man there is the reflection
of a woman, and within every woman there is the reflection of a man,"
writes the American Indian Hyemeyohsts Storm, who is stating not his
own personal opinion, but an ancient American Indian belief.[2] The
ancient alchemists agreed: "Our Adamic hermaphrodite, though he appears in masculine form, nevertheless carries about with him Eve, or
his feminine part, hidden in his body."[3]

The idea that the original human being was male and female is found
in numerous traditions. It is a thought expressed most succinctly, perhaps, in Plato's *Symposium*. Here Plato's character Aristophanes retells an
ancient Greek myth about the original human beings, who were perfectly
round, had four arms and four legs, and one head with two faces, looking
opposite ways. These human spheres possessed such marvelous qualities
and great intelligence that they rivaled the gods, who, acting out of envy
and fear, cut the spheres in two in order to reduce their power. The original, spherical beings fell apart into two halves, one feminine and one
masculine. Ever since then, so the story goes, the two severed parts of the
original human being have been striving to reunite. "And when one of
them meets his other half," Aristophanes informs us, "the actual half
of himself, . . . the pair are lost in an amazement of love and friendship
and intimacy, and one will not be out of the other's sight . . . even for

a moment: these are the people who pass their whole lives together; yet they could not explain what they desire of one another."[4]

Storm's intuition that each man contains the reflection of a woman, and vice versa, is also reflected in shamanism. The shaman, the primitive healer or "medicine man," often has a tutelary spirit who assists him in the work of healing and teaches and instructs him in the healing arts. In the case of a male shaman, this tutelary spirit is female and acts like a spirit wife to him. In the case of a shamaness the tutelary spirit is male, and is her spirit husband, whom she has in addition to her flesh-and-blood husband. The shaman is unique partly because he or she has cultivated a special relationship to the other half of his or her personality, which has become a living entity, a real presence.

So the idea of man's androgynous nature is an old one that has often been expressed in mythology and by the great intuitive spirits of times past. In our century, C. G. Jung is the first scientist to observe this psychological fact of human nature, and to take it into account in describing the whole human being.

Jung called the opposites in man and woman the *anima* and the *animus*. Empirical evidence for the reality of the anima and animus can be found wherever the psyche spontaneously expresses itself. The anima and animus appear in dreams, fairy tales, myths, the world's great literature, and most important of all, in the varying phenomena of human behavior. For the anima and animus are the invisible partners in every human relationship, and in every person's search for individual wholeness. Jung called them *archetypes*, because the anima and animus are essential building blocks in the psychic structure of every man and woman. If something is archetypal, it is typical. Archetypes form the basis for instinctive, unlearned behavior patterns that are common to all mankind, and represent themselves in human consciousness in certain typical ways.

Naturally, in any such discussion as this we come up against the question of what is meant by "masculine" and "feminine." Is there a difference between the masculine and feminine? Are the apparent differences between men and women due to archetypal, underlying psychological dissimilarities, or are they entirely the result of socially assigned roles and conditioning? In support of the latter idea it can be argued that the roles men and women play sometimes seem to be designated by the particular cultures in which they exist. It can be argued that men and women do what they do only because society assigns them that particular role or task. According to this point of view, there is no essential psychological difference between men and women, and it is only cultural influence that produces the apparent dissimilarities between the male and the female. In support of this contention is the fact that men can perform most of the functions women usually perform, except the biological functions associated with childbearing, of course, and women can also perform the way men do. The fact that women do not usually do what men do, and vice versa, is laid at the door of social expectation. In addition, there is the admitted difficulty of defining what is masculine and what is feminine, for as soon as a definition is offered there is always an objection, "But women (or men) sometimes act that way too."

On the other side of the discussion, the question of whether or not there is an archetype for the masculine and for the feminine—that is, whether essential psychological differences exist between the sexes and between the psychological polarities within each sex—is a matter to be decided by empirical evidence. Jung's view is that, while undoubtedly the cultural and social expectations and roles greatly influence the ways men and women live their lives, there are nevertheless underlying archetypal psychological patterns.

As for differentiating between what is the masculine and what is the feminine, it is perhaps best to talk in terms of images rather than in terms of psychological functioning. To speak of male and female is a way of saying that psychic energy, like all forms of energy, flows between two poles. Just as electricity flows between a positive and a negative pole, so psychic energy flows between two poles that have been called masculine and feminine. The ancient Chinese terminology of yang and yin is often more satisfactory because yang and yin are not defined in terms of role, or even in terms of psychological qualities, but by means of images. "Yang means 'banners waving in the sun,' that is, something 'shone upon' or bright." Yang is designated by heaven, the sky, the bright, the creative, the south side of the mountain (where the sun shines) and the north side of the river (which also receives the sunlight). On the other hand, "In its primary meaning yin is 'the cloudy, the overcast.'" Yin is designated by the earth, the dark, the moist, the receptive, the north side of the mountain and the south side of the river.[5] Of course the Chinese also speak of yang as the masculine and yin as the feminine, but basically yang and yin represent the two spiritual poles along which all life flows. Yang and yin exist in men and women, but they are also cosmic principles, and their interaction and relationship determine the course of events, as the Chinese wisdom book, the *I Ching*, clearly shows.

We might wonder why, if men and women have always had a feminine and a masculine component, this fact has eluded the awareness of mankind in general for so many years. Part of the answer is that self-knowledge has never been one of our strong points. But there also is another factor that makes knowledge of the anima or animus so elusive: These psychic factors within us are usually projected. Projection is a psychic mechanism that occurs whenever a vital aspect of our personality of which we are unaware is activated. When something is projected we see it outside of us, as though it belongs to someone else and has nothing to do with us. Projection is an unconscious mechanism. We do not decide to project something, it happens automatically. If we decided to project something it would be conscious to us and then, precisely because it is conscious to us, it could not be projected. Only unconscious contents are projected.

So the anima and animus have, for the millennia of mankind's history, been projected onto mythological figures, onto the gods and goddesses who have peopled our spiritual world, and, perhaps most important of all, onto living men and women. The gods and goddesses of Greek mythology can be understood as personifications of different aspects of the masculine or the feminine archetype. Mythology has long been the way in which the human psyche personified itself, and as long as people believed in the living reality of their gods and goddesses they could, through appropriate ritual and worship, effect some sort of relationship to their psychic world.

When the anima and animus are projected onto other people our perception of them is remarkably altered. For the most part, man has projected the anima onto woman, and woman has projected the animus onto man. Woman has carried for man the living image of his own feminine soul or counterpart, and man has carried for woman the living image of her own spirit. This has led to many unusual and often unfortunate consequences, since these living realities within ourselves often have a peculiarly powerful or irritating effect.

Because the anima and animus are projected, we do not usually recognize that they belong to us, for they *appear* to be outside of us. On the other hand, once the phenomenon of projection is recognized, these projected images can, to a certain extent, be taken back into ourselves, for we can use projections as mirrors in which we see the reflection of our own psychic contents. If we discover the anima or animus image has been projected onto a man or a woman, that makes it possible for us to see in reflection contents of our own psyche that otherwise might escape us. The contra-sexual element within us is so psychologically elusive that it escapes our complete awareness, therefore it always is projected, at least in part. As far as self-knowledge is concerned, it is a matter of utilizing projections as mirrors.

All of this has important implications for the relationship between the sexes. Men, identified with their masculinity, typically project their feminine side onto women, and women, identified with their feminine nature, typically project their masculine side onto men. These projected psychic images are the invisible partners in every man/woman relationship, and greatly influence the relationship, for wherever projection occurs the person who carries the projected image is either greatly overvalued or greatly undervalued. In either case, the human reality of the individual who carries the projection for us is obscured by the projected image. This is especially the case with the anima and animus since these archetypes are so numinous. This means that they are charged with psychic energy, so that they tend to grip us emotionally. Consequently these projected images have a magnetic effect on us, and the person who carries a projection will tend to greatly attract or repel us, just as a magnet attracts or repels another metal.

Like all archetypes, the anima and animus have positive and negative aspects. That is, sometimes they appear to be highly desirable and attractive, and sometimes destructive and infuriating. In this they resemble the gods and goddesses who could shower mankind with gifts, but could also turn on mankind destructively. If the positive aspect of the anima image is projected by a man onto a woman, she then becomes highly desirable to him. A woman who carries this projection for a man readily becomes the object of his erotic fantasies and sexual longings, and it seems to the man that if he could only be with her and make love to her he would be fulfilled. Naturally, a woman who carries such a powerful anima projection is pleased, at least at first. She feels flattered and valued, and, though she may be only dimly aware of it, enjoys a feeling of considerable power.

The woman usually regrets the situation in time, however, as she experiences the disagreeable side of being the carrier of another person's soul. She may find that he resents it when she is not immediately and always available to him, and this gives an oppressive quality to their relationship. She will also discover that the man resents any attempt on her part to develop her individual personality in such a way that it goes beyond the anima image he has placed on her, for, in fact, he sees her not as she actually is, but as he *wants* her to be. So she may find herself living in his box, fenced in by his determination that she fulfill his projection for him, and she may discover that the shadow side of his seeming love for her is a possessiveness and restrictiveness on his part that thwarts her own natural tendency to become an individual. When she insists on being herself she may find her man jealous, resentful, and pouting. She may also begin to dread his sexual advances, which, she begins to suspect, are not functions of the relationship between them, but have a compulsive, unrelated quality to them. Indeed, the two easily wind up at loggerheads regarding sex. The man is compulsively drawn to sexual relationship with the woman who carries his feminine image for him, and feels the relationship is complete only after coitus, when he feels a sense of momentary oneness with her. The woman, on the other hand, wants to work out the human relationship first and then give herself sexually to the man, and many devils whirl around this difference between them.

Moreover, the opposite projection can replace the positive one suddenly and without warning. The woman who at one time carried the projection of the positive anima, the soul image, for a man, may suddenly receive the projection of the negative anima, the image of the witch. All a man has to do is blame her for his own bad moods and suddenly he will see her in this light, and men, unfortunatley, are notorious for putting the responsibility for their bad moods on women.

The same projections are made by women onto men, of course. If a woman projects onto a man her positive animus image, the image of the savior, hero, and spiritual guide, she overvalues that man. She feels completed only through him, as though it were through him that she found her soul. Such projections are especially likely to be made onto men who have the power of the word. A man who uses words well, who has power with ideas and is effective in getting them across, is an ideal figure to carry such animus projections from a woman. When this happens he then becomes bigger-than-life to her, and she is quite content to be the loving moth fluttering around his flame. In this way she misses the creative flame within herself, having displaced it onto the man.

If both a man and a woman project their positive images onto each other at the same time, we have that seemingly perfect state of relationship known as being in love, a state of mutual fascination. The two then declare that they are "in love with each other" and are firmly convinced that they have now found the ultimate relationship. There is much to be said for falling in love. Most of us can probably remember the first time we were in love, and what unexpected and powerful emotions were released. To have the experience of falling in love is to become open to matters of the heart in a wonderful way. It can be the prelude to a valuable expansion of personality and emotional life. It is also an important experience because it brings the sexes together and initiates relationship. Whether this leads to happy or unhappy consequences, life is kept moving in this way. A life that has not known this experience is no doubt impoverished.

The fact is, however, that a relationship founded exclusively on the being-in-love state can never last. The inability of the state of being in love to endure the stress of everyday human life is recognized by all great poets. This is why the relationship of Romeo and Juliet had to end in death. It would have been unthinkable for Shakespeare to have concluded his great love story by sending his loving couple to Sears to buy pans for their kitchen. They would have quarreled in an instant over what frying pan to choose and how much it was going to cost, and the whole beautiful love story would have evaporated. Great poets leave such love stories where they belong: in the hands of the gods. Or, if the human pair insists on living out the love fantasy, they may bring everything down around their heads in ruin. This is what Lancelot and Guinevere did in *Camelot*. Having fallen in love, they insisted on trying to make their love relationship a personal matter, to try to found their lives on it no matter what. As they tried to identify with and possess each other, and fulfill their love fantasies in a human sexual relationship, they brought down around them the ruin of Camelot.

It should now be clear that to the extent that a relationship is founded on projection, the element of human love is lacking. To be in love with someone we do not know as a person, but are attracted to because they reflect back to us the image of the god or goddess in our souls, is, in a sense, to be in love with oneself, not with the other person. Real love begins only when one person comes to know another for who he or she really is as a human being, and begins to like and care for that human being.

No human being can match the gods and goddesses in all their shimmer and glory and, at first, seeing the person whom we love for who she or he is, rather than in terms of projections, may seem uninteresting and disappointing, for human beings are, on the whole, rather an ordinary lot. Because of this many people prefer to go from one person to another, always looking for the ultimate relationship when the projections wear off and the in-loveness ends. It is obvious that with such shallow roots no real, permanent love can develop.

This is not to say that projection is a bad thing. In itself, the projection of the anima and the animus is a perfectly natural event that will always occur. Each time projection occurs there is another opportunity for us to know our inner, invisible partners, and that is a way of knowing our own souls. There is also the fact that, as has already been noted, projection is often the factor that first draws the sexes together. Man and woman are so unlike that it takes quite a power of attraction to bring them together in the first place; projection provides this influence because of the fascination with which it endows the member of the other sex. For this reason most love relationships begin with projection, and this serves life for then life moves. The question is, what happens then? Does that relationship become a vehicle for the development of consciousness, or do we give in to our infantile nature and go on and on through life insisting that somewhere there must be a relationship that offers us perfect bliss and fulfillment? Projection in itself is neither good nor bad; it is what we do with it that counts.

NOTES

[1]The word *androgynous* comes from two Greek words, *andros* and *gynos*, meaning "man" and "woman" respectively, and refers to a person who combines both male and female elements within himself or herself. The word *hermaphrodite* is an analogous word. It comes from the Greek god Hermaphroditus, who was born of the union of Hermes and Aphrodite and embodied the sexual characteristics of both of them.

[2]Storm (1962), p. 14.

[3]From the alchemical treatise *Hermetis Trismegisti Tractatus vere Aureus*, 1610. Quoted in Jung (1973), p. 443.

[4]Plato, *Symposium* (1928), p. 356.

[5]Wilhelm (1950), p. xxxvi.

Cosmic Masculine and Feminine

Sukie Colegrave

The story of human consciousness begins with humanity's fall from innocence, from a pre-conscious identity with the whole universe. Its early
history is presided over by the image of the Great Mother who contains
all things and people in her embrace. Slowly the impulse towards independence acquires the necessary strength and momentum to challenge
and overthrow the old consciousness and introduce a polarized vision of
the world. Mythology represents this battle as the struggle of the son
against the mother, but the association of consciousness with either the
male or female begs certain questions about the nature of "masculinity"
or "femininity." We need to know what these concepts describe. The
researches of anthropologists suggest that the links between sex and gender are considerably more tenuous than was once assumed; the cultural
definitions of gender are too diverse to permit a genitally determined
definition of masculinity and femininity.

Gender is increasingly acknowledged to be as much a product of
culture as of biology. This awareness has performed the valuable function
of freeing people, to some extent, from traditional role stereotypes.
Women and men are less obliged to perceive and experience themselves,
and to model their behavior according to traditional definitions of "male"
and "female." However, the desire to be free from the restrictive sexual
role stereotyping can become as much an inhibition to the development
of individuality as what preceded it, particularly when this desire takes

the form of rejecting difference in the pursuit of sameness. Psychological "unisex" may have the laudable objective of recognizing people first as individuals and only second as sexually differentiated, but it can have the less salutary consequence of denying the existence of the masculine and feminine principles as a crucial polarity of body and psyche. The growth of self-knowledge depends not on restricting discussions of sexuality to cultural patterns or to the arena of chromosomes and hormones, but on exploring the sexual principles at every level of human nature.

The meaning and nature of sexuality, of masculine and feminine as nouns as well as adjectives, remains central to an understanding of the individual. The difficulty lies in finding a framework within which to explore the question. Here is the attraction of yin-yang theory. It regards biology as merely one expression of a primordial sexual polarity which lies at the foundation of all existence, cosmic and human, biological and psychological, organic and inorganic. Hence it offers a more productive way of understanding "masculinity" and "femininity" and their relation to individual development, as well as providing a framework within which to examine the relationship between sexuality and consciousness.

The history of yin-yang theory begins in the obscurity of legend and gradually unfolds during three or four thousand years until its full flowering in the minds of the Neo-Confucian philosophers of the Sung dynasty (A.D. 960–1279).

The extreme simplicity of yin-yang theory is reminiscent of the saying in *I Corinthians* 1:18 that "God hath chosen the foolish things of the world to confound the wise." While it is the pivotal theory in traditional Chinese thought, so that no aspect of Chinese civilization, philosophy, government, art, medicine, architecture, personal relationships, sex, or ethics has escaped its influence, its salient points can be summarized quite briefly. It teaches that everything is the product of two forces, principles, or archetypes, yin and yang, whose interaction generates the five elements (metal, wood, water, fire, and earth), which, in various combinations, constitute the foundation of the cosmos in all its forms. Yin and yang are the polar manifestations of the Supreme Ultimate, the Tao, which by definition, defies description. The process of generation is conceived of as cyclical, an endless beginning and ending, in which everything is constantly changing into its polar opposite. This is yin-yang theory in brief. For a clearer understanding of it and the concept of change it implies it is necesssary to turn to the *I Ching* (*Book of Changes*).

The structure of the hexagrams in the *I Ching* express the conception of all situations created out of the interaction of yin and yang. The sixty-four symbols are built up out of different combinations of the yin and yang lines, but the first two are composed exclusively from six yang and six yin lines respectively. It is these which reveal most about the different natures of the two principles:

Ch'ien   K'un

Ch'ien is usually translated as the Creative and K'un as the Receptive, but these translations reveal more about the values of Confucian thinking than about the essential meaning of yin and yang. This is a general problem in seeking to understand the masculine and feminine principles; their essence is frequently obscured by the variety of symbols with which they are associated. It is necessary to distinguish their fundamental qualities from the values attached to the two principles during different historical periods and stages of consciousness. "Creativity" is an unsatisfactory translation of Ch'ien because it is only in certain circumstances that creativity is a monopoly of the masculine. At other times it is the feminine which is creative, and more often both, as in much artistic and cerebral work.

According to the commentaries on the Ch'ien hexagram, the masculine is an active, strong force whose energy is unrestricted by any fixed conditions in space and is, therefore, conceived of as motion. In this function it is associated with the rain: "The clouds pass and the rain does its work, and all individual beings flow into their forms."[1] The masculine is the principle which leads through its powers of conservation to the "continuous actualization and differentiation of form."[2] Its course alters and shapes all things until each attains its true, specific nature. To live in accordance with Ch'ien is to bring peace and security to the world through one's activity in creating order. It brings the possiblity of seeing with "great clarity causes and effects." As the principle of leadership, of order, of differentiation, of individuality, of motion in time and of cause and effect, Ch'ien is the polar opposite of K'un.

The feminine is the principle of relatedness. It nourishes and embraces all things, giving them uncritical protection and support. "Embracing all things it becomes bright and shines forth. Its essential characteristic is glad acceptance."[3] K'un is the principle of the earth in that it receives the seeds from Ch'ien and brings them to birth. "While the success of the Creative (Ch'ien) lies in the fact that individual beings receive their specific forms, the success of the Receptive (K'un) causes them to thrive and unfold."[4] In its devotion it carries all things good and evil without exception. It is the principle of calmness, of reserve, of yielding and of moderation. The movement of *K'un* is an opening out in space in contrast to the idea of direction implicit in *Ch'ien*. "In the resting, closed state, it embraces all things as though in a vast womb."[5] It has no need of purpose; everything becomes, through it, spontaneously what it should rightly be. Its characteristics are gentle and accommodating. It is the principle of devotion and the force which gathers things and people together rather than dividing them. One of its symbols is water, the element which creates uniformity and equality, which covers and embraces all things in its still, dark depths.

It is now possible to construct a list of the essential qualities of the two principles:

Yin	*Yang*	*Yin*	*Yang*
relationship	individualization	nourisher	fertilizer
space	time	unity	polarity
community	hierarchy/order	acausal	causal
not judging	judging	spontaneous	planned
purposeless	purpose	oneness	differentiation

It is interesting to supplement the Chinese definitions of the two principles with two other views on this polarity, both of which originated in twentieth-century Switzerland and both of which strikingly endorse the ancient Chinese intuitions. The first comes from Carl Jung; the second from Rudolf Steiner.

Jung's approach to psychology was predominantly empirical. He observed that all human beings have a contrasexual element within their psyches: men, a feminine "anima" and women, a masculine "animus." But implicit in Jung's work is also the notion of the anima and animus as archetypes which cannot be attributed to or located exclusively within the psyche of either sex, but are common to both men and women.

The anima and animus constitute a polarity in all human beings, but they are rarely brought into harmonious relationship with each other; usually one is emphasized to the detriment of the second. This accounts for the psychological imbalance which most of us have, and for which we unconsciously compensate by our attractions and dependencies on people or ideologies which represent the undeveloped aspect of our own psyches. Psychological maturity depends, according to Jung, on finding a relationship between these two principles within ourselves. This is the sacred marriage which forms the central motif of many religions and philosophies, and which is the highest mark of psychological development. It cannot take place before the complete differentiation of the masculine and feminine from each other.

Steiner's description of the masculine and feminine principles corroborates and elucidates both those of the *I Ching* and of analytical psychology. He identified the masculine as the principle of differentiation, the individualizing principle in contrast to the maternal principle of resemblance. "Forces that bring about resemblances are inherent in the female principle, while all that reduces it, that creates differences, lies within the male principle."[6] The masculine individualizes, specializes and separates, while the feminine tends to generalization.

In a series of lectures on the *Study of Man* he describes a polarity working within all psyches. He calls it the polarity of sympathy and antipathy. Sympathy is the force which involves us in the world and with other people, whether by love or hate or anything in between. Antipathy separates us from the world, creating the possibility for memory, perception, and cognition. In animals, Steiner says, the forces of sympathy are much stronger than that of antipathy. So if human beings had no more antipathy for their environment than the animal, they should be much more intimately connected to nature than they are.

From Steiner's comments, antipathy seems to be a different description of the principle which emerged during the Great Mother stage of consciousness, bringing about an increasing separation of humanity from its environment and a corresponding development of individual consciousness. Antipathy is the losing which is a precondition of new finding, or the differentiation which is a prerequisite of a new relationship and unity. The formulation of yin-yang theory could not have taken place without this birth of the masculine principle and the polarity in consciousness it created.

Yin-yang theory, which receives some affirmation and elucidation from analytical psychology, argues that there are two cosmic principles, the masculine and the feminine, inherent in all phenomena and responsible, by their interactions, for the emergence and dissolution of all things. Sexuality is, therefore, a cosmic or archetypal phenomenon, which expresses itself, in different forms, in all creation, from the level of the inorganic through to the level of human consciousness. Since yin and yang are responsible for both the manifest and nonmanifest worlds, they describe a world in which mind and body, space and form, constitute different expressions of one continuum, rather than irreconcilable opposites. Since, also, they are the polar manifestations of the Tao, the principle lying behind all creation, the pursuit of physical and mental health, as well as wisdom, depends on the attainment of a harmonious relationship between the two principles. Human nature can only reveal itself in its essential wholeness when yin and yang are brought into conscious communion with each other. It is a development in which the Tao is divided into yin and yang by the active, separating energy of yang, which, in turn, calls forth its polar opposite, the feminine principle.

There is an important disadvantage in relying exclusively on either the masculine or feminine consciousness: it can inhibit the development of consciousness itself. Neither principle can realize its full potential without continual reference to its opposite. This expresses itself psychologically in a number of ways. "If a man fails to develop his relation to . . . (the) female element in himself, he suffers at least a partial diminution of being and at worst, a serious mental illness."[7] The same is true of women. A person excessively controlled by the masculine discriminating principle may feel, at a certain point, that life has lost its meaning. He or she may oscillate violently between arrogance and despair, experiencing a growing alienation from other people and from the self, as the masculine continues to differentiate unaided by the complementary influence of the feminine to reveal connections and relationships. Such a person becomes psychologically marooned, incapable of building bridges either to the neglected areas of the psyche or to other people and nature. Psychological growth becomes impossible because new insights, feelings, and ideas are prevented from entering consciousness by the rigid, divisive influence of the masculine. The psyche stagnates. Aridity, meaninglessness and a total lack of any sense of direction ensue. At such a point only the feminine attributes of listening, yielding, accepting, waiting, and trusting, and the capacity of surrender to the outside world as well as to the inner promptings of the unconscious, can revitalize the psyche. The feminine alone can nourish the lonely dried-up ego and create the necessary relationships to inner and outer nature as well as to other people which can restore meaning and purpose to life.

A similar psychological stagnation and imbalance can result from an excessive reliance by the conscious mind on the feminine principle. It drags consciousness into a mystical ocean of sameness, a bog in which all differences are submerged, all identities lost. An awakening of the masculine principle is necessary to give the person a sense of self, of independence, and the ability to discriminate, essential for understanding. And as with the masculine, by relying too heavily on the feminine we eventually lose it. It can only live and develop in consciousness by being continually explored and developed in relation to its opposite; otherwise it is not the feminine which expresses itself in the psyche, but an undifferentiated chaos. We need the masculine to be able to focus and understand the different feminine qualities.

Instinctively we may express some aspects of the feminine, but to know her nature and, more importantly, to learn to recognize the appropriate moments to allow her expression, we must have already acquired a good relationship to the masculine in consciousness. To understand the feminine at every level of our nature, and thereby to have a free, rather than obsessive, or compulsive relationship to her, depends on continual reference to her opposite. "Over-awareness of diffuse feminine values may paralyze us and make action impossible, in the outer world. On the other hand a too-focused consciousness may render the wisdom from the feminine layer of our psyche, invisible, and burn it up with too bright a flame."[8] It seems that the feminine in consciousness is dependent, for its realization and maturity, on a prior development of the masculine. The conventional saying that the masculine leads and the feminine follows—which, in its identification with gender has caused considerable oppression to both sexes—acquires in the specific sense of the relation between the two principles, new and important value.

A notable example of the dangers inherent in the search for the feminine unassisted by the masculine skills of analysis and discrimination is the identification of the matriarchal consciousness with the feminine. The discovery of the feminine depends, first of all, on the capacity to distinguish her from the matriarchal experience. The Great Mother rules over a pre-polarized consciousness, a time or stage of psychological development when everything appears to be embraced in one undifferentiated unity. Under her there is no need for relationship, as the masculine consciousness has not yet split human awareness into subject and object, mother and child, or male and female. The Great Mother consciousness does not know individual identities, but experiences everything as part of the whole. But with the birth of the masculine consciousness this ancient way of seeing is overthrown by the introduction of an "I" and "Thou" experience. Through this, individuals gradually become conscious of a distance between their conscious and unconscious minds, between the inner and outer worlds and between humanity and nature. This initial separation has two important consequences for the development of human consciousness: internally, it generates the capacity to say "I" to oneself and "You" to others, which is an expression of self-consciousness; externally, it leads to an emphasis on exploring the world in terms of differences rather than unities. This is a psychological precondition of the creation of social, political, and economic structures. The emergence of a feminine consciousness whose salient characteristics are those of recognizing and helping to create relationships, of being receptive and recognizing harmony, depends on a prior differentiation by the masculine principle of human awareness; we cannot receive, integrate, and harmonize before discovering the separate parts both in the outside world and within our own psyches.

If "marriage" is understood not in its outer sense as a system of rules designed to organize and control relationships *between* the sexes, but in the inner psychological sense of the union of the masculine and feminine principles *within* each psyche, then far from being a fetter on freedom, such a "marriage" within each individual becomes the way to freedom. Psychological "marriage" of the feminine and masculine within each person imbues its practices with new meaning and life. The injunction that the man must initiate and the woman follow, highly oppressive to many individual women and men in their relationship with each other, can be recognized as wisdom for self-development. For the way of the masculine is actively to organize and initiate, while the way of the feminine is to yield, receive, and harmonize. Both are valued equally. The prohibitions against "divorce" in such a psychological "marriage" become valuable statements about the way of androgyny which depends for its realization on the continual interaction of the two principles. To "divorce" one from the other is to deny our own nature. The idea of fulfillment of marriage through the procreation of children acquires new meaning once the word is interpreted as an inner process. Physically the union of the male and female may produce a child. Psychologically the union of the masculine and the feminine can also result in conception, not of another human being, but of a new self.

Christianity as well as the ancient Chinese both point to this inner marriage as the way to the true self, the realization of the Tao, or God within. Early Gnostic texts contain numerous references to androgyny as the nature of Christ and the potential of the human being. In one of these, Jesus says, "When you make the two become one, you will become the son of Man."[9] According to the *Second Epistle of Clement*, when Jesus was asked at what moment the Kingdom would come, He replied: "When the two shall be one, outside like the inside, the male with the female, neither male nor female."[10]

Through the centuries of Christian tradition the idea of the androgyny of Christ as the goal of human endeavor was kept alive by different groups and emerged from time to time in different forms. For instance, it constituted a central part of European alchemy and appeared again in the writing of many of the German Romantics. Ritter, a friend of Novalis, said that the human being of the future would be, like Christ, androgynous, and Schlegel wrote that the goal towards which the human race should strive is a progressive reintegration of the sexes which should end in androgyny.

The search for androgyny entails exchanging a partial self for a complete self through the discovery that we can see further than we have seen, know more than we have known, feel deeper than we have felt and love more than we have loved, that we are, in truth, far more than we knew.

Loss initiates the journey towards androgyny. As humanity awoke millennia ago from its instinctive at-oneness with the cosmos, so each individual emerges, at some moment, from his or her pre-conscious identity with the Mother. This initial loss coincides with the birth of human consciousness. It is followed by a struggle between the desire for freedom and knowledge and the longing for wholeness and peace. The tension between these two impulses propels the restless psyche ever onwards in search of a kingdom in which freedom and unity belong together, in which understanding and peace are no longer in conflict.

Just as the union of the physical male and female is described as making love, so the union of the masculine and feminine principles within the psyche allows for an inner experience of love, which is the hallmark of the androgynous consciousness. It becomes more possible to love others for what they are rather than for the unrealized aspects of oneself they provide. Jacobi describes the implications of this stage of psychological development:

In a sense we are alone, for our "inner freedom" means that a love relation can no longer fetter us; the other sex has lost its magic power over us, for we have come to know its essential traits in the depths of our own psyche. We shall not easily "fall in love," for we can no longer lose ourselves in someone else, but we shall be capable of a deeper love, a conscious devotion to the other.[11]

Such love in its freedom from possession is not free from pain. We learn that, however whole and free we may be, we are, at another level, no stronger than the weakest member of humanity, no freer than the most imprisoned; that their pain is our pain, their burdens our burdens. Source of this knowledge is love itself, or what the Chinese call "human-heartedness." It, alone, is the teacher.

NOTES

[1]Wilhelm (1950), p. 4
[2]*Ibid.*, p. 5.
[3]*Ibid.*, p. 4.
[4]*Ibid.*, p. 387.
[5]*Ibid.*

[6]Steiner (1973), p. 155.
[7]Ulanov (1971), p. 166.
[8]de Castillejo (1974), p. 16.
[9]*The Gospel of Thomas* in J. Doresse, *Les Livres Secrets des Gnostiques d'Egypte*, Vol. II. Quoted in Eliade (1969), p. 106.
[10]*Ibid.*, pp. 106–107.
[11]Jacobi (1973), p. 123.

What Men Really Want

Robert Bly & Keith Thompson

Keith Thompson: After exploring the way of the goddess and the matriarchy for many years, lately you've turned your attention to the pathways of *male* energy—the bond between fathers and sons, for example, and the initiation of young males. You're also writing a book relating some of the old classic fairy tales to men's growth. What's been going on with men?

Robert Bly: No one knows! Historically, the male has changed considerably in the past thirty years. Back then there was a person we could call the fifties male, who was hard-working, responsible, fairly well disciplined: he didn't see women's souls very well, though he looked at their bodies a lot. Reagan has this personality. The fifties male was vulnerable to collective opinion: if you were a man, you were supposed to like football games, be aggressive, stick up for the United States, never cry, and always provide. But this image of the male lacked feminine space. It lacked some sense of flow; it lacked compassion in a way that led directly to the unbalanced pursuit of the Vietnam war, just as the lack of feminine space inside Reagan's head led to his callousness and brutality toward the poor in El Salvador, toward old people here, the unemployed, schoolchildren, and poor people in general. The fifties male had a clear vision of what a man is, but the vision involved massive inadequacies and flaws.

Then, during the sixties, another sort of male appeared. The waste and anguish of the Vietnam war made men question what an adult male really is. And the women's movement encouraged men to actually *look* at women, forcing them to become conscious of certain things that the fifties male tended to avoid. As men began to look at women and at their concerns, some men began to see their own feminine side and pay attention to it. That process continues to this day, and I would say that most young males are now involved in it to some extent.

Now, there's something wonderful about all this—the step of the male bringing forth his own feminine consciousness is an important one—and yet I have the sense there is something wrong. The male in the past twenty years has become more thoughtful, more gentle. But by this process he has *not* become more free. He's a nice boy who now not only pleases his mother, but also the young woman he is living with.

I see the phenomenon of what I would call the "soft male" all over the country today. Sometimes when I look out at my audiences, perhaps half the young males are what I'd call soft. They're lovely, valuable people—I like them—and they're not interested in harming the earth, or starting wars, or working for corporations. There's something favorable toward life in their whole general mood and style of living.

But something's wrong. Many of these men are unhappy. There's not much energy in them. They are life-preserving, but not exactly *life-giving*. And why is it you often see these men with strong women who positively radiate energy? Here we have a finely tuned young man, ecologically superior to his father, sympathetic to the whole harmony of the universe, yet he himself has no energy to offer.

Thompson: It seems as if many of these soft young men have come to equate their own natural male energy with being macho. Even when masculine energy would clearly be life-giving, productive, of service to the community, many young males step back from it. Perhaps it's because back in the sixties, when we looked to the women's movement for leads as to how we should be, the message we got was that the new strong women *wanted* soft men.

Bly: I agree. That's how it felt. The women did play a part in this. I remember a bumper sticker at the time that read: "WOMEN SAY YES TO MEN WHO SAY NO." We know it took a lot of courage to resist, or to go to Canada, just as it took some courage also to go to Vietnam. But the women were definitely saying that they preferred the softer receptive male, and they would reward him for being so: "We will sleep with you if you are not too aggressive and macho." So the development of men was disturbed a little there: nonreceptive maleness was equated with violence, and receptivity was rewarded.

Also, as you mention, some energetic women chose soft men to be their lovers—and in a way, perhaps, sons. These changes didn't happen by accident. Young men for various reasons wanted harder women, and women began to desire softer men. It seems like a nice arrangement, but it isn't working out.

Thompson: How so?

Bly: Recently I taught a conference for men only at the Lama Community in New Mexico. About forty men came, and we were together ten days. Each morning I talked about certain fairy tales relating to men's growth, and about the Greek gods who embody what the Greeks considered different kinds of male energy. We spent the afternoons being quiet or walking and doing body movement or dance, and then we'd all come together again in the late afternoon. Often the younger males would begin to talk and within five minutes they would be weeping. The amount of grief and anguish in the younger males was astounding! The river was deep.

Part of the grief was a remoteness from their fathers, which they felt keenly, but part, too, came from trouble in their marriages or relationships. They had learned to be receptive, and it wasn't enough to carry their marriages. In every relationship, something fierce is needed once in a while: both the man and the woman need to have it. At the point when it was needed, often the young man didn't have it. He was nurturing, but something *else* was required—for the relationship, for his life. The male was able to say, "I can feel your pain, and I consider your life as important as mine, and I will take care of you and comfort you." But he could not say what *he* wanted and stick by it: that was a different matter.

In *The Odyssey*, Hermes instructs Odysseus, when he is approaching a kind of matriarchal figure, that he is to lift or show Circe his sword. It was difficult for many of the younger males to distinguish between showing the sword and hurting someone. Do you understand me? They had learned so well not to hurt anyone that they couldn't lift the sword, even to catch the light of the sun on it! Showing a sword doesn't mean fighting; there's something joyful in it.

Thompson: You seem to be suggesting that uniting with their feminine side has been an important stage for men on their path toward wholeness, but it's not the final one. What *is* required?

Bly: One of the fairy tales I'm working on for my *Fairy Tales for Men* collection is a story called "Iron John." Though it was first set down by the Grimm Brothers around 1820, this story could be ten or twenty thousand years old. It talks about a different development for men, a further stage than we've seen so far in the United States.

As the story starts, something strange has been happening in a remote area of the forest near the king's castle: when hunters go into this area, they disappear and never come back. Three hunters have gone out and disappeared. People are getting the feeling that there's something kind of weird about that part of the forest and they don't go there anymore.

Then one day an unknown hunter shows up at the castle and says, "What can I do around here? I need something to do." And he is told, "Well, there's a problem in the forest. People go out there and they don't come back. We've sent in groups of men to see about it and they disappear. Can you do something?"

Interestingly, this young man does not ask for a group to go with him—he goes into the forest alone, taking only his dog. As they wander about in the forest, they come across a pond. Suddenly a hand reaches up from the pond, grabs the dog, and drags it down. The hunter is fond of the dog, and he's not willing to abandon it in this way. His response is neither to become hysterical, nor to abandon his dog. Instead, he does something sensible: he goes back to the castle, rounds up some men with buckets, and then they bucket out the pond.

Lying at the bottom of the pond is a large man covered with hair all the way down to his feet, kind of reddish—he looks a little like rusty iron. So they capture him and bring him back to the castle, where the king puts him in an iron cage in the courtyard.

Now, let's stop the story here for a second. The implication is that when the male looks into his psyche, not being instructed what to look for, he may see beyond his feminine side, to the other side of the "deep pool." What he finds at the bottom of his psyche—in this area that no one has visited in a long time—is an ancient male covered with hair. Now, in all of the mythologies, hair is heavily connected with the instinctive, the sexual, the primitive. What I'm proposing is that every modern male has, lying at the bottom of his psyche, a large, primitive man covered with hair down to his feet. Making contact with this wildman is the step the seventies male has not yet taken; this is the process that still hasn't taken place in contemporary culture.

As the story suggests very delicately, there's a little fear around this ancient man. After a man gets over his initial skittishness about expressing his feminine side, he finds it to be pretty wonderful. He gets to write poetry and go out and sit by the ocean, he doesn't have to be on top all the time in sex anymore, he becomes empathetic—it's a beautiful new world. But Iron John, the man at the bottom of the lake, is quite a different matter. This figure is even more frightening than the interior female, who is scary enough. When a man succeeds in becoming conscious of his interior woman, he often feels warmer, more alive. But when he approaches what I'll call the "deep male," that's a totally different situation.

Contact with Iron John requires the willingness to go down into the psyche and accept what's dark down there, including the sexual. For generations now, the business community has warned men to keep away from Iron John, and the Christian Church is not too fond of him either. But it's possible that men are once more approaching that deep male.

Freud, Jung, and Wilhelm Reich are three men who had the courage to go down into the pond and accept what's there, which includes the hair, the ancientness, the rustiness. The job of modern males is to follow them down. Some of that work has already been done, and in some psyches (or on some days in the whole culture) the Hairy Man or Iron John has been brought up and stands in a cage "in the courtyard." That means he has been brought back into the civilized world, and to a place where the young males can see him.

Now, let's go back to the story: One day the king's eight-year-old son is playing in the courtyard and he loses his beloved golden ball. It rolls into the cage, and the wildman grabs it. If the prince wants his ball back, he's going to have to go to this rusty, hairy man who's been lying at the bottom of the pond for a very long time, and ask for it. The plot begins to thicken.

Thompson: The golden ball, of course, is a recurrent image in many fairy stories. What does it symbolize in general, and what is its signficance here?

Bly: The golden ball suggests the unity of personality that we have as children—a kind of radiance, a sense of unity with the universe. The ball is golden, representing light, and round, representing wholeness; like the sun, it gives off a radiant energy from inside.

Notice that in this story, the boy is eight. We all lose something around the age of eight, whether we are girl or boy, male or female. We lose the golden ball in grade school if not before; high school finishes it. We may spend the rest of our lives trying to get the golden ball back. The first stage of that process, I guess, would be accepting—firmly, definitively—that the ball has been lost. Remember Freud's words? "What a distressing contrast there is between the radiant intelligence of the child and the feeble mentality of the average adult."

So who's got the golden ball? In the sixties, males were told that the golden ball was the feminine, in their own feminine side. They found the feminine, and still did not find the golden ball. The step that both Freud and Jung urged on males, and the step that men are beginning to undertake now, is the realization that you *can't* look to your own feminine side, because that's not where the ball was lost. You can't go to your wife and ask for the golden ball back; she'd give it to you if she could because women are not hostile in this way to men's growth, but she doesn't have it anyway, and besides, she has lost her own. And heaven knows you can't ask your mother!

After looking for the golden ball in women and not finding it, then looking in his own feminine side, the young male is called upon to consider the possibility that the golden ball lies within the magnetic field of the wildman. Now, that's a very hard thing for us to conceive; the possibility that the deep nourishing and spiritually radiant energy in the male lies not in the feminine side, but in the deep masculine. Not the shallow masculine, the macho masculine, the snowmobile masculine, but the *deep* masculine, the hairy instinctive one who's underwater and who has been there we don't know how long.

Now, the amazing thing about the "Iron John" story is that it doesn't say that the golden ball is being held by some benign Asian guru or by a kind young man named Jesus. There's something connected with getting the golden ball back that is incompatible with niceness. In the story of "The Frog Prince" it's the frog, the un-nice one, the one everyone says "Ick!" to, who brings the golden ball back. And the frog only turns into a prince when it is thrown against the wall in a fit of what New Age people might call "negative energy." New Age thought has taught young men to kiss frogs. That doesn't always work. You only get your mouth wet. The women's movement has helped women learn to throw the frog against the wall, but men haven't had this kind of movement yet. The kind of energy I'm talking about is not the same as macho, brute strength, which men already know enough about; it's forceful action undertaken not without compassion, but with resolve.

Thompson: It sounds as if contacting the wildman would involve in some sense a movement against the forces of "civilization."

Bly: It's true. When it comes time for a young male to have a conversation with the wildman, it's not the same as a conversation with his minister or his guru. When a boy talks with the hairy man, he is not getting into a conversation about bliss or mind or spirit, or "higher consciousness," but about something wet, dark, and low—what James Hillman would call "soul."

And I think that today's males are just about ready to take that step; to go to the cage and ask for the golden ball back. *Some* are ready to do that. Others haven't gotten the water out of the pond yet—they haven't yet left the collective male identity and gone out into the wilderness alone, into the unconscious. You've got to take a bucket, several buckets. You can't wait for a giant to come along and suck out all the water for you: all that magic stuff isn't going to help you. A weekend at Esalen won't do it either! You have to do it bucket by bucket. This resembles the slow discipline of art: it's the work that Rembrandt did, that Picasso and

Yeats and Rilke and Bach all did. Bucket work implies much more discipline than many males have right now.

Thompson: And of course it's going to take some persistence and discipline, not only to uncover the deep male, but to get the golden ball back. It seems unlikely that this "un-nice" wildman would just hand it over.

Bly: You're right: what kind of story would it be if the wildman answered: "Well, okay, here's your ball—go have your fun"? Jung said that in any case, if you're asking your psyche for something, don't use yes-or-no questions—the psyche likes to make deals. If part of you, for example, is very lazy and doesn't want to do any work, a flat-out New Year's resolution won't do you any good: it will work better if you say to the lazy part of yourself, "You let me work for an hour, then I'll let you be a slob for an hour—deal?" So in "Iron John," a deal is made: the wildman agrees to give the golden ball back if the boy opens the cage.

At first, the boy is frightened and runs off. Finally, the third time the wildman offers the same deal, the boy says, "I couldn't open it even if I wanted to, because I don't know where the key is." The wildman now says something magnificent: he says, "The key is under your mother's pillow."

Did you get that shot? The key to let the wildman out is lying not in the toolshed, not in the attic, not in the cellar—it's under his mother's pillow! What do you make of that?

Thompson: Would it suggest that the young male has to take back the power he has given to his mother and get away from the force field of her bed? He must direct his energies away from pleasing Mommy and toward the search for his own instinctive roots.

Bly: That's right, and we see a lot of trouble right there these days, particularly among spiritual devotees. A guru may help you skip over your troubled relations with your mother, but one doesn't enter the soul by skipping: one's personal history is also history in the larger sense. In the West our way has been to enter the soul by consciously exploring the relationship with the mother—even though it may grieve us to do it, even though it implies the incest issue, even though we can't seem to make any headway in talking with her.

Thompson: Which would explain why the boy turns away twice in fright before agreeing to get the key from his mother's bed. Some longtime work is involved in making this kind of break.

Bly: Yes. And it also surely accounts for the fact that, in the story, the mother and father are away on the day that the boy finally obeys the wildman. Obviously, you've got to wait until your mother and father have gone away. This represents not being so dependent on the collective, on the approval of the community, on being a nice person, or essentially being dependent on your own mother. Because if you went up to your mother and said, "I want the key so I can let the wildman out," she'd say, "Oh no, you just get a job," or "Come over here and give Mommy a kiss." There are very few mothers in the world who would release that key from under the pillow, because they are intuitively aware of what would happen next—namely, they would lose their nice boys. The possessiveness that some mothers exercise on sons—not to mention the possessiveness that fathers exercise toward their daughters—cannot be overestimated.

And then we have a lovely scene in which the boy succeeds in opening the cage and setting the wildman free. At this point, one could imagine a number of things happening. The wildman could go back to his pond, so that the split happens over again: by the time the parents come back, the wildman is gone and the boy has replaced the key. He could become a corporate executive, an ordained minister, a professor; he might be a typical twentieth-century male.

But in this case, what happens is that the wildman comes out of the cage and starts toward the forest, and the boy shouts after him, "Don't run away! My parents are going to be very angry when they come back." And Iron John says, "I guess you're right; you'd better come with me." He hoists the boy up on his shoulders and off they go.

Thompson: What does this mean, that they take off together?

Bly: There are several possible arrangements in life that a male can make with the wildman. The male can be separated from the wildman in his unconscious by thousands of miles and never see him. Or the male and the wildman can exist together in a civilized place, like a courtyard, with the wildman in a cage, and then they can carry on a conversation with one another which can go on for a long time. But apparently the two can never be united in the courtyard: the boy cannot bring the wildman with him into his home. When the wildman is freed a little, when the young man feels a little more trust in his instinctive part after going through some discipline, then he can let the wildman out of the cage. And since the wildman can't stay with him in civilization, he must go off with the wildman. This is where the break with the parents finally comes. As they go off together, the wildman says, "You'll never see your mother and father again," and the boy has to accept that the collective thing is over. He must leave his parents' force field.

Thompson: In the ancient Greek tradition a young man would leave his family to study with an older man the energies of Zeus, Apollo, or Dionysus. We seem to have lost the rite of initiation, and yet young males have a great need to be introduced to the male mysteries.

Bly: This is exactly what has been missing in our culture. Among the

Hopis and other Native Americans of the Southwest, a boy is taken away at age twelve and led down into the kiva (down!): he stays down there for six weeks, and a year and a half passes before he sees his mother. He enters completely into the instinctive male world, which means a sharp break with both parents. You see, the fault of the nuclear family isn't so much that it's crazy and full of double-binds (that's true in communes, too—it's the human condition); the issue is that the son has a difficult time breaking away from his parents' field of energy, especially the mother's field. Our culture has made no provision for this initiation.

The ancient societies believed that a boy becomes a man only through ritual and effort—that he must be initiated into the world of men. It doesn't happen by itself; it doesn't happen just because he eats Wheaties. And only men can do this work of initiation.

Thompson: We tend to picture initiation as a series of tests that the young male goes through, but surely there's more to it.

Bly: We can also imagine initiation as that moment when the older males together welcome the younger male into the male world. One of the best stories I've heard about this kind of welcoming is one which takes place each year among the Kikuyus in Africa. When a young man is about ready to be welcomed in, he is taken away from his mother and brought to a special place the men have set up some distance from the village. He fasts for three days. The third night he finds himself sitting in a circle around the fire with the older males. He is hungry, thirsty, alert, and frightened. One of the older males takes up a knife, opens a vein in his arm, and lets a little of his blood flow into a gourd or bowl. Each man in the circle opens his arm with the same knife as the bowl goes around, and lets some blood flow in. When the bowl arrives at the young male, he is invited in tenderness to take nourishment from it.

The boy learns a number of things. He learns that there is a kind of nourishment that comes not from his mother only, but from males. And he learns that the knife can be used for many purposes besides wounding others. Can he have any doubt now that he is welcome in the male world?

Once that is done, the older males can teach him the myths, the stories, the songs that carry male values: not fighting only, but spirit values. Once these "moistening myths" are learned, they lead the young male far beyond his personal father and into the moistness of the swampy fathers who stretch back century after century.

Thompson: If young men today have no access to initiation rites of the past, how are they to make the passage into their instinctive male energy?

Bly: Let me turn the question back to you: as a young male, how are *you* doing it?

Thompson: Well, I've heard much of my own path described in your remarks about soft young men. I was fourteen when my parents were divorced, and my brothers and I stayed with our mom. My relationship with my dad had been remote and distant anyway, and now he wasn't even in the house. My mom had the help of a succession of maids over the years to help raise us, particularly a wonderful old country woman who did everything from changing our diapers to teaching us to pray. It came to pass that my best friends were women, including several older, energetic women who introduced me to politics and literature and feminism. These were platonic friendships on the order of a mentor-student bond. I was particularly influenced by the energy of the women's movement, partially because I had been raised by strong yet nurturing women and partially because my father's absence suggested to me that men couldn't be trusted. So for almost ten years, through about age twenty-four, my life was full of self-confident, experienced women friends and men friends who, like me, placed a premium on vulnerability, gentleness, and sensitivity. From the standpoint of the sixties–seventies male, I had it made! Yet a couple of years ago, I began to feel that something was missing.

Bly: What was missing for you?

Thompson: My father. I began to think about my father. He began to appear in my dreams, and when I looked at old family photos, seeing his picture brought up a lot of grief—grief that I didn't know him, that the distance between us seemed so great. As I began to let myself feel my loneliness for him, one night I had a powerful dream, a dream I had actually had before and forgotten. In the dream I was carried off into the woods by a pack of she-wolves who fed and nursed and raised me with love and wisdom, and I became one of them. And yet, in some unspoken way, I was always slightly separate, different form the rest of the pack. One day after we had been running through the woods together in beautiful formation and with lightning speed, we came to a river and began to drink. When we put our faces to the water, I could see the reflection of all of them but I couldn't see my own! There was an empty space in the rippling water where I was supposed to be. My immediate response in the dream was panic—was I really *there*, did I even *exist*? I knew the dream had to do in some way with the absent male, both within me and with respect to my father. I resolved to spend time with him, to see who we are in each other's lives now that we've both grown up a little.

Bly: So the dream deepened the longing. Have you seen him?

Thompson: Oh yes. I went back to Ohio a few months later to see him. He and my mom are both remarried and still live in our hometown. For the first time, I spent more time with my dad than with my mom.

One long afternoon he and I spent driving to old familiar places—the pond where we fished, the county reservoir where we skated each winter, my grandfather's old farm, which is now owned by someone outside our family. The old windmill stood in the field, rusting, same as it ever was. When we got back to my dad's house, I called my mom and said, "I'm having dinner and spending the night over here at Dad's. See you later." That would *never* have happened a few years earlier.

Bly: That dream is the whole story. What has happened since?

Thompson: Since reconnecting with my father I've been discovering that I have less need to make my women friends serve as my sole confidantes and confessors. I'm turning more to my men friends in these ways, especially those who are working with similar themes in their lives. What's common to our experience is that not having known or connected with our fathers and not having older male mentors, we've tried to get strength secondhand through women who got *their* strength from the women's movement. It's as if many of today's soft young males want these women, who are often older and wiser, to initiate them in some way.

Bly: I think that's true. And the problem is that, from the ancient point of view, women *cannot* initiate males: it's impossible.

When I was lecturing about the initiation of males, several women in the audience who were raising sons alone told me they had come up against exactly that problem. They sensed that their sons needed some sort of toughness, or discipline, or hardness—however it is to be said— but they found that if they tried to provide it, they would start to lose touch with their own femininity. They didn't know what to do.

I said that the best thing to do when the boy is twelve is send him to his father. And several of the women just said flatly, "No, men aren't nourishing, they wouldn't take care of him." I told them that I had experienced tremendous reserves of nourishment that hadn't been called upon until it was time for me to deal with my children. Also, I think a son has a kind of body-longing for the father which must be honored.

One woman told me an interesting story. She was raising a son and two daughters. When the son was fourteen or so, he went off to live with his father, but stayed only a month or two and then came back. She said she knew that, with three women, there was too much feminine energy in the house for him—it was unbalanced, so to speak, but what could she do? One day something strange happened. She said gently, "John, it's time to come to dinner," and he knocked her across the room. She said, "I think it's time to go back to your father." He said, "You're right." The boy couldn't bring what he needed into consciousness, but his body knew it. And his body acted. The mother didn't take it personally either: she understood it was a message. In America there are so many big-muscled high-school boys hulking around the kitchen rudely, and I think in a way they're trying to make themselves less attractive to their mothers.

Separation from the mother is crucial. I'm not saying that women have been doing the wrong thing, necessarily. I think the problem is more that the men are not really doing their job.

Thompson: Underneath most of the issues we've talked about is the father, or the absence of the father. I was moved by a statement you made in *News of the Universe*, that the love-unit most damaged by the Industrial Revolution has been the father-son bond.

Bly: I think it's important that we not idealize past times, and yet the Industrial Revolution does present a new situation, because as far as we know, in ancient times the boy and his father lived closely with each other, at least in the work world after age twelve.

The first thing that happened in the Industrial Revolution was that boys were pulled away from their fathers and other men, and placed in schools. D. H. Lawrence described what this was like in his essay "Men Must Work and Women as Well." What happened to his generation, as he describes it, was the appearance of the idea that physical labor is bad. Lawrence recalls how his father enjoyed working in the mines, enjoyed the camaraderie with the other men, enjoyed coming home and taking his bath in the kitchen. But in Lawrence's lifetime the schoolteachers arrived from London to teach him and his classmates that physical labor is a bad thing, that boys and girls both should strive to move upward into more "spiritual" work—higher work, mental work. With this comes the concept that fathers have been doing something wrong, that men's physical work is low, that the women are right in preferring white curtains and a sensitive, elegant life.

When he wrote *Sons and Lovers*, Lawrence clearly believed the teachers: he took the side of "higher" life, his mother's side. It was not until two years before he died, when he had tuberculosis in Italy, that he began to notice the vitality of the Italian working men, and to feel a deep longing for his own father. He began to realize it was possible that his mother hadn't been right on this issue.

A mental attitude catches on like a plague: "Physical work is wrong." And it follows from that that if Father is wrong, if Father is crude and unfeeling, then Mother is right and I must advance upward, and leave my father behind. Then the separation between fathers and sons is further deepened when *those* sons go to work in an office, become fathers, and no longer share their work with their sons. The strange thing about this is not only the physical separation, but the fact that the father is not able to explain to the son what he's doing. Lawrence's father could show his son what he did, take him down in the mines, just as my own father, who was a farmer, could take me out on the tractor, and show me around. I knew what he was doing all day and all the seasons of the year.

In the world of offices, this breaks down. With the father only home in the evenings, and women's values so strong in the house, the father loses the son five minutes after birth. It's as if he had amnesia and can't remember who his children are. The father is remote: he's not in the house where we are, he's somewhere else. He might as well be in Australia.

And the father is a little ashamed of his work, despite the "prestige" of working in an office. Even if he brings his son there, what can he show him? How he moves papers? Children take things physically, not mentally. If you work in an office, how can you explain how what you're doing is important, or how it differs from what the other males are doing?

The German psychologist Alexander Mitscherlich writes about this situation in a fine book called *Society Without the Father*. His main idea is that if the son does not understand clearly, physically, what his father is doing during the year and during the day, a hole will appear in the son's perception of his father, and into the hole will rush demons. That's a law of nature: demons rush in, because nature hates a vacuum. The son's mind then fills with suspicion, doubt, and a nagging fear that the father is doing evil things.

This issue was dramatized touchingly in the sixties when rebellious students took over the president's office at Columbia, looking for evidence of CIA involvement with the university. It was a perfect example of taking the fear that your father is demonic and transferring the fear to some figure in authority. I give the students all the credit they deserve for their bravery, but on a deeper level they weren't just making a protest against the Vietnam war; they were looking for evidence of their fathers' demonism. A university, like a father, looks upright and decent on the outside, but underneath, somewhere, you have the feeling that he's doing something evil. And it's an intolerable feeling, that the inner fears should be so incongruous with the appearances. So you go to all the trouble to invade the president's office to make the outer look like the inner, to find evidence of demonic activity. And then, naturally, given the interlocking relationships between establishments, you *do* discover letters from the CIA, and demonic links *are* found!

But the discovery is never really satisfying, because the image of the demons inside wasn't real in the first place. These are mostly imagined fears; they come in because the father is *remote*, not because the father is wicked. Finding evidence doesn't answer the deep need we spoke to in the first place—the longing for the father, the confusion about why I'm so separate from my father, where is my father, doesn't he love me, what is going on?

Thompson: Once the father becomes a demonic figure in the son's eyes, it would seem that the son is prevented from forming a fruitful association with *any* male energy, even positive male energy. Since the father serves as the son's earliest role model for male ways, the son's doubts will likely translate into doubts toward the masculine in general.

Bly: It's true: the idea that male energy, when in authority, could be good has come to be considered impossible. Yet the Greeks understood and praised that energy. They called it Zeus energy, which encompasses intelligence, robust health, compassionate authority, intelligent, physically healthy authority, good will, leadership—in sum, positive power accepted by the male in the service of the community. The Native Americans understood this, too—that this power only becomes positive when exercised for the sake of the community, not for personal aggrandizement. All the great cultures, except ours, have lived with images of this energy.

Zeus energy has been disintegrating steadily in America. Popular culture has destroyed it mostly, beginning with the "Maggie and Jiggs" and "Dagwood" comics of the 1920s, in which the male is always foolish. From there the stereotype went into animated cartoons, and now it shows up in TV situation comedies. The young men in Hollywood writing these comedies have a strong and profound hatred for the Zeus image of male energy. They may believe that they are giving the audience what it wants, or simply that they're working to make a buck, whereas in fact what they are actually doing is taking revenge on their fathers, in the most classic way possible. Instead of confronting their father in Kansas, these television writers attack him long distance from Hollywood.

This kind of attack is particularly insidious because it's a way of destroying not only all the energy that the father lives on, but the energy that he has tried to pass on. In the ancient tradition, the male who grows is one who is able to contact the energy coming from older males—and from women as well, but especially male spiritual teachers who transmit positive male energy.

Thompson: I find in your translations of the poems of Rainer Maria Rilke, as well as in your most recent book of poems, *The Man in the Black Coat Turns*, a willingness to pay honor to the older males who have influenced you—your own father and your spiritual fathers. In fact, in the past few years, you seem to have deliberately focused on men and the masculine experience. What inspired this shift in emphasis away from the feminine?

Bly: After a man has done some work in recovering his wet and muddy feminine side, often he still doesn't feel complete. A few years ago I began to feel diminished by my lack of embodiment of the fruitful male, or the "moist male." I found myself missing contact with the male—or should I say my father?

For the first time, I began to think of my father in a different way. I began to think of him not as someone who had deprived me of love or attention or companionship, but as someone who himself had been deprived, by his mother or by the culture. This process is still going on. Every time I see my father I have different and complicated feeings about how much of the deprivation I felt with him came willfully and how much came against his will—how much he was aware of and unaware of. I've begun to see him more as a man in a complicated situation.

Jung made a very interesting observation: he said that if a male is brought up mainly with the mother, he will take a feminine attitude toward his father. He will see his father through his mother's eyes. Since the father and the mother are in competition for the affection of the son, you're not going to get a straight picture of your father out of your mother. Instead, all the inadequacies of the father are well pointed out. The mother tends to give the tone that civilization and culture and feeling and relationship are things which the mother and the son and the daughter have together, whereas what the father has is something inadequate, stiff, maybe brutal, unfeeling, obsessed, rationalistic, money-mad, uncompassionate. So the young male often grows up with a wounded image of his father—not necessarily caused by the father's actions, but based on the mother's view of these actions.

I know that in my own case I made my first connection with feeling through my mother: she gave me my first sense of human community. But the process also involved picking up a negative view of my father and his whole world.

It takes a while for a man to overcome this. The absorption with the mother may last ten, fifteen, twenty years, and then, rather naturally, a man turns toward his father. Eventually, when the male begins to think it over, the mother's view of the father just doesn't hold up.

Another way to put all this is to say that if the son accepts his mother's views of the father, he will look at his own masculinity from a feminine point of view. But eventually the male must throw off this view and begin to discover for himself what the father is, what masculinity is.

Thompson: What can men do to get in touch with their male energy—their instinctive male side? What kind of work is involved?

Bly: I think the next step for us is learning to visualize the wildman. And to help that visualization, I feel we need to return to the mythologies that today we only teach children. If you go back to ancient mythology,

you find that people in ancient times have already done some work in
helping us to visualize the wildman. I think we're just coming to the place
where we can understand what the ancients were talking about.

In the Greek myths, for example, Apollo is visualized as a golden
man standing on an enormous accumulation of dark, dangerous energy
called Dionysus. The Bhutanese bird men with dog's teeth are another
possible visualization. Another is the Chinese tomb-guardian: a figure
with enormous power in the music and the will, and a couple of fangs
sticking out of his mouth. In the Hindu tradition this fanged aspect of the
Siva is called the Bhairava: in his Bhairava aspect, Shiva is not a nice boy.
There's a hint of this energy with Christ going wild in the temple and
whipping everybody. The Celtic tradition gives us Cuchulain—smoke
comes out of the top of his head when he gets hot.

These are all powerful energies lying in ponds we haven't found yet.
All these traditions give us models to help us sense what it would be
like for a young male to grow up in a culture in which the divine is associated not only with the Virgin Mary and the Blissful Jesus, but with
the wildman covered with hair. We need to tap into these images.

Thompson: These mythological images are strong, almost frightening. How would you distinguish them from the strong but destructive
male chauvinist personality that we've been trying to get *away* from?

Bly: The male in touch with the wildman has true strength: he's able
to shout and say what he wants in a way that the sixties–seventies male is
not able to. The approach to his own feminine space that the sixties–
seventies male has made is infinitely valuable, and not to be given up. But
as I say in my poem "A Meditation on Philosophy": "When you shout at
them, they don't reply. They turn their face toward the crib wall, and die."

However, the ability of a male to shout and to be fierce is *not* the
same as treating poeple like objects, demanding land or empire, expressing aggression—the whole model of the fifties male. Getting in touch
with the wildman means religious life for a man in the broadest sense of
the phrase. The fifties male was almost wholly secular, so we are not
talking in any way of a movement back.

Thompson: How would you envision a movement forward?

Bly: Just as women in the seventies needed to develop what is known
in the Indian tradition as Kali energy—the ability to really say what they
want, to dance with skulls around their neck, to cut relationships when
they need to—what males need now is an energy that can face this energy
in women, and *meet* it. They need to make a similar connection in their
psyches to their "Kala" energy—which is just another way to describe the
wildman at the bottom of the pond. If they don't, they won't survive.

Thompson: Do you think they can?

Bly: I feel very hopeful. Men are suffering right now—young males especially. But now that so many men are getting in touch with their feminine side, we're ready to start *seeing* the wildman and to put its powerful, dark energy to use. At this point, many things can happen.

Robert Bly and Keith Thompson have begun collaborating on a book, tentatively titled *Conversations on the Wildman,* on the relations between fathers and sons, stages in the development of the male psyche, and the absence of male initiation. In response to those who expressed alarm that they were counselling men to regress to primitive monsters, they attempt to make a strong distinction between the wildman and what might be called the "savage man" in their forthcoming work.

On Being a Man

D. H. Lawrence

Man is a thought-adventurer.

Which isn't the same as saying that man has an intellect. In intellect there is skill, and tricks. To the intellect the terms are given, as the chessmen and rules of the game are given in chess. Real thought is an experience. It begins as a change in the blood, a slow convulsion and revolution in the body itself. It ends as a new piece of awareness, a new reality in mental consciousness.

On this account, thought is an adventure, and not a practice. In order to think, man must risk himself doubly. First, he must go forth and meet life in the body. Then he must face the result in his mind.

The risk is double, because man is double. Each of us has two selves. First is this body which is vulnerable and never quite within our control. The body with its irrational sympathies and desires and passions, its peculiar direct communication, defying the mind. And second is the conscious ego, the self I KNOW I am.

The self that lives in my body I can never finally know. It has such strange attractions, and revulsions, and it lets me in for so much irrational suffering, real torment, and occasional frightening delight. That me that is in my body is like a jungle in which dwells an unseen me, like a black panther in the night, whose two eyes glare green through my dreams, and, if a shadow falls, through my waking day.

Then there is this other me, that is fair-faced and reasonable and sensible and complex and full of good intentions. The known me, which can be seen and appreciated. I say of myself: "Yes, I know I am impatient and rather intolerant in ideas. But in the ordinary way of life I am quite easy and really rather kindly. My kindliness makes me sometimes a bit false. But then I don't believe in mechanical honesty."

This is the known me, having a talk with itself. It sees a reason for everything it does and feels. It has a certain unchanging belief in its own good intentions. It tries to steer a sensible and harmless course among all the other people and "personalities" around itself.

To this known me, everything exists as a term of knowledge. A man is what I know he is. England is what I know it to be. I am what I know I am. To the known me, nothing exists beyond what I know. True, I am always adding to the things I know. But this is because, in my opinion, knowledge begets knowledge. Not because anything has entered *from the outside*. There *is* no outside. There is only more knowledge to be added. People go to Spain, and "know" Spain. People study entomology, and "know" insects. Lots of people "know" me.

And this is how we live. We proceed from what we know already to what we know next. If we don't know much about the moon, we have only to get the latest book on that orb, and we shall be *au courant*.

All this is the adventure of knowing and understanding. But it isn't the thought-adventure.

The thought adventure starts in the blood, not in the mind.

Take the case of men and women. A man, proceeding from his known self, likes a woman because she is in sympathy with what he knows. He feels that he and she know one another. They marry. And then the fun begins. In so far as they know one another they can proceed from their known selves, they are as right as ninepence. Loving couple, etc. But the moment there is real blood contact, as likely as not a strange discord enters in. She is not what he thought her. He is not what she thought him. It is the other, primary or bodily self—appearing very often like a black demon, out of the fair creature who was erst the beloved.

The man who before marriage seemed everything that is delightful, after marriage begins to come out in his true colors, a son of the old and rather hateful Adam. And she, who was an angel of loveliness and desirability, gradually emerges as an almost fiendlike daughter of the snake-frequenting Eve.

What has happened?

Marriage is the great puzzle of our day. It is our sphinx-riddle. Solve it, or be torn to bits, is the decree.

We marry from the known self, taking the woman as an extension of our knowledge—an extension of our known self. And then, almost invariably, comes the jolt. The woman of the known self is fair and lovely. But the woman of the dark blood looks, to man, most malignant and horrific. In the same way, the fair daytime man of courtship days leaves nothing to be desired. But the husband, horrified by the Eve of the blood, obtuse and arrogant in his Adam obstinacy, is an enemy pure and simple.

Solve the puzzle. The quickest way is for the wife to smother the serpent-advised Eve which is in her, and for the man to talk himself out of his old arrogant Adam. Then they make a fair and above-board combination, called a successful marriage.

But Nemesis is on our track. The husband forfeits his arrogance, the wife has her children and her way to herself. But lo, the son of one woman is husband to the woman of the next generation! And oh, women, beware the mother's boy! Or else the wife forfeits her nature and becomes the instrument of the man. And then, oh young husband of the next generation, prepare for the daughter's revenge.

What's to be done?

The thought-adventure! We've got to take ourselves as we are, not as we know ourselves to be. I am the son of the old red-earth Adam, with a black touchstone at the centre of me. And all the fair words in the world won't alter it. Woman is the strange serpent-communing Eve, inalterable. We are a strange pair, who meet, but never mingle. I came, in the bath of birth, out of a mother. But I arose the old Adam, with the black old stone at the core of me. She had a father who begot her, but the column of her is pure enigmatic Eve.

In spite of all the things I know about her, in spite of my knowing her so well, the serpent knows her better still. And in spite of my fair words, and my goodly pretences, she runs up against the black stone of Adam which is in the middle of me.

Know thyself means knowing at last that you *can't* know yourself. I can't know the Adam of red-earth which is me. It will always do things to me, beyond my knowledge. Neither can I know the serpent-listening Eve which is the woman, beneath all her modern glibness. I have to take her at that. And we have to meet as I meet a jaguar between the trees in the mountains, and advance, and touch, and risk it. When man and woman *actually* meet, there is always terrible risk to both of them.

There is always risk, for him and for her. Take the risk, make the adventure. Suffer and enjoy the change in the blood. And, if you are a man, slowly, slowly make the great experience of realizing. Fully conscious realization. If you are a woman, the strange, slumbrous serpentine realization, which knows without thinking.

But with men, it is a thought-adventure. He risks his body and blood. And in a new adventure he dares take thought. And daring to take thought, he ventures on, and realizes at last.

To be a man! To risk your body and your blood first, and then to risk your mind. All the time, to risk your known self, and become once more a self you could never have known or expected.

To be a man, instead of being a mere personality. Today men don't risk their blood and bone. They go forth, panoplied in their own idea of themselves. Whatever they do, they perform it all in the full armor of their own idea of themselves. Their known bodily self is never for one moment unsheathed. All the time, the only protagonist is the known ego, the self-conscious ego. And the dark self in the mysterious labyrinth of the body is cased in a tight armor of cowardly repression.

You dare anything, except being a man. So intense and final is the modern and white man's conviction, his internal conviction, that he is *not* a man, that he dares anything on earth except be a man. There his courage drops to its grave. He daren't be a man: the old Adam of red earth, with the black touchstone at the middle of him.

He knows he's not a man. Hence his creed of harmlessness. He knows he is not a man of living red earth, to live onward through strange weather into new springtime. He knows there is extinction ahead: for nothing but extinction lies in wait for the conscious ego. Hence his creed of harmlessness, of relentless kindness. There should be no danger in life *at all*, even no friction. This he asserts, while all the time he is slowly, malignantly undermining the tree of life.

The Neglected Child Within

Robert Stein

Marriage is no marriage if it is not based on the essential maleness and femaleness of husband and wife. As soon as the male/female polarity begins to become indistinct, the marriage relationship deteriorates. This condition is probably the source of most of the dissatisfactions in modern marriages.

Pure maleness and pure femaleness are strongly attracted to each other. They are not enemies, not hostile opponents, as they seem to be in most marital relationships nowadays. What, then, is causing the breakdown in the vital flow between husband and wife? I believe it is principally because the *neglected inner child within both partners tends to rule the relationship*. That is, this neglected and unfulfilled child is continually demanding care and attention.

While the unformed maleness and femaleness of a child begins to emerge as soon as it is born—as soon as it is conceived, really—the child does not attain its own sexual identity until it becomes sexually conscious. And this cannot occur before its bodily centers of sexuality are fully awakened, not before its consciousness develops sufficiently to receive the dark mystery of sexual passion. In most cultures, the transition rites into manhood and womanhood center mainly around the mysteries of sexuality and sexual identity. Mankind has always found it necessary to help the child through this dangerous passage with the aid of complex rituals. Few of us nowadays have successfully completed this psychological passage into manhood and womanhood; thus, the uninitiated and fearful child within us cries out continually for help and instruction. And this neglected child so dominates the marriage relationship that it quickly deteriorates into the asexual comfort and security of the parent-child relationship.

Not until the child has been initiated into the mysteries of manhood or womanhood will it be ready for marriage. Not until the child has become man or woman can it contain the mystery of its own dark sexual nature. Only then do husband and wife emerge into the full splendor and dignity of their own maleness and femaleness. Only then can they once again experience the powerful attraction of sexual polarity which the soul needs.

What is to be done for this neglected and dissatisfied child so that it may become truly man or woman? Obviously some initiation or healing rite is needed. Analysis, I believe, can be such a rite. But it is a long, slow, and still inadequate ritual. With or without analysis, the troubled child need not dominate if each partner at least attempts to assume responsibility for the care of his own inner child.

The demanding child is one who has encountered too much destructive resistance to its own development, who has been made to feel guilty and ashamed about the uniqueness of his own nature. The child inside the adult needs desperately to experience the full acceptance of its nature, and to be absolved from the crippling guilt which has arrested its development. Unfortunately, the demanding child usually evokes criticism and censure from others, especially when it speaks out of the body of an adult. What this child really wants is to be allowed to live spontaneously and naturally. But when we ourselves are critical and rejecting of the child within us, how can we expect others to accept it? Besides, even when others have compassion for it, the negative parent archetype within our own psyches is even more rejecting than others; consequently the child's need for approval becomes insatiable and is never really gratified.

When the demanding child in us cries out to another person, it often provokes the other person to fall into the negative parent role. We then experience rejection and betrayal, and an even deeper sense of inadequacy and humiliation. When this happens in marriage, the flow of eros is totally obstructed. Clearly, it is crucial to the re-awakening of the male/female connection to develop the capacity to contain the sufferings of the demanding child. We only prolong the process of its transformation each time we subject this child to further rejection and humiliation.

Containing the painful needs of the demanding child is difficult because they always seem so simple, so right, and unpretentious to us: "Surely every human being has a right to a little love and understanding? Why should I suffer and contain a basic need which is so easy to fulfill?

Now give me an important or meaningful cause and I'll show you what I can take! But why should I suffer just because you refuse to make a proper meal or keep the house properly? Why should I endure the pain I experience because of the way you sexually frustrate me? Why should I suffer because of your coldness and lack of understanding for my very simple, basic needs? A stranger would show more feeling for me than you do. I just won't tolerate it! You can talk all you like about meaningful suffering, shout it from the roof tops, but I know what I have a right to expect and simple human kindness is not too much to demand . . . and so forth."

So there you are. Do we have the right to deprive a baby of its milk? to deprive our loved ones of the milk of human kindness, of simple understanding? Well, an infant or child certainly has a right to expect certain basic needs to be fulfilled by its parents. A husband and wife, however, are not parents to each other; to expect more than honesty and openness kills the flow of love between them. And if the inner child still persists in demanding its rights from the other, the marriage will remain stuck in a parent-child pattern. There is no possibility for any vital male/female connection, then, and no real sex. So my answer to the man or woman who sees no reason to endure the "rightful" demands of his or her own neglected and frustrated child is this: there is no hope for any real change in your marriage, no hope for reconnecting to the great natural rhythms of your own being and of the cosmos, unless you do; until this is fully realized and lived, your marriage can be only a sterile prison or a battlefield.

Now, the transformation of the demanding child cannot occur without a parallel internal change occurring in the negative parent archetype. As soon as one demands from another what one feels to be one's "right," the critical, rejecting negative parent is activated in the other person. I will take this one step further: the negative parent is also constellated within oneself as soon as we even *begin* to feel hurt or anger toward another for letting us down, for not giving us what we feel we have a "right" to expect.

Let me describe how I think the negative parent works internally. It enters as soon as the inner child begins to demand its rights, its simple needs for love, compassion, and understanding. The negative parent makes us feel guilty about having such infantile and immature needs: "Are you not capable of standing on your own two feet? You are a worthless, dependent child—a nobody." So we are crushed by words such as these, and we make a determined effort to pull ourselves up by our own bootstraps. In the process, we reject the needs of our inner child. But the child is persistent and soon returns with its demands, even stronger than before. Now the battle is on in full fury and we are caught between these two opposing forces—the child of our own nature and the antilife force of the negative parent. And we become devitalized, paralyzed by it all, not knowing which way to go. If we go with the negative parent, the life force within us falls into its iron grip and we feel imprisoned. But if we go with the demanding child in an attempt to get others to fulfill its needs, we only encounter the same negative parent reaction externally. This dilemma can only be resolved once we gain the capacity to contain the struggle. This makes it possible for the internal negative parent to be ultimately transformed into a positive parent who supports and nourishes the child. Then this inner child begins to receive the compassion it needs and we can discover the best possible means of fulfilling its neglected instinctual needs.

Fears of Intimacy

Lillian Rubin

Separation and unity—the excitement and fear, the triumph and anxiety they generate—will remain continuing themes in adult life. In adulthood, when we find ourselves in an intimate relationship, we each experience again, even if only in highly attenuated form, those early struggles around separation and unity—the conflict between wanting to be one with another and the desire for an independent, autonomous self. For each woman and man who comes into a marriage stirs the yearnings from an unremembered but still powerfully felt past; each brings with her or him two people—the adult who says, "I do," and the child within who once knew both the agony and the ecstasy of a symbiotic union. Ecstasy, because in the mother's arms the infant could experience the bliss of unity and the security that accompanies it. Agony, because from birth onward life seems a series of separations—each one an insistent reminder of those past and those yet to come, each one experienced as a threat to survival itself.

Of course, as adults we know there's no return to the old symbiotic union; of course, survival is no longer at stake in separation. But the child within feels as if this were still the reality. And the adult responds to the archaic memory of those early feelings even though they're far from consciousness. Thus, we don't usually know what buffets us about—what makes us eager to plunge into a relationship one moment and frightens us into anxious withdrawal the next. We know only that we long for closeness and connection with another, and that we feel unaccountably uncomfortable when we get it—that, without warning, we begin to feel anxious in some ill-defined and indefinable way.

The process by which a child separates is a complicated one, including within it several major developmental tasks. Paramount among them is the need to develop an independent, coherent, and continuing sense of self.

In this process, two things are central: the crystallization of a gender identity and the maintenance of what psychologists call "ego boundaries"—those personal psychological boundaries of the self that serve to set us off from the rest of the world. This, in large part, is what a child's separation struggle is all about—a struggle that's different for boys and for girls just because it's a woman who has mothered them both.

It's not that the lot of one is easier than the other; growing up is hard for children of either gender. But the problems they encounter with each developmental task are different and, depending upon the issue in process at any given time, are sometimes harder for girls, sometimes for boys. Thus, when the task is to establish the boundaries of self, the identity between mother and daughter makes that more complicated for a girl than for a boy. Just because they are the same gender, it's more difficult for a girl to separate, harder for her or her mother to know where one ends and the other begins. On the other hand, when we look at another central issue in this developing selfhood—the establishment of a gender identity, which means the internalization and consolidation of the knowledge that says, "I am a girl"; "I am a boy"—the identity between mother and daughter is a help not a hindrance, while the difference between mother and son makes it a much more difficult and complicated issue for a boy.

It's obvious that the experience of *being* male and *being* female is different. But what has been less clear until now is how the *process* of developing and internalizing a gender identity—so different in girls and in boys because of the structure of parenting—affects the development of ego boundaries and, therefore, determines the shape of feminine and masculine personality in adulthood.

When a boy who has been raised by a woman confronts the need to establish his gender identity, it means a profound upheaval in his internal world. Now, in order to identify with his maleness, he must renounce this connection with the first person outside self to be internalized into his inner psychic world—the one who has been so deeply embedded in his psychic life as to seem a part of himself—and seek instead a deeper attachment and identification with father. But this father with whom he is expected to identify has, until this time, been a secondary character in his internal life, often little more than a sometimes pleasurable, sometimes troublesome shadow on the consciousness of the developing child.

It's a demanding, complicated, and painful process that takes its toll on a boy who must grow into a man. Although they happen at different times in the life of the infant and are two separate psychological processes, identification and attachment are so closely linked that the child can't give up one without an assault on the other. With the repression of the identification with mother, therefore, the attachment to her becomes ambivalent. He still needs her, but he can't be certain anymore that she will be there, that she can be trusted.

For girls, the process of developing an independent sense of self presents a wholly different set of obstacles. Just as the fact that there are no obvious differences between a girl and her mother makes the process of establishing a gender identity easier for girls than for boys, the problem of separating—of defining and experiencing self as an autonomous, bounded individual—is harder.

In the normal developmental course, the formation of a gender identity in a girl requires no wrenching breaks with the past. She's a girl, mother's a woman; the one, she understands intuitively, leads quite naturally to the other. There's no need to build defenses against feeling and attachment, therefore, no need for the kind of rigid boundaries a man develops as a means of protecting and maintaining those defenses. This means that, as a woman, she'll develop ego boundaries that are more permeable than a man's—a fact of paramount importance in the management of both her internal life and her external one.

It is in this part of the developmental scenario that we see the birth of the empathic capacities for which women are so justly known. The context within which separation takes place and identity is forged means that a girl never has to separate herself as completely and irrevocably as a boy must. Her sense of herself, therefore, is never as separate as his; she experiences herself always as more continuous with another; and the maintenance of close personal connections will continue to be one of life's essential themes for her. As a result, she will preserve the capacity, born in the early symbiotic union, for participating in another's inner life, for sensing another's emotional states almost as if they were her own—the capacity that, in an adult, we call empathy.

The conventional wisdom says that women want intimacy, men resist it. Women complain to each other all the time about not being able to talk to their men about the things that matter most to them—about what they themselves are thinking and feeling, about what goes on in the hearts and minds of the men they're relating to. And men, less able to expose themselves and their conflicts—those within themselves or those with the women in their lives—either turn silent or take cover by holding women up to derision. It's one of the norms of male camaraderie to poke fun at women, to complain laughingly about the mystery of their minds, wondering about their ways. Even Freud did it when, in exasperation, he asked mockingly, "What do women want? Dear God, what do they want?"

Commitment is not a problem for a man; he's good at that. He can spend a lifetime living in the same family, working at the same job—even one he hates. And he's not without an inner emotional life. But when a relationship requires the sustained verbal expression of that inner life and the full range of feelings that accompany it, then it becomes burdensome for him. He can act out anger and frustration inside the family, it's true. But ask him to express his sadness, his fear, his dependency—all those feelings that would expose his vulnerability to himself or to another—and he's likely to close down as if under some compulsion to protect himself.

All requests for such intimacy are difficult for a man, but they become especially complex and troublesome in relations with women. It's another of those paradoxes. For, to the degree that it's possible for him to be emotionally open with anyone, it is with a woman—a tribute to the power of the childhood experience with mother. Yet it's that same early experience and his need to repress it that raises his ambivalence and generates his resistance.

He moves close, wanting to share some part of himself with her, trying to do so, perhaps even yearning to experience again the bliss of the infant's connection with a woman. She responds, woman style—wanting to touch him just a little more deeply, to know what he's thinking, feeling, fearing, wanting. And the fear closes in—the fear of finding himself again in the grip of a powerful woman, of allowing her admittance only to be betrayed and abandoned once again, of being overwhelmed with denied desires.

So he withdraws, [as one husband describes:]

Well, it can go something like this. Molly can come into the room, take one look, and know something's wrong. So she'll ask: "What's the matter?" And then the craziest damn thing happens. Instead of saying, "I'm feeling really terrible, and I need to talk to you," what do I do? I stick my head deeper into the paper I'm reading and grunt something unintelligible. She'll say again, "Hey, what's the matter? Is anything wrong?" I'll just mutter, "Nothing." Then she'll say, "It doesn't sound like nothing; you sound angry at me. Are you?" I'll say, "I'm not angry at you." But the truth is, the vibes say I'm sitting there smoldering. But I don't give an inch. It's like she's going to take some-

thing priceless from me, that's how hard I hold on to it. But I don't even know what the "it" is. I just know it's like when my mother would keep harping on me: "Where you going? What you doing? Who you seeing?" It's really nuts. There's some part of me that doesn't want her to leave me alone, like I want her to push me so maybe I won't feel so bad. But when she does I freeze up, like I have to protect myself from her.

To a woman, the world men live in seems a lonely one—a world in which their fears of exposing their sadness and pain, their anxiety about allowing their vulnerability to show, even to a woman they love, is so deeply rooted inside them that, most often, they can only allow it to happen "late at night in the dark."

Partly that's a result of the ways in which boys are trained to camouflage their feelings under cover of an exterior of calm, strength, and rationality. Fears are not manly. Emotions, above all, are not for the strong, the sane, the adult. Women suffer them, not men—women, who are more like children with what seems like their never-ending preoccupation with their emotional life. But the training takes so well because of their early childhood experience when, as very young boys, they had to shift their identification from mother to father and sever themselves from their earliest emotional connection. Put the two together and it does seem like suffering to men to have to experience that emotional side of themselves, to have to give it voice.

That's his side of the ambivalence that leads to the approach-avoidance dance we see so often in relations between men and women. What about her side?

On the surface, she seems to have little problem in dealing with closeness in a relationship. She's the one who keeps calling for more intimacy, who complains that he doesn't share himself fully enough, doesn't tell her what he's thinking and feeling. And while there's partial truth in this imagery, the reality is more complex. Thus, when, as is sometimes the case, a woman meets a man who seems capable of the kind of intimacy she longs for, dreams about, we see that it's not just a matter of a woman who keeps asking for more in a relationship and a man who keeps protesting. Instead, we hear the other side of the story, as these words from a thirty-year-old patient show:

I can't figure out what's happening to me. I try to read a book, and I find myself thinking of him. But it's not loving thoughts; it's critical, picky thoughts—anything negative, just to get me out of the relationship. Then, once I've convinced myself, I wonder: Why did I love him yesterday? And, if I did, how can it feel so miserable today? I get so confused I want to run and hide just to get away. But now I understand better what I'm scared of; I know it's my problem. I can't tolerate the intimacy. How could it be such a burden to be loved?

Then there are the women who present the semblance of intimacy without much substance. We all know them—women who seem to have an ineffable ability to attract people, who develop a kind of court around themselves. They walk in an atmosphere that radiates warmth and openness, that promises an intense and intimate closeness. But the husband of one such woman spoke bleakly about what it's like to be married to her:

Everybody gets a piece of the action but me. She looks like she's wonderful at closeness just so you don't get too close. She's got a million friends and they all think she's great. Everyone comes to her for advice or to cry on her shoulder, and she loves it all. It makes her feel like the queen bee—always in the center of a swarm. But the truth is, she uses it to bind people to her, gets them to need her; that's the only way she feels secure.

Surprised at the bitterness of the outburst from this quiet, contained man, I commented, "Yet you've been married to her for twenty-three years. What keeps you here?" With a small, sad smile, he replied:

I guess the same thing that keeps others around—the seduction. There's always the hope that she'll deliver what she promises, and that if she ever does, it'll be worth the wait.

Despite the cant about women being available for intimacy and men being unavailable, they are both likely to experience problems and pressures in an intimate relationship. But, given the combination of the social roles for which they were trained, and their early developmental experiences inside the family, what makes intimacy feel risky is different for each of them.

For a woman, the problem of finding and maintaining the boundary between self and a loved other is paramount. The continuity of identification with mother means that the tie is never quite severed—an invisible cord that fastens them to each other in a powerful bond that doesn't exist between mother and son.

This fusion of identities and the struggle a girl engages in to break those bonds foretells the future of her adult emotional relationships. "The basic feminine sense of self is connected to [others in] the world," writes Nancy Chodorow, "the basic masculine sense of self is separate." Compared to a man, therefore, a woman remains more preoccupied with relational issues, gives herself more easily to emotional relationships, and reaches for attachment and emotional connection with an insistence and intensity that often startles her as well as the man in her life.

But this need for intimacy and connection is not without its paradoxical side. Because her boundaries can be so easily breached, she begins to fear that she's losing some part of herself—not just because someone is taking something from her but because, unless she's constantly vigilant, she's all too likely to give it away. For her, therefore, maintaining herself as a separate person in the context of an intimate relationship is the dominant issue, the one she'll wrestle with from girlhood on.

How the conflicts are handled depends on the couple—on the ability of the individuals involved to tolerate both closeness and distance, to establish the boundaries of self while, at the same time, permitting a satisfactory level of emotional connection and attachment; in essence, on their capacity to move comfortably between separation and unity. But, however well or badly they are dealt with, these problems will be there, requiring resolution. And they will be felt most keenly in any relationship that has the aura of permanence, that recreates the old family.

For men, who come to define themselves in terms of the denial of the original connection, the issue of unity is the most pressing. The problem that plagues their emotional relationships is their difficulty in allowing another to penetrate the boundaries sufficiently to establish the communion, the unity, that's necessary for a deep and sustained intimacy with another.

For women, it's the other way around. Because they come to define themselves by affirming that original connection, the problem of separation is in the forefront. Their more permeable boundaries and greater relational concerns make women less certain that they can maintain the hard-won separation, even that they want to maintain it. The possibility of merger with another, therefore, remains both a threat and a promise— a persistent strain in their relationships as they move ambivalently from the fear of violation and invasion to the hunger for that old symbiotic union.

In relating to men, women rarely have to face the conflict inside themselves squarely, precisely because men take care of the problem for them by their own unmistakable difficulties with closeness and connection—because men tend to be so self-contained and protected from intrusion, except in the matter of sex. This, more than any other, is the area in which the conflicts of both—their differences and similarities—can be seen most clearly.

Feminine Genius

Ariel Ruth Hoebel

The archetypal relationship between man and woman seems ideal and beautiful on the surface, and we are all taken in by its glamor. But where is the individual in the tragic tale of Tristan and Isolde, of Romeo and Juliet, of the prince and princess who live happily ever after? The individual stands far outside the tale, because it is an analogy, a symbol of what goes on within himself. Male and female within the individual must battle with each other in opposition until they achieve union. But the actual man and woman who live in the world and love each other must not lose sight of their true identity in the battle and the union. They must not mistake this one symbol for the whole story of their lives. There must be surrender, surely, in the act of union, in the bliss of love, in the hell of hate, but one's individuality is more precious than any archetype.

But there are few individuals, few who have emerged from the primordial ooze enough to stand outside these archetypal dramas. Men and women who are asleep, who have no real individuality, find themselves compelled to be like the polar opposites of masculinity and femininity, like stereotypes, regardless of whether that is who they are. Men feel they must be dominant, aggressive, and active, and women feel they must be submissive, passive, and receptive. They cultivate the qualities of the archetype rather than their own peculiarities.

Since we live in a patriarchy, masculine values based on masculine qualities are the prescribed modes of thinking. Women take on the dark side of this. If the masculine world would open itself to feminine knowledge there would be a *hieros gamos* on a large scale, a union of opposites, a marriage between art and science, between poetry and philosophy. This alchemical union takes place on the individual plane in a few people but rarely, and these people attain to something like genius of being. So, though the masculine mind rejects the feminine, on the individual plane this most despised thing, the stone rejected by the builders, is actually the cornerstone of the alchemical work.

What is the feminine part of the psyche? It is a blind spot, so it is difficult to see. Let us say the intellect is masculine; it is ordered, structured, and finite. Objectivity and rationality, we shall also say are masculine. And therefore, what lies outside these masculine realms is feminine territory: intuition, subjectivity, and irrationality. It is not this simple though, because objectivity is very subjective, rationality is very irrational, and the borders between intellect and intuition cannot be found. And here lies the threat of the feminine point of view: it forever beholds the folly of pure rationality, pure intellect, pure objectivity. But given the strict duality of the male/female myth, men are rational, objective, and intellectual; women are irrational, subjective, and intuitional. We who have lived under the yoke of this myth for thousands of years have become like the creatures of the myth. This is a sad state of affairs because intellect without intuition is a stale rigid trap.

Men need the qualities they project onto women. We believe because of our conditioning that a man is not a man if he has any of the qualities he gets rid of by claiming they are exclusively female. He knows unconsciously that he needs those qualities—that is why he is drawn to certain women, women who display outwardly the qualities he has hidden within himself, in the dark shadows of his psyche. It is no wonder a man wants to possess a woman, he really wants to reclaim that lost part of himself, to be whole again. He must have or imagine he has a woman who is all of those qualities he is missing. She will be an extension of himself, devoid of individuality. This is how she fulfills her role as mate to her man.

The tragedy of this situation strikes at both sides. A man may seem to have individuality and dignity but he is not himself if he has repressed part of himself. The tragedy on the other side is that a woman doesn't even have this false individuality and dignity. She is only a part of the man, like Adam's rib. She has individuality and dignity vicariously. She must repress the part of her psyche that demands these things and project this part onto her man. He opens all doors for her, he blazes a path through the world for both of them. One wonders what men do with their emotions and what women do with their aggressions. What does a man do inside himself when he would weep? What does a woman do inside herself when she would be forceful and take over a situation? There must be murders and imprisonments inside, amputations and other tortures, punishments and deformities.

Where then do we find men and women who are truly individuals, who are truly themselves? Artists and poets, and other outsiders are escapees from our tragic conditioning. The outsiders experiment with what they have: visions and premonitions, intuitions, hoping to regain the lost paradise of the psyche when it is whole. Men and women use what they have: each other, to regain this lost inner paradise. One need only look at the other to see what is missing in himself. Men must learn to listen to women. Women must find their voice because they must describe a taboo in such a way that it will be accepted again by those who fear it most. They must defend their part of the psyche, bring it out into the light and let everyone become familiar with it. They must learn to write and sing and paint and philosophize from man's opposite pole: messages from the shadow people.

What is the feminine view of the world? It is a preoccupation with the relationship between things rather than with the things themselves. Men believe they are objective because they take careful note of individual things but they are coming more to realize that the object is not alone, it is inseparable from all the objects around it. In fact, it is the whole that must be understood before any one object can be understood. This is a more feminine point of view. In conversation, a woman is more occupied with the way things are said, the tone of voice, gesture, body language, than is a man. A man is more occupied with the content of the words. In modern psychology, body language is studied by intuitive persons because they find that words can lie but the body cannot. This is a field in which women are unconscious adepts.

Because of her peculiar orientation, woman has developed talents to see where men cannot see, to see from angles he cannot see from. In this patriarchy, what men see is what mankind sees. Woman is silent about what she sees. She does not see what she sees. Now is the time when we are beginning to look at ourselves and reassess our possibilities.

Why is it there have been no women of genius, only an occasional one who even aspired? Because woman has always had to play a part for man's sake. She has had to be his missing part, so that he can be whole and survive his own unbalanced state. The danger of woman's desire for independence, for a life of her own, has always been felt by those who train her for this role. "Oh, my child," the old crones seem to say, "get that look of aspiring independence out of your eyes, or you'll upset the apple cart." Let us hope we can heal a universal neurosis, that we can effect an alchemy that will give back to man his soul, his emotions, his imagination, all that he now sees in woman, and free woman to enjoy her individuality.

I foresee a renaissance for woman. Once her creativity is allowed to come forth boldly and with its own peculiar mark of femininity, we will see women of genius, who will once and for all destroy the stupid myths about sex. By female genius I mean that it does not act in spite of being female, it comes out of being female. It is the flowering of experience from a particular point of view of an individual who is courageous enough to experience life deeply, to experience all the pangs and joys, the awesome vision of death and infinity. Genius and madness and sainthood are all entwined in the vision of life being greater than oneself, and if one can stand the vision and speak of it, though never really capturing it in words and symbols, that is the work of the genius. One can see the mark of psychic courage in these words. They seem to demand that one have such a vision oneself. They haunt one and lead one on to unimaginable goals, like fairy paths through an enchanted forest.

A woman, unburdened of her role as psychic crutch to man, can stand shining in her own individuality, can experience at last what she has always had to put aside: herself. What do we know of this female self: All we know of it is what it is in the shadow of men. What it is in itself, free of these considerations, we have yet to see. What I glimpse is inspiring: individuality so noble and radiant.

The Alchemy of Man and Woman

Eleanor Bertine

Now that the barriers against women are largely broken down, the tide which carried their sex into all sorts of activities, suitable and unsuitable, is receding and women are looking for their proper sphere. But they are no longer quite sure what that is. Their excursion into the man's world has given them criteria for judgment which may not be suitable in their own—prestige, power, purely rational standards and principles, which somehow do not seem to do justice to the realm where human relationships play the dominant part. While the feminists stressed the common humanity of both men and women, thereby releasing women from a too traditionalized role, their modern sisters are now trying to become aware of and to develop those differences which constitute the specific feminine character. For it is by virtue of their inherent difference that women are able to complement men in a truly organic fashion, a fact of no small importance to both sexes.

Women of today have learned the value of freedom, not only for their individual development, but also for the fullest experience of love. One of the most widespread archetypes of femininity is the virgin goddess of the earth or the moon. Virgin means "one in herself," that is, whole, free, not existing solely as the anima of a man. Olive Schreiner, a distinguished South African writer, published a little book called *Dreams*. I will quote one of them:

I saw a woman sleeping. In her sleep she dreamt Life stood before her and held in each hand a gift—in the one, Love, in the other, Freedom. And she said to the woman, "Choose!"

And the woman waited long, and she said, "Freedom!" And Life said, "You have well chosen. If you had said Love, I would have given you what you asked for; and I would have gone from you, and returned no more. Now the day will come when I shall return. In that day I shall bear both gifts in one hand."

I heard the woman laugh in her sleep.[1]

That dream expresses in a nutshell the basic truth of eros.

Emerson has said, "The condition which high friendship demands is ability to do without it." The same thing applies to love. If we cannot do without the friend or lover, it means either that we have been using him to satisfy our own wishes, or else to stuff up a hole in our mandala. Neither belongs to relatedness. Woman is learning that, in her relation to her man, she must, at the same time, keep in touch with a strong independence in herself, so that she may dare to face squarely and accept the inner truth of the situation, whether it should lead to a deeper togetherness or to a breakup of everything.

In a truly magnificent paper on Amor and Psyche, Dr. Neumann has gone right to the heart of the woman's problem in relationship, which, he realizes, is for the partners to find each other as individuals. The myth itself is a gem, expressing the anonymous approach of the masculine partner to sexuality, which is taken by Neumann as a nonpersonal ecstasis, a "paradise in the dark," as he calls it, a momentary union of two strangers, with no touch of human relatedness in it. It may have a terrific poignancy, passion, sublimity even, but it just happens to him, without his being aware, either of the meaning of the experience to himself or of the individuality of the woman who is his partner. He may treat coitus as though it were no more than the king of indoor sports. Or it is the ultimate mystery of life, which he may drink quite impersonally from the woman.

In the myth, Psyche, against the express command of her unknown lover Eros, that they were to be together only in the darkness of the night, lights a lamp in order to discover who he really is and finds that he is the god. She had felt compelled to see him so that she could know and relate to him. Neumann writes:

. . . we must not forget that Eros himself did not want such a Psyche! He threatened her, he fervently implored her to remain in the paradise-darkness, he warned her that she would lose him forever by her act. The tendency toward

consciousness (here toward consciousness in the love relationship) was stronger in Psyche than everything else, even her love for Eros—or so, at least, the masculine Eros would have said. But wrongly so, for though the Psyche of the paradisiacal state was subservient to Eros, though she had yielded to him in the darkness, she had not loved him. Something in her, which may be designated as a tendency toward consciousness and a fulfillment precisely of her feminine nature, drove her to emerge from the darkness. It is in the light of knowledge, the knowledge of Eros, that she begins to love.[2]

It was the drop of flaming oil dripping from Psyche's lamp which in the myth awakened Amor and caused him to depart.

The oil as essence of the plant world, as essence of the earth . . . is significant as the basis of light, and to give light it must kindle and burn. Similarly in psychic life, it is the heat, the fire of passion, the flame and ardor of emotion that provides the basis of illumination, that is, of an illumined consciousness, which rises from the combustion of the fundamental substances and enhances it.[3]

The myth continues with Psyche, desperate at the departure of her lover, setting out to find him. She asks help of the great goddess in vain, until Aphrodite, mother of Eros, who was terribly jealous of the girl, promises success if she is able to perform a series of impossible tasks, each one so dangerous that it will almost certainly prove fatal. However, various kindly spirits warn Psyche and tell her how to avoid the risk and yet attain her end. But, after fulfilling the last task, she disobeys the goddess, and as a result falls into a deathlike trance. When Eros learns of this, he rushes back to her and awakens her. There is a reunion of the lovers, but this time in the full light of consciousness and shared love.

Thus we see that the love which begins as a tremendously passionate desirousness, may, for spiritually sensitive people, be but the first act of a drama whose beginning is on the level of nature, where the human being is caught in forces that threaten to overwhelm him. But sooner or later circumstances arise, often produced unintentionally by himself, in which this passionate libido has to be sacrificed. This is tantamount to a death, as in the trance of Psyche. But the death may lead to a rebirth, in which the libido becomes no longer a blind force of nature, but is the expression also of a transcendent choice, in which the conscious will and the nonpersonal forces are reconciled. Such an experience is felt to be deeply religious, though no theology may be involved.

Of this Neumann writes:

With Psyche, then, there appears a new love principle, in which the en-counter between feminine and masculine is revealed as the basis of individua-tion. From the standpoint of Aphrodite as a nature principle, the union of feminine with masculine is not essentially different in man and in the animals, from the snakes and wolves to the doves. But once the relation between Psyche and Eros has transcended this stage through Psyche's act, it represents a psy-chology of encounter; a uniquely loving one fulfills his existence through this love, which embraces suffering and separation.[4]

After this excursion into this myth, let us take another look at mod-ern woman. As a result of her relatively new emphasis on the individualis-tic side of her nature, she has lost contact with the archetypal woman in herself. This should be her conscious principle, as her grandmother knew instinctively, and it seems ironic that she should have to learn it again at all. Yet it is a common experience that those things which have been lived unconsciously since the beginning of time may have to die as automatic or natural responses, in order to be reborn as conscious knowledge and voluntary action. One does not go directly from purely natural automa-tisms to a conscious control in that same area. On the contrary, the spiral movement goes over to the opposite side of its round and comes back on a new level. It was so with Psyche, who could not change from the stage of the "paradise-in-the-dark" to a conscious love. Instead, she had to lose love entirely and work on alone. Then, when she herself was trans-formed, so also was her love. And so also it has been with modern women. They had to learn to think independently, which, of course, is the only kind of real thinking there is. And for that they had to free them-selves from identification to men, which, for a while, involved the sacri-fice of love. But when the tool of thinking is made conscious, it can be used in the service of eros instead of against it.

But, while the typical modern woman needs to reconnect with nature on a more conscious level, there are still plenty of the old-fashioned ones who have never extricated so much as a little finger from the archetypal matrix of yin. For many women even today, the relation to this collective core of themselves is one of total identity. They are unaware of themselves as in any way differentiated from it. I have had such patients, and they are just like water. You try to get them to stand up for themselves in the open, or to put themselves consciously on record, and they simply can't do it; it is just unimaginable to them. They are essentially indirect in their methods, and always seem to be pulling invisible wires. If they knew what they were doing, I would have no objection, but often their course of action is not intentional at all. Their constant desire seems to be to get, and hold, the approval and liking of the person they are with. They are naturals as anima carriers.

Fortunately, the undiluted anima attitude went pretty much out of style in the suffragette generation, principally because it smacked too much of the hated subservience to men, but also because it was in conflict with a meticulous honesty which refused to use any wiles or artificial means to attract. "I want to be loved just for myself," these women said.

But now a few women, no longer blind to the archetypal reverberations in human relationships, are learning to use from the right motives means which they had rejected before because the motives were frequently ambiguous, if not positively reprehensible. The desire to attract comes from the basic feminine principle which is expressed by the Moon Goddess, from whom comes also that element in love which transcends the common workaday reality, and connects the lovers with the gods themselves. Indeed, it was this very desire to attract which was the redeeming error which led Psyche, disobeying the prohibition of Aphrodite, to open the vial of beauty ointment, which she was bringing back from Persephone, in order to make herself even more lovely for her beloved. When the animus makes a woman insist upon being "just herself," she loses her magic. She may be an excellent comrade, but the archetypal experience will not be found with her. For there is a vast difference between the eros woman and the anima woman. The latter is just an empty little vessel, waiting to be filled up with the libido of the man, while the former is connected with her own feminine nature and its archetypal depths in such a way that the mystery and magic of life can live in her. She submits to the projection of the anima; she even makes it easy by developing every attraction God gave her, but without losing or falsifying herself.

The very nature of yin makes it possible for a woman to become merely the feminine counterpart of a man. Her impulses readily make her adapt, adjust, fit in. The archetypal yin wants to submit in love. So it is not necessarily an overadaptation to the man or a falsification of herself when a woman wants to submit. But it must be to something worthwhile in him, and not to mere masculine vanity or ego power. For the submissiveness of the woman stands over against her independence in a theoretically irreconcilable conflict.

In any relation between a man and a woman that touches the deeper levels, the conscious interchange between them is accompanied by an obligato from the archetypal world which offers them a chance to be lifted out of their banal and limited selves and to participate in the fateful experience of life's august suprapersonal powers—powers which have always been worshipped, or placated, as gods. In *Sparkenbroke*, a novel by Charles Morgan, the hero who is himself a poet seeks to discover how this suprapersonal level of consciousness may be reached, and he comes to the conclusion that there are three roads to it. These are the experience of love, of death, and of poetry. Not the love in friendship, where human companionship plays the leading role; but the love in passion, where a nonpersonal, daemonic factor takes possession, raising the participants to a level of intensity beyond that of their daily lives. The loss of this daemonic aspect of love is what the woman risks who too heavily stresses the comradely aspect of her relations with men, or tries to obliterate the archetypal differences between the sexes in favor of an undifferentiated common humanity.

This is especially true in the sex act itself, in which the personalities of the participants are momentarily suspended in an experience they share with all but the most primitive forms of life. Intercourse is not primarily an experience of personal love, as women try to make it, but of the gods, which yet happens through the union of the two. The love comes before as a preparation, or after, as a result. But the love is then changed. The partner is no longer felt to be limited to the familiar conscious personality, but has become also the gateway to the infinite mystery of life. Projection? Yes, partly. Yet a projection that must be treated very tenderly, for it may lead to the most precious kind of love. So we begin to see how, quite apart from the all-too-common duplicity of a woman's efforts to attract and hold men, there is also a secret art of knowing how the libido of two ordinary people can be freed to leap across the abyss of sex polarity, so that each may, for a moment, find in the other, not only a nice, dear person, but the reflection of the soul itself. This art does not come from the strictly personal self of the woman but from the archetypal moon nature within, to which she becomes, as it were mediumistic. This inner connection enables her to carry to some extent, or at least not reject, the role in which she may find herself cast in the eyes of her lover—of Eve or Hertha or Helen of Troy or Carmen—but without ever violating her own truth. If she has integrity, she will never enact these roles for the effect they produce, but her closer contact with the unconscious will make it possible for the man to find them in her because they are universal images which are potentially part of erotic experience and express the nonpersonal truth of a particular moment.

You will have no illusion that this depth of awareness in the love experience is at all common. I am speaking here of the woman who has passed through the phase of collecting the projections of men, has, perhaps, revolted indiscriminately against the things she had done in that stage in an effort to get a more real personal relationship, but has finally come to see in the unconscious the nonpersonal, organic patterns of life which are constellated in the relation and may greatly enrich it.

She began as the anima woman, reflecting the feelings of the man instead of relating to them, went on to find her own true reactions and the inner patterns from which they sprang, and finally was able, through this connection with her collective roots, to become the mediator between the man and the collective unconscious, which, as anima holder, she had previously been, but then in a blind, instinctive way. Thus, the transcendence of the anima woman leads to the true eros woman, who stands half in the light and half in darkness and unites the two. The end is a return to the unconscious in a completed cycle, but this time in freedom and with vision and a gay humorousness. But this kind of feminine consciousness is still very rare.

In developing a conscious relationship, the woman will need the yin qualities of pliancy and devotion, but the yang qualities of clarity and independence are also essential. Obviously she can accomplish little alone. If the man is not deeply involved with her, he will lose interest rather than face anything that might prove difficult or unpleasant. But if his love is strong, then she has a real chance to foster the bit of life between them. It should, however, be recognized that this is as great and creative an accomplishment as writing a book or painting a picture. The medium is not ink or pigments but the very fabric of human life. And most men I have talked with who have had the experience of an individual relationship willingly admit that it was thanks to the love and tact of the woman. Here it is that she makes her unique contribution. And this means more than the outer achievement, because the consciousness of those concerned evolves with the relationship, slowly gaining breadth and solidity and form. Thus, the work upon the relationship in itself helps the lovers to become capable of carrying a much stronger current of life than before. Clearly, if life is meant to be fully lived, this is a furtherance of its purpose; for the higher the voltage that the carriers can bear without disintegrating, the deeper is the experience. The urgent masculine sexual impulse furnishes the drive, and the feminine power of nurture and conservation gives it enduring effect.

The problem of men and women boils down to the development of human relationship and of the ability to love. When two people fall in love, they are not yet truly loving but are caught in a tidal wave of nature which, for the time being, lifts them up and hurls them together. But it will just as surely set them down again in disillusionment, unless, in the moment of togetherness, they have built a solid bridge of communication and relatedness. For modern man this must be a new kind of relationship, one which incorporates whatever increase of consciousness has been achieved during this era of struggle and transition.

I remember the enormous impression made upon me some years ago by an exhibit of manmade lightning. This consisted of millions of volts roaring and crackling across the gap between one electric pole and another. As I watched, spellbound and in awe, it became the image of the overwhelming emotions that may be constellated between a man and a woman. This is something quite beyond the small sphere controlled by the human will. It belongs to the drama of the gods or cosmic forces. The poles through which the torrential energy flows, however, are human business. If either of them is shoddy or should fuse under the impact of such a current, not only would the pole be destroyed forever, but the whole dynamic process would be stopped short or turned to disaster. In early maturity the man and woman who are the poles are too soft, too childish, too greedy and ignorant to be able to carry on a relation of great intensity without danger of cracking if something goes wrong. It is indeed a stern fate to be the medium through which the lightning elects to flow. Yet it is just that fate that has compelled many a person to make the ascent from psychological childhood to maturity. The energy of intense desire either turns destructive, or it heats the retort for the alchemical transformation.

The desire of the man for a moment of complete fullfillment with the woman is, *au fond*, a longing for an experience of the nonpersonal. The woman, on the other hand, is seeking personal relatedness. The former is, as a consequence, oriented to the electric current, the latter to the poles. But the current is impossible without the poles; the poles meaningless without the current. The man and woman must each bow to the utter indispensability of the complementary principle in the other, while firmly maintaining his own. The woman who takes sexuality on the same easy, impersonal basis as the man fails to hold up the feminine side, and so the potential drops. For if the poles are the same, both positive or both negative, no current will flow. Similarly, the man who is so tied to one woman that he cannot see any other is apt to become quite a bore, even to the lady of his choice. And so again the current fails. For its existence there must be an adequate difference of potential, in psychological terms, a strong yang-yin polarization. If a spirited woman is to be fired enough to follow a man's lead devotedly, she must see in him a true spark of the creative masculine quality and impersonal truth, and he must be able to carry something of this archetype without using it to enhance his ego or to exploit the woman. And likewise the woman must allow the man to find in her the repose and renewal of the earth principle and the delicate colorfulness of that of the moon. Then he can bring to her his deepest reality, for she stimulates his strength but also accepts his weakness. A man once asked his beloved: "Why do you care for me so much? Is it for my clever mind and the books I have written?" Her answer was that of a real woman: "Not a bit of it! I love you because you are such an old stupid!" Thus she playfully deflected the conversation from flattery of his ego to the deeper truth that love is not for personal assets or qualities, but for the being of the beloved. Had there been no basis of respect, she could not have answered that way without giving offense. But when there is, the human weaknesses may be more endearing than the strength.

Sexual union is fundamentally symbolic and this is its deepest meaning. It expresses the *coniunctio*, that mystic inner marriage which was the goal of the alchemical work. By its process *Sol* and *Luna*, gold and silver, logos and eros, were no longer to be estranged but were to be brought together and united.

The *coniunctio* is a completely nonpersonal process, as separate from the ego of the individual in whom it takes place as is the flash of lightning from the electric pole which may appear to give it rise. Yet the individual must be able to endure the fire. In the *coniunctio*, love and truth are reconciled. The woman adores the spirit embodied for her in the man, and he in turn comes to realize that spirit must incarnate as love. So the human union is paralleled and completed by the mystic marriage of the opposite principles within the psyche.

Now please do not get the idea that this really happens consciously except in rare instances. Yet back of the relations of a man and a woman, there lies in the unconscious the image of this transcendent union, waiting to be wakened into life. Though a really complete relationship is a great and rare achievement, fortunately full success in the outer sphere is not necessary to bring about the inner result; nor is the outer success of a happy marriage, in itself, any guarantee that a high psychological goal has been attained. Indeed, it is a striking fact that frustration seems to be the fate of most great lovers. Perhaps just the suffering and the struggle are the *conditio sine qua non*, the vital condition, for the production of redeemed love or the philosopher's gold. The alchemists advise sometimes the use of a gentle heat on the retort, which would correspond to brooding and introverting on the situation. But sometimes the directions call for the application of intense heat. The psychological equivalent of this could hardly be less than the full intensity of passionate conflict and emotion, and passion mounts when it meets a barrier. Only then, if at all, does the alchemical process begin.

NOTES

[1] Olive Schreiner, *Dreams* (London: Unwin, 1890), p. 79.
[2] Neumann (1956), p. 80 f.
[3] Ibid., p. 84.
[4] Ibid., p. 90 f.

Woman and Solitude

Anne Morrow Lindbergh

This is a snail shell, round, full, and glossy as a horse chestnut. Comfortable and compact, it sits curled up like a cat in the hollow of my hand. Now it is the moon, solitary in the sky, full and round, replete with power. Now it is an island, set in ever-widening circles of waves, alone, self-contained, serene.

We are all, in the last analysis, alone. And this basic state of solitude is not something we have any choice about. It is, as the poet Rilke says, "not something that one can take or leave. We *are* solitary. How much better it is to realize that we are so, yes, even to begin by assuming it. Naturally," he goes on to say, "we will turn giddy."

Naturally. How one hates to think of oneself as alone. How one avoids it. It seems to imply rejection or unpopularity. An early wallflower panic still clings to the word. One will be left, one fears, sitting in a straight-backed chair *alone*, while the popular girls are already chosen and spinning around the dance floor with their hot-palmed partners. We seem so frightened today of being alone that we never let it happen. Even if family, friends, and movies should fail, there is still the radio or television to fill up the void. When the noise stops there is no inner music to take its place. We must re-learn to be alone.

It is a difficult lesson to learn today—to leave one's friends and family and deliberately practice the art of solitude for an hour or a day or a week. For me, the break is the most difficult. Parting is inevitably painful, even for a short time. It is like an amputation, I feel. And yet, once it is done, I find there is a quality to being alone that is incredibly precious. Life rushes back into the void, richer, more vivid, fuller than before. It is as if in parting one did actually lose an arm. And then, like the star-fish, one grows it anew; one is whole again, complete and round—more whole, even, than before, when the other people had pieces of one.

For a full day and two nights I have been alone. I lay on the beach under the stars at night alone. I made my breakfast alone. Alone I watched the gulls at the end of the pier, dip and wheel and dive for the scraps I threw them. A morning's work at my desk, and then, a late picnic lunch alone on the beach. And it seemed to me, separated from my own species, that I was nearer to others: the shy willet, nesting in the ragged tide-wash behind me; the sand piper running in little unfrightened steps down the shining beach rim ahead of me; the slowly flapping pelicans over my head, coasting down wind.

I felt a kind of impersonal kinship with them and a joy in that kinship. Beauty of earth and sea and air meant more to me. I was in harmony with it, melted into the universe, lost in it, as one is lost in a canticle of praise, swelling from an unknown crowd in a cathedral.

Yes, I felt closer to my fellow men too, even in my solitude. For it is not physical solitude that actually separates one from other men, not physical isolation, but spiritual isolation. It is not the desert island nor the stony wilderness that cuts you off from the people you love. It is the wilderness in the mind, the desert wastes in the heart through which one wanders lost and a stranger. When one is a stranger to oneself then one is estranged from others too. If one is out of touch with oneself, then one cannot touch others. How often in a large city, shaking hands with my friends, I have felt the wilderness stretching between us. Both of us were wandering in arid wastes, having lost the springs that nourished us—or having found them dry. Only when one is connected to one's own core is one connected to others, I am beginning to discover. And, for me, the core, the inner spring, can best be refound through solitude.

I walked far down the beach, soothed by the rhythm of the waves, the sun on my bare back and legs, the wind and mist from the spray on my hair. Into the waves and out like a sandpiper. And then home, drenched, drugged, reeling full to the brim with my day alone. There is a quality to fullness that the Psalmist expressed: "My cup runneth over." Let no one come—I pray in sudden panic—I might spill myself away!

Is this then what happens to woman? She wants perpetually to spill herself away. All her instinct as a woman—the eternal nourisher of children, of men, of society—demands that she give. Her time, her energy, her creativeness drain out into these channels if there is any chance, any leak. Eternally, woman spills herself away in driblets to the thirsty, seldom being allowed the time, the quiet, the peace, to let the pitcher fill up to the brim.

Here is a strange paradox. Woman instinctively wants to give, yet resents giving herself in small pieces. Basically is this a conflict? Or is it an over-simplification of a many-stranded problem? I believe that what woman resents is not so much giving herself in pieces as giving herself purposelessly. What we fear is not so much that our energy may be leaking away through small outlets as that it may be going "down the drain." If it is woman's function to give, she must be replenished too. But how?

Solitude, says the moon shell. Every person, especially every woman, should be alone sometime during the year, some part of each week, and each day. How revolutionary that sounds and how impossible of attainment. If women were convinced that a day off or an hour of solitude was a reasonable ambition, they would find a way of attaining it. As it is, they feel so unjustified in their demand that they rarely make the attempt.

As far as the search for solitude is concerned, we live in a negative atmosphere as invisible, as all-pervasive, and as enervating as high humidity on an August afternoon. The world today does not understand, in either man or woman, the need to be alone.

How inexplicable it seems. Anything else will be accepted as a better excuse. If one sets aside time for a business appointment, a trip to the hairdresser, a social engagement, or a shopping expedition, that time is accepted as inviolable. But if one says: I cannot come because that is my hour to be alone, one is considered rude, egotistical, or strange. What a commentary on our civilization, when being alone is considered suspect; when one has to apologize for it, make excuses, hide the fact that one practices it—like a secret vice!

Actually these are among the most important times in one's life— when one is alone. Certain springs are tapped only when we are alone. The artist knows he must be alone to create; the writer, to work out his thoughts; the musician, to compose; the saint, to pray. But women need solitude in order to find again the true essence of themselves: that firm strand which will be the indispensable center of a whole web of human relationships. She must find that inner stillness which Charles Morgan describes as "the stilling of the soul within the activities of the mind and body so that it might be still as the axis of a revolving wheel is still."

This beautiful image is to my mind the one that women could hold before their eyes. This is an end toward which we could strive—to be the still axis within the revolving wheel for relationships, obligations, and activities. Solitude alone is not the answer to this; it is only a step toward it, a mechanical aid, like the "room of one's own" demanded for women, before they could make their place in the world. The problem is not entirely in finding the room of one's own, the time alone, difficult and necessary as this is. The problem is more how to still the soul in the midst of its activities. In fact, the problem is how to feed the soul.

For it is the spirit of woman that is going dry, not the mechanics that are wanting. Mechanically, woman has gained in the past generation. Certainly in America, our lives are easier, freer, more open to opportunities, thanks—among other things—to the feminist battles. But these hard-won prizes are insufficient because we have not yet learned how to use them. With our garnered free time, we are more apt to drain our creative springs than to refill them.

Mechanically we have gained, in the last generation, but spiritually we have, I think, unwittingly lost. In other times, women had in their lives more forces which centered them whether or not they realized it; sources which nourished them whether or not they consciously went to these springs. Their very seclusion in the home gave them time alone. Many of their duties were conducive to a quiet contemplative drawing together of the self. Woman's life today is tending more and more toward the state William James describes so well in the German word, "Zerrissenheit—torn-to-pieces-hood." She cannot live perpetually in "Zerrissenheit." She will be shattered into a thousand pieces. On the contrary, she must consciously encourage those pursuits which oppose the centrifugal forces of today. It need not be an enormous project or a great work. But it should be something of one's own. Arranging a bowl of flowers in the morning can give a sense of quiet in a crowded day—like writing a poem, or saying a prayer. What matters is that one be for a time inwardly attentive.

Woman must be the pioneer in this turning inward for strength. In a sense she has always been the pioneer. Less able, until the last generation, to escape into outward activities, the very limitations of her life forced her to look inward. And from looking inward she gained an inner strength which man in his outward active life did not as often find. But in our recent efforts to emancipate ourselves, to prove ourselves the equal of man, we have, naturally enough perhaps, been drawn into competing with him in his outward activities, to the neglect of our own inner springs. Why have we been seduced into abandoning this timeless inner strength of woman for the temporal outer strength of man?

Moon shell, who named you? Some intuitive woman I like to think. I shall give you another name—Island shell. I cannot live forever on my island. But I can take you back to my desk in Connecticut. You will sit there and fasten your single eye upon me. You will remind me that I must try to be alone for part of each year, even a week or a few days; and for part of each day. You will remind me that unless I keep the island-quality intact somewhere within me, I will have little to give my husband, my children, my friends, or the world at large. You will remind me that woman must be still as the axis of a wheel in the midst of her activities; that she must be the pioneer in achieving this stillness, not only for her own salvation, but for the salvation of family life, of society, perhaps even of our civilization.

III. Marriage as a Path

Introduction

In exploring the relationship of man and woman, one inevitably has to confront the question of marriage, which most cultures have regarded, along with birth and death, as one of life's major passages. Although some of the best minds of our generation have tried to dismiss marriage as an outdated artifact of a dying social order, marriage does not seem to go away all that easily. It continues to be a central reference point between men and women, no matter how much they try to ignore or downgrade it. Since falling in love is an inherently unstable condition, it is inevitable that lovers will want to stabilize their relationships in a living arrangement that can foster intimacy, caring, and commitment.

The arguments against marriage are legion. It is undeniable that marriage has been used for centuries as an instrument of social repression—to curtail individual freedom, growth, and self-expression and to enforce dominant ideologies of a man's and a woman's "place." Many have argued as well that monogamy is monotony, and that monogamous marriage is an invitation to disaster, because it goes against the natural appetites. ("Open" marriages do not seem to fare any better, however.) Others argue that marriage creates a state of co-dependence, where both people use each other to avoid facing their real aloneness and their individual paths in life through an enforced togetherness that entails continual compromise.

What then is the point of marriage? Is it purely a social convention designed to provide for child-rearing, to subjugate women, or to give couples an illusion of security in an insecure world? Apart from child-rearing, is there an intrinsic need for men and women to marry? Does marriage answer deeply felt psychological and spiritual needs? Can marriage help two people become more themselves by providing a container or alchemical vessel in which their natures are steadily refined through the heat of their proximity and daily interaction? What does marriage need to develop into if it is to serve as an instrument of love's urge toward greater awareness, freedom, and truth, instead of serving as an instrument of torture, suppression, or deadening routine? These are the difficult questions we face today, which the writers in this section begin to address.

Guggenbühl-Craig distinguishes between marriage as a path to happiness and marriage as a path to "salvation"—i.e., discovering what is most meaningful in one's life. He argues provocatively that the happy marriage is dead (if it ever existed at all), and that those who want to find happiness should seek elsewhere. Only if marriage is understood as a path toward deeper meaning and truth is it possible to find the strength to endure the hells it puts one through. As a path of self-knowledge, Guggenbühl-Craig argues, marriage is clearly not for everyone.

D. H. Lawrence sees marriage as formal recognition of the sacredness of the man/woman bond, which is a microcosm of the interaction of larger forces in the greater cosmos. However, this sacredness is lost when couples relate to each other primarily as personalities. Then their magnetic polarity is diminished by what he calls "little needs"—for entertainment, excitement, security, admiration, and so on. The real magic of love can only happen when a couple's connection reflects the dynamic interplay of energies in the cosmos at large.

Lawrence defends the sacredness of marriage both from stylish youth who turn the relations of men and women into counterfeit imitations of media images, and from the puritanical old guard, who had banned his books in England. To illustrate the bloodless belief in "functional sexuality" that Lawrence is fighting against here, it might be useful to quote from an English philosopher, whose words were recently published in a book on "spiritual relationships":

A mutual attraction is no proper basis for a human relationship between a man and a woman. . . . The sexual relationship is a simple organic function to be used like all the others for the expression of personality. . . . Sex must fall within the life of the personality. . . . When people enjoy themselves through each other, that is merely mutual lust.[1]

Since Lawrence is speaking primarily as a poet, it is often hard to know exactly what he means—as, for instance, when he writes of man as

"Adam of red-earth" with a "black touchstone" at his center, woman as "serpent-advised Eve of the blood," or marriage as a "correspondence of blood." In reading Lawrence I have found it more useful to see what such statements stir within me than to debate his accuracy or precision. At his best, Lawrence speaks from and appeals to some ancient place inside. He does not try to take an objective or detached view of the mysteries of the man/woman bond. In speaking directly from the center of those mysteries, his style often embodies many of the intense, passionate, irritating, and contradictory qualities of the very man/woman relations he is writing about.

Speaking in the more measured tone and style often associated with the Greek god Saturn, Wendell Berry sees marriage as a communal form that connects us with larger patterns of history, cultural lineage, and the search for meaning. It is precisely this form that allows us to enter the unknown terrain of sexual love without losing our way entirely. The form of marriage is, like the earth, a common ground that transcends individuals while also connecting them across generations. It forces us to work hard and to mold a relationship into a shape that has meaning, just as poetic form is a container that allows words to take on creative import. Like Lawrence, Berry also implies that marriage is sacred because it connects us with the larger cycles of life.

Even if we respect the form of marriage, however, the need to mate is only one half of the equation, suggests Robert Stein; the need to be single, free, and independent is equally strong. Often one partner winds up as the spokesman for one of these needs, while the other partner is the spokeswoman for the opposite one. The resulting struggle has destroyed many marriages. Stein argues that we need to find a way to include both these needs in a marriage, while not getting exclusively identified with either one of them. This is an important point, for it suggests a way out of the deadlock between those who argue for the lifelong monogamous marriage and those who argue against the marriage commitment. Clearly, neither the need for a mate nor the need for greater freedom and flexibility in relationships is soon going to disappear. We somehow have to allow for and recognize both needs if we are to evolve new forms and understandings of marriage that are suited to the changing times.

J. G. Bennett writes about the inner meaning of marriage as a "union of wills" whose ultimate fruition is service to all beings. In order to be able to serve others, we first have to learn to serve one other, to consider another person's well-being before our own. It is important to realize, according to Bennett, that this kind of service and acceptance does not mean subordinating ourselves or blinding ourselves to the other's weaknesses. The most fully realized marriage is one in which a couple regard this mutual acceptance as a real discipline and practice that bring about union on the subtler levels of their beings. They are held together by this "work," which refines their natures so that they can serve life as a whole.

Elizabeth Bugental concludes this section with a brief personal account of this mutual acceptance, and of how allowing ourselves to be fully "seen" in a marriage helps us live more fully in the present. And yet, the more fully we love in the present, the more keenly we feel the ever-present possibility of death. The paradox of marriage is that the more fully one loves another, the more one has to practice letting go. Love and death are always intimately related.

NOTES

[1] John MacMurray, "Reason and Emotion." In Miners (1984), p. 28, 29, 31.

Marriage Is Dead, Long Live Marriage!

Adolf Guggenbühl-Craig

It requires no particularly original or keen spirit to discern that family and marriage are today caught up in a state of dissolution, even though many people still get married with great enthusiasm. But in all countries where laws do not make it too difficult to obtain a divorce, many marriages are being dissolved.

It would be tiresome to give statistics on frequency of divorce in various countries, cultures, and social strata. It is much more impressive for the individual to let pass through his mind acquaintances, relatives, and friends who are somewhat over forty-five years old. In doing this one realizes with sadness—or with secret satisfaction if one is himself divorced—that many marriages which began auspiciously are no longer in existence. Often the marriages ended, childless, after several years; often there were already children present. Everyone also knows married couples who dissolve their family after fifteen, twenty, or twenty-five years of marriage. And just when one has calmly concluded that at least that old schoolfriend Jack and his wife Louise are enjoying a happy marriage, the telephone rings and Jack shares his decision to get a divorce.

All these divorces would not be so bad if one could at least discern unalloyed happiness and joy among the undivorced. But this is not the case. One knows from general studies as well as from personal experience that many married people manage to hold the family together only with great difficulty, by denying themselves everything that is dear to them. Here and there, nevertheless, one does meet married people who are genuinely satisfied with each other. At least they themselves think that this is the case. The objective observer often has another opinion: the marriage seems to function so well only because at least one of the partners sacrifices himself completely and neglects his own development. Either the wife sacrifices all of her personal and cultural claims for the sake of her husband's professions and comfort; or—and this is becoming ever more frequently the case—the husband serves his wife and hardly dares express his own opinions in her presence. He sacrifices his friends and his professional opportunities and practically allows his power-addicted wife to use him as a servant. How often one observes how interesting, witty, and animated the married person is when alone, but then with the marriage partner present, every sign of liveliness vanishes. Many marriage partners who have a good marriage from an external point of view in fact virtually cripple one another.

Despite armies of psychologists and marriage counselors, not only do divorces continue to occur with great frequency, but even the marriages that still exist often seem to be nothing but growth-stunting situations. It is often doubted whether marriage and family in their contemporary form are still meaningful institutions. Is not marriage, as social revolutionaries explain it, mostly just an instrument of society used to stupefy the people?

Even psychiatrists andd psychologists who do not share this radical viewpoint add debits daily to the case against marriage and family. In the cases of most neurotic patients, the cause of emotional suffering is traced back to the sick marriage compromises of their parents, to a suppressed mother or to a henpecked father, to every kind of unhappy family constellation.

If one looks at the institution of marriage and family with complete impartiality and fairness, the following picture emerges: if, using great psychological acuity, one were to dream up a social institution which would be unable to function in every single case and which was meant to torment its members, one would certainly invent the contemporary marriage and the institution of today's family. Two people of different sex, usually with extremely different images, fantasies, and myths, with differing strength and vitality, promise one another to be with each other night and day, so to speak, for a whole lifetime. Neither of them is supposed to spoil the other's experience, neither is supposed to control the other, both of them should develop all their potentials fully. This mighty oath is often declared, however, only because of an overwhelming sexual intoxication. Such an intoxication is wonderful, but is it a solid groundwork for a lifetime together?

It is well-known that most people get on each other's nerves even when they undertake only a fourteen-day trip together. The two marriage partners, however, promise to live their whole lives (thirty, forty, fifty, sixty years) together in the greatest physical, spiritual, and psychological intimacy. And this lifelong commitment they make to each other in their youth! Perhaps in ten years they are both completely different people. They make this promise at an age when they neither know who they are themselves nor who the other is. Above all, no one knows how one or the other is later going to develop. The charming, adaptable young girl turns into—who would guess it?—a power-intoxicated matron. The romantic young man with such lofty plans for the future behaves later perhaps like an irresponsible weakling.

That a decent, responsible society not only allows, but actually encourages, young people in their complete ignorance to bind themselves permanently to the psychological problems which their vows entail, seems incomprehensible.

The more life-expectancy increases, the more grotesque this situation becomes. Two hundred years ago people did not grow so very old, and most marriages ended after ten or twenty years with the death of one of the marriage partners. Today many unbroken marriages last fifty, or even sixty, years.

Marriage as conceived under the image of well-being has become, for countless people, the greatest disappointment. The so-called happy marriage is unequivocally finished. Marriage as a welfare institution has no justification anymore. Psychologists who feel themselves committed to the goal of well-being would do better, if they really took their standpoint seriously, to recommend and suggest other forms of living together, rather than to waste their energy trying to patch up a fundamentally impossible institution with a lot of technical treatment modalities.

The tenacity of marriage as an institution, the fact that it continues to be popular despite its pain-inflicting structure, becomes easier to understand if we turn our attention to images that have nothing to do with well-being.

The central issue in marriage is not well-being or happiness; it is salvation. Marriage involves not only a man and a woman who happily love each other and raise offspring together, but rather two people who are trying to individuate, to find their "soul's salvation."

The concept of salvation is familiar to us from its religious context. The Christian religion, for example, sought to bring salvation to mankind. This has to do not simply with a happy, relaxed earthly existence. In the context of religious language, salvation means seeking and finding contact with God. In philosophy one speaks of the search for meaning, for an experience of the meaning of life. Salvation involves the question of life's meaning, and this question can never be ultimately answered.

Just as there are innumerable philosophies and religions, so there are innumerable ways to salvation. In the last analysis, every individual person must seek and find salvation in his own way. All paths to salvation have, nevertheless, certain features in common. I know of none in which a confrontation with suffering and death is not necessary.

We can hardly ever say precisely, or even imagine, just what salvation is. We know only the various pathways. The state of salvation as such can perhaps only be intuited in a human life during the brief moments of religious or philosophical peak experiences. For just a few seconds, while watching a sunset, or standing in the shower, or in a church at a baptism, or at an annual festival, one believes suddenly that he knows the meaning of life; one makes contact with his own spark of divinity.

As goals, salvation and well-being contradict each other. The path to happiness does not necessarily include suffering. For the sake of our well-being we are urged to be happy and not to break our heads with questions that have no answer. A happy person sits at his family table among his loved ones and enjoys a hearty meal. A person who seeks salvation wrestles with God, the devil, and the world, and he confronts death, even if all of this is not absolutely necessary at that precise moment. The civil state is obliged to concern itself with the well-being of its citizens, but it is not in a position to offer anyone salvation. It can only provide each citizen with the freedom to seek salvation as the spirit moves him to do so. It is the churches and religious communities that occupy themselves with salvation.

In Jungian psychology and psychotherapy a fairly sharp distinction is drawn between well-being and salvation. To promote well-being involves helping the patient to adapt to his environment and to learn to make his way successfully through the world. It also has to do with freeing him so far as possible from neurotic patterns. But we speak further of "individuation" in Jungian psychology. This does not necessarily concern mental health, well-being, or a sense of happiness. Individuation involves the striving of a person to find his own pathway of salvation.

For us the question is, has marriage to do with well-being or with salvation? Is marriage, this *opus contra naturam*, a path to individuation or a way to well-being?

The following may give us a clue: all marriage ceremonies contain certain religious elements and overtones. A purely civil marriage, so-called, is practically nonexistent. One may object that in most cultures a great many human undertakings are accompanied by some kind of religious ceremony, such as merely eating, hunting, embarking in a ship, etc. Nevertheless, it is noteworthy that not much in the course of life is as surrounded by religious ceremonies as is marriage; only birth and death are taken with equal seriousness.

Is the presence of references to transcendence in most marriage ceremonies perhaps an indication that marriage has much more to do with salvation than with well-being? Is this why marriage is a kind of difficult "unnatural institution"?

The lifelong dialectical encounter between two partners, the bond of man and woman until death, can be understood as a special path for discovering the soul, as a special form of individuation. One of the essential features of this pathway is the absence of avenues for escape. Just as the saintly hermits cannot evade themselves, so the married persons cannot avoid their partners. In this partially uplifting, partially tormenting evasionlessness lies the specific character of this path.

Everyone has to search for his own pathway. A painter finds it in painting, an engineer in building, etc. Often people set out on a pathway which later proves not to be the one for them. Many have believed themselves to be artists and later found out that their vocation lay elsewhere.

Is marriage, then, a pathway to salvation for everyone? Are there not people whose psychological development is not furthered by marriage? We do not require that everyone find his salvation in music, for example. Is it not then equally questionable that many think they must find their salvation in marriage? Here one can make the following objection: to be sure there are numerous pathways, but this fact does not apply to marriage; it occurs to no one that the majority of the population should become painters, but it is expected that a normal person will marry after a certain age. Not to marry, it is supposed, is abnormal. Older people who are single are described as infantile problematical developments: older unmarried men are suspected of homosexuality, and women who have not married are thought to be in this position because of a lack of attractiveness ("The poor thing couldn't find a man"). There exists a virtual terror about everyone's having to marry. Perhaps in this attitude lies one of the biggest problems with respect to modern marriage. Innumerable people are married today who have no business in marriage.

Despite many modern movements to the contrary, marriage, from the purely social point of view, remains more highly prized than the situation of being single. This was not always the case. In the Middle Ages, for example, the unmarried state was highly regarded. The vocation of nun or priest was approvingly regarded.

It is high time to promote the possibilities of the unmarried life for people who seek their salvation elsewhere than in marriage. This would also function to make marriage more valuable. The social position and the material security of single people must be improved, and it should become possible and acceptable for people to have children outside of marriage. The goal would be to reserve marriage only for those people who are especially gifted in finding their salvation in the intensive, *continuous* relationship and dialectical encounter between man and woman.

The modern marriage is possible only when this special pathway is desired and wished for. The collective, however, continues to herd people toward marrying for the sake of well-being. Many girls marry to evade the pressure of a career and to find someone who will take care of them. Only a few marriages can last "until death" if marriage is understood as a welfare institution.

But people are continually being taught by psychiatrists, psychologists, marriage counselors, etc., that only happy marriages are good marriages or that marriages *should* be happy. In fact, however, every path to salvation leads through hell. Happiness in the sense that it is presented to married couples today belongs to well-being, not to salvation. Marriage above all is a soteriological institution, and this is why it is filled with highs and lows; it consists of sacrifices, joys, *and* suffering. For instance, a married person may bump up against the psychopathic side of his partner, namely that part of his partner's character which is not amenable to change and which has tormenting consequences for both of them; if the marriage is not to break up at this point, one partner (usually the less psychopathic one) is going to have to give in. Should one of them be emotionally cold, for example, there is no alternative except for the other to continue to show loving feelings, even if the partner reacts to these weakly and inadequately. All of the well-intentioned advice to men and women in the vein of "That just won't do," or "You must not tolerate that," or "A man (or woman) must not let that happen to himself," are therefore false and deleterious.

A marriage only works if one opens himself to exactly that which he would never ask for otherwise. Only through rubbing oneself sore and losing oneself is one able to learn about oneself, God, and the world. Like every soteriological pathway, that of marriage is hard and painful.

A writer who creates meaningful works does not want to become happy, he wants to be creative. Likewise married people can seldom enjoy happy, harmonious marriages, as psychologists would force it upon them and lead them to believe. The image of the "happy marriage" causes great damage.

For those who are gifted for the soteriological pathway of marriage, it, like every such pathway, naturally offers not only trouble, work, and suffering, but the deepest kind of existential satisfaction. Dante did not get to heaven without traversing hell. And so also there seldom exist "happy marriages."

Marriage is not comfortable and harmonious; rather, it is a place of individuation where a person rubs up against himself and against his partner, bumps up against him in love and in rejection, and in this fashion learns to know himself, the world, good and evil, the heights and the depths.

Marriage and the Living Cosmos

D. H. Lawrence

There are few married people today, and few unmarried, who have not felt an intense and vivid hatred against marriage itself, marriage as an institution and an imposition upon human life. Far greater than the revolt against governments is this revolt against marriage. Do we, then, want to break marriage? Is marriage a great help to the fulfilment of man and woman, or is it a frustration? It is a very important question indeed, and every man and woman must answer it.

The Old Church knew best the enduring needs of man, beyond the spasmodic needs of today and yesterday. The rhythm of life itself was preserved by the Church hour by hour, day by day, season by season, year by year, epoch by epoch, down among the people. We feel it, in the south, in the country, when we hear the jangle of the bells at dawn, at noon, at sunset, marking the hours with the sound of mass or prayers. It is the rhythm of the daily sun. We feel it in the festivals, the processions, Christmas, the Three Kings, Easter, Pentecost, St. John's Day, All Saints, All Souls.

This is the wheeling of the year, the movement of the sun through solstice and equinox, the coming of the seasons, the going of the seasons. And it is the inward rhythm of man and woman, too, the sadness of Lent, the delight of Easter, the wonder of Pentecost, the fires of St. John, the candles on the graves of All Souls, the lit-up tree of Christmas, all representing kindled rhythmic emotions in the souls of men and women. And men experience the great rhythm of emotion man-wise, women experience it woman-wise, and in the unison of men and women it is complete.

Augustine said that God created the universe new every day: and to the living, emotional soul, this is true. Every dawn dawns upon an entirely new universe, every Easter lights up an entirely new glory of a new world opening in utterly new flower. And the soul of man and the soul of woman is new in the same way, with the infinite delight of life and the ever-newness of life. So a man and a woman are new to one another throughout a lifetime, in the rhythm of marriage that matches the rhythm of the year.

Sex is the balance of male and female in the universe, the attraction, the repulsion, the transit of neutrality, the new attraction, the new repulsion, always different, always new. The long neuter spell of Lent, when the blood is low, and the delight of the Easter kiss, the sexual revel of spring, the passion of midsummer, the slow recoil, revolt, and grief of autumn, greyness again, then the sharp stimulus of winter of the long nights. Sex goes through the rhythm of the year, in man and woman, ceaselessly changing: the rhythm of the sun in his relation to the earth. Oh, what a catastrophe for man when he cut himself off from the rhythm of the year, from his unison with the sun and the earth. Oh, what a catastrophe, what a maiming of love when it was made a personal, merely personal feeling, taken away from the rising and the setting of the sun, and cut off from the magic connection of the solstice and the equinox! This is what is the matter with us. We are bleeding at the roots, because we are cut off from the earth and sun and stars, and love is a grinning mockery, because, poor blossom, we plucked it from its stem on the tree of Life, and expected it to keep on blooming in our civilized vase on the table.

Marriage is the clue to human life, but there is no marriage apart from the wheeling sun and the nodding earth, from the straying of the planets and the magnificence of the fixed stars. Is not a man different, utterly different, at dawn from what he is at sunset? and a woman too? And does not the changing harmony and discord of their variation make the secret music of life?

And is it not so throughout life? A man is different at thirty, at forty, at fifty, at sixty, at seventy: and the woman at his side is different. But is there not some strange conjunction in their differences? Is there not some peculiar harmony, through youth, the period of childbirth, the period of florescence and young children, the period of the woman's change of life, painful yet also a renewal, the period of waning passion but mellowing delight of affection, the dim, unequal period of the approach of death, when the man and woman look at one another with the dim apprehen-

sion of separation that is not really a separation: is there not, throughout
it all, some unseen, unknown interplay of balance, harmony, completion,
like some soundless symphony which moves with a rhythm from phase to
phase, so different, so very different in the various movements, and yet
one symphony, made out of the soundless singing of two strange and incompatible lives, a man's and a woman's? This is marriage, the mystery of
marriage, marriage which fulfils itself here, in this life.

But—and this *but* crashes through our heart like a bullet—marriage
is no marriage that is not basically and permanently phallic, and that is
not linked up with the sun and the earth, the moon and the fixed stars
and the planets, in the rhythm of days, in the rhythm of months, in the
rhythm of quarters, of years, of decades, and of centuries. Marriage is no
marriage that is not a correspondence of blood. For the blood is the substance of the soul, and of the deepest consciousness. It is by blood that
we are: and it is by the heart and liver that we live and move and have our
being. In the blood, knowing and being, or feeling, are one and undi-
vided. So that only when the conjunction is of the blood, is marriage
truly marriage. The blood of man and the blood of woman are two eternally different streams, that can never be mingled. Even scientifically we
know it. But therefore they are the two rivers that encircle the whole of
life, and in marriage the circle is complete, and in sex the two rivers touch
and renew one another, without ever commingling or confusing. We
know it. The phallus is a column of blood that fills the valley of blood of a
woman. The great river of male blood touches to its depths the great
river of female blood—yet neither breaks its bounds. It is the deepest of
all communions, as all the religions, in practice, know. And it is one of
the greatest mysteries, in fact, the greatest, as almost every initiation
shows, showing the supreme achievement of the mystic marriage.

And this is the meaning of the sexual act: this Communion, this
touching on one another of the two rivers, Euphrates and Tigris—to use
old jargon—and the enclosing of the land of Mesopotamia, where Paradise was, or the Park of Eden, where man had his beginning. This is marriage, this circuit of the two rivers, this communion of the two blood
streams, this, and nothing else: as all the religions know

Two rivers of blood are man and wife, two distinct eternal streams,
that have the power of touching and communing and so renewing, making new one another, without any breaking of the subtle confines, any
confusing or commingling. And the phallus is the connecting link between the two rivers, that establishes the two streams in a oneness, and
gives out of their duality a single circuit, forever. And this, this oneness
gradually accomplished throughout a lifetime in twoness, is the highest

achievement of time or eternity. From it all things human spring, children and beauty and well-made things; all the true creations of humanity.

Man dies, and woman dies, and perhaps separate the souls go back to the Creator. Who knows? But we know that the oneness of the blood-stream of man and woman in marriage completes the universe, as far as humanity is concerned, completes the streaming of the sun and the flowing of the stars.

There is, of course, the counterpart to all this, the counterfeit. There is counterfeit marriage, like nearly all marriage today. Modern people are just personalities, and modern marriage takes place when two people are "thrilled" by each other's personality: when they have the same tastes in furniture or books or sport or amusement, when they love "talking" to one another, when they admire one another's "minds." Now this, this affinity of mind and personality is an excellent basis of friendship between the sexes, but a disastrous basis for marriage. Because marriage inevitably starts the sex-activity, and the sex-activity is, and always was and will be, in some way hostile to the mental, *personal* relationship between man and woman. It is almost an axiom that the marriage of two *personalities* will end in a startling physical hatred. People who are personally devoted to one another at first end by hating one another with a hate which they cannot account for, which they try to hide, for it makes them ashamed, and which is nonetheless only too painfully obvious, especially to one another. In people of strong individual feeling the irritation that accumulates in marriage increases only too often to a point of rage that is close akin to madness. And, apparently, all without reason.

But the real reason is, that the exclusive sympathy of nerves and mind and personal interest is, alas, hostile to blood-sympathy, in the sexes. The modern cult of personality is excellent for friendship between the sexes, and fatal for marriage. On the whole, it would be better if modern people didn't marry. They could remain so much more true to what they are, to their own personality.

But marriage or no marriage, the fatal thing happens. If you have only known personal sympathy and personal love, then rage and hatred will sooner or later take possession of the soul, because of the frustration and denial of blood-sympathy, blood-contact. In celibacy, the denial is withering and souring, but in marriage, the denial produces a sort of rage. And we can no more avoid this, nowadays, then we can avoid thunderstorms. It is part of the phenomenon of the psyche. The important point is that sex itself comes to subserve the personality and the fulfilment. In fact, there is probably far more sexual activity in a "personal" marriage than in a blood-marriage. Woman sighs for a perpetual lover:

and in the personal marriage, relatively, she gets him. And how she comes to hate him, with his never-ending desire, which never gets anywhere or fulfils anything!

It is a mistake I have made, talking of sex I have always inferred that sex meant blood-sympathy and blood-contact. Technically this is so. But as a matter of fact, nearly all modern sex is a pure matter of nerves, cold and bloodless. This is personal sex. And this white, cold, nervous, "poetic" personal sex, which is practically all the sex that moderns know, has a very peculiar physiological effect, as well as psychological. The two bloodstreams are brought into contact, in man and woman, just the same as in the urge of blood-passion and blood-desire. But whereas the contact in the urge of blood-desire is positive, making a newness in the blood, in the insistence of this nervous, personal desire the blood-contact becomes frictional and destructive, there is a resultant whitening and impoverishment of the blood. This is one of the many reasons for the failure of energy in modern people; sexual activity, which ought to be refreshing and renewing, becomes exhaustive and debilitating.

And the other, the warm blood-sex that establishes the living and revitalizing connection between man and woman, how are we to get that back? It will be by the arising of a new blood-contact, a new touch, and a new marriage. It will be a phallic rather than a sexual regeneration. For the phallus is only the great old symbol of godly vitality in a man, and of immediate contact.

It will also be a renewal of marriage. . . . And still further, it will be marriage set again in relationship to the rhythmic cosmos. The rhythm of the cosmos is something we cannot get away from without bitterly impoverishing our lives. The Early Christians tried to kill the old pagan rhythm of cosmic ritual, and to some extent succeeded. They killed the planets and the zodiac, perhaps because astrology had already become debased to fortune-telling. They wanted to kill the festivals of the year. But the Church, which knows that man doth not live by man alone, but by the sun and moon and earth in their revolutions, restored the sacred days and feasts almost as the pagans had them, and the Christian peasants went on very much as the pagan peasants had gone, with the sunrise pause for worship, and the sunset, and noon, the three great daily moments of the sun: then the new holy-day, one in the ancient seven-cycle: then Easter and the dying and rising of God, Pentecost, Midsummer Fire, the November dead and the spirits of the grave, then Christmas, then Three Kings. For centuries the mass of people lived in this rhythm, under the Church. And it is down in the mass that the roots of religion are eternal. When the mass of a people loses the religious rhythm, that people is dead, without hope. But Protestantism came and gave a great blow to the religious and ritualistic rhythm of the year, in human life. Nonconformity *almost* finished the deed. Now you have a poor, blind, disconnected people with nothing but politics and bank-holidays to satisfy the eternal human need of living in ritual adjustment to the cosmos in its revolutions, in eternal submission to the greater laws. And marriage, being one of the greater necessities, has suffered the same from the loss of the sway of the greater laws, the cosmic rhythms which should sway life always. Mankind has got to get back to the rhythm of the cosmos, and the permanence of marriage.

Man has little needs and deeper needs. We have fallen into the mistake of living from our little needs till we have almost lost our deeper needs in a sort of madness. There is a little morality, which concerns persons and the little needs of man: and this, alas, is the morality we live by. But there is a deeper morality, which concerns all womanhood, all manhood, and nations, and races, and classes of men. This greater morality affects the destiny of mankind over long stretches of time, applies to man's greater needs and is often in conflict with the little morality of the little needs. The greatest need of man is the renewal forever of the complete rhythm of life and death, the rhythm of the sun's year, the body's year of a lifetime, and the greater year of the stars, the soul's year of immortality. This is our need, our imperative need. It is a need of the mind and soul, body, spirit, and sex: all.

It is a question, practically, of relationship. We *must* get back into relation, vivid and nourishing relation to the cosmos and the universe. The way is through daily ritual, and the re-awakening. We *must* once more practice the ritual of dawn and noon and sunset, the ritual of the kindling fire and pouring water, the ritual of the first breath, and the last. This is an affair of the individual and the household, a ritual of day. The ritual of the moon in her phases, of the morning star and the evening star is for men and women separate. Then the ritual of the seasons, with the Drama and the Passion of the soul embodied in procession and dance, this is for the community, an act of men and women, a whole community, in togetherness. And the ritual of the great events in the year of stars is for nations and whole peoples. To these rituals we must return: or we must evolve them to suit our needs. For the truth is, we are perishing for lack of fulfilment of our greater needs, we are cut off from the great sources of our inward nourishment and renewal, sources which flow eternally in the universe. Vitally, the human race is dying. It is like a great uprooted tree, with its roots in the air. We must plant ourselves again in the universe. Let us prepare now for the death of our present "little" life, and the re-emergence in a bigger life, in touch with the moving cosmos.

Poetry and Marriage: The Use of Old Forms

Wendell Berry

The meaning of marriage begins in the giving of words. We cannot join ourselves to one another without giving our word. And this must be an unconditional giving. The promise must be absolute, for in joining ourselves to one another we join ourselves to the unknown. We can join one another *only* by joining the unknown.

Because the condition of marriage is worldly and its meaning communal, no one party to it can be solely in charge. What you alone think it ought to be, it is not going to be. Where you alone think you want it to go, it is not going to go. It is going where the two of you—and marriage, time, life, history, and the world—will take it. You do not know the road; you have committed your life to a way.

In marriage as in poetry, the given word implies the acceptance of a form that is never entirely of one's own making. When understood seriously enough, a form is a way of accepting and living within the limits of creaturely life. These forms are artificial; if they exist, they have to be made. Sexual love is natural, but marriage is not. The impulse to sing is natural, but language and the form of song are not.

These forms are also initially arbitrary, because at the outset they can always be argued against. Until the wedding vows are said, the argument that one might find a better spouse has standing because there is no argument or evidence that can be produced against it; statistical probability would seem to support it: given the great number of theoretically possible choices, one *might* make a better choice.

Similarly, before the poem, there is no necessity governing the choice of form. The forms then, are arbitrary *before* they are entered upon. Afterward, they have the same undoubtable existence and standing as the forms of an elm or a river. A poet such as Spenser evidently entered upon the form of a poem as solemnly as he entered upon any other cultural form— that of public service, say, or that of marriage. He understood it both as enablement and as constraint, and he meant not to break it, for in keeping the form he did not merely obey an arbitrarily imposed technical requirement, but maintained his place in his cultural lineage, as both inheritor and bequeather, which saved him from loneliness and enabled him to mean.

It is often assumed, as if under the influence of the promises of advertisements, that need or desire, ambition or inspiration may proceed straight to satisfaction. But this is false, contrary to the nature of form and the nature of discipline, as it is to common experience. Impulses dependably come to fruition only by encountering the resistances of form, by being balked, baffled, forced to turn back and start again. They come to fruition by error and correction. Form is the means by which error is recognized, and the means by which correctness is recognized.

There are, it seems two Muses: the Muse of Inspiration, who gives us inarticulate visions and desires, and the Muse of Realization, who returns again and again to say, "It is yet more difficult than you thought." This is the muse of form.

The first muse is the one mainly listened to in a cheap-energy civilization, in which "economic health" depends on the assumption that everything desirable lies within easy reach of anyone. It is the willingness to hear the second muse that keeps us cheerful in our work. To hear only the first is to live in the bitterness of disappointment.

Properly used, a verse form, like a marriage, creates impasses, which the will and present understanding can solve only arbitrarily and superficially. These halts and difficulties do not ask for immediate remedy; we fail them by making emergencies of them. They ask, rather, for patience, forbearance, inspiration—the gifts and graces of time, circumstance and faith.

Marriage too is an attempt to rhyme, to bring two different lives— within the one life of their troth and household—periodically into agreement or consent. The two lives stray apart necessarily, and by desire come together again: to "feel together," to "be of the same mind." Difficult virtues are again necessary. And failure, permanent failure, is possible. But it is this possibility of failure, together with the formal bounds, that turns us back from fantasy, wishful thinking, and self-pity into the real terms and occasions of our lives.

It may be, then, that form serves us best when it works as an obstruction to baffle us and deflect our intended course. It may be that when we no longer know what to do, we have come to our real work, and that when we no longer know which way to go, we have begun our real journey. The mind that is not baffled is not employed. The impeded stream is the one that sings.

Part of the nature of a form seems to be that it is communal—that it can be bequeathed and inherited, that it can be taught, not as an instance (a relic), but as a way still usable. Both its validity and its availability depend upon our common understanding that we humans are all fundamentally alike.

Forms are broken, usually, on the authority of the opposing principle that we are all fundamentally or essentially different. Each individual, each experience, each life is assumed to be unique—hence, each individual should be "free" to express or fulfill his or her unique self in a way appropriately unique.

To adopt a communal form with the idea of changing or discarding it according to individual judgment is hopeless, the despair and death of meaning. To keep the form is an act of faith in possibility, not of the form, but of the life that is given to it; the form is a question addressed to life and time, which only life and time can answer. But a necessary corollary of the faith is that the individual must not answer for the community.

The analogy I have been working with here is most readily apparent if we think of marriage and poetic forms as *set forms*—that is, forms that in a sense *precede* the content, that are in a sense *prescriptive*. These set forms are indispensable, I believe, because they accommodate and serve that part of our life which is cyclic, drawing minds and lives back repeatedly through the same patterns, as each year moves through the same four seasons in the same order.

The work of poetic form is coherence, joining things that need to be joined, as marriage joins them—in words by which a man or a woman can stand, words confirming acts. Forms join, and this is why forms tend to be analogues of each other and to resonate with each other. Forms join diverse things that they contain; they join their contents to their context; they join to themselves; they join us to each other; they join writers and readers; they join generations together, the young and the old, the living and the dead. Thus, for a couple, marriage is an entrance into a timeless community. So, for the poet (or a reader), is mastery of poetic form. Joining the form, join all that the form has joined.

Coupling/Uncoupling

Robert Stein

As powerful as the human need for coupling is the need to be free and unattached. The tension between the needs to be coupled and to be single has become an increasing problem in our times. Our urban-industrial society wreaks havoc on marriage, family and kinship community. As a consequence nuclear families atomize and couples become increasingly dependent on each other and their children for intimacy and security. This dependence has put enormous pressure on the marriage relation to fulfill all needs for intimacy and security, of course intensifying the soul's need to be free.

Since the 1960s we have seen sexual freedom, open, multiple or communal marriages, unmarried unions, democratic or patriarchal communes, religious and non-religious communities, explored. And it appears that in spite of the external changes, psychologically the younger generation have encountered the same oppressive patterns in their relationships, and seem just as incapable as older generations of resolving the polarization between the need to be bound and attached, and the need to be free and unattached. The sixties revolution has not reaped many new fruits in marriage and relationship. When the tension between the opposites becomes unbearable, separation or divorce is still the prevailing solution.

Let us briefly review some of the ways in which the polarization *within* marriage has been dealt with historically. In our Western monogamous culture the dominant pattern has been the illicit, extramarital love affair or prostitution. In polygamous cultures, multiple marriages or concubinage, in primitive cultures, polygamy, ritual orgies, ritual sharing of wives are some of the patterns. Much has been written about comparative cultural patterns of marriage. My intention is only to show that none of these solutions attend to the soul's need to be separate, free and unattached. An illicit love affair is eventually as binding and confining as legitimate marriage. The same can be said for multiple marriages in a polygamous culture. Though all these patterns allow for variations on the theme of coupling, and may relieve the oppressive tension of the exclusive, monogamous marriage, they do little to heal the split. Neither does the more modern pattern of sequential marriage and divorce. The need to be coupled soon returns in full force, and a high percentage of divorced people remarry.

The sacred marriage (*hieros gamos*) between Zeus and Hera presents a model for human monogamy. It is told that they celebrated their mating for three hundred blissful years. Only after the royal honeymoon was over did Zeus begin his wandering infidelities. Hera is recognized in Greek religion as the goddess of marriage, as the guardian of the sacrament of coupling. Her jealousy, wrath and vindictiveness toward her husband's infidelities with other goddesses and mortals are well known. To the present day the myth of unfaithful husband and abandoned, faithful wife, devoted to the sanctity of the marriage bed, continues to be enacted, though changes are evident as a result of women's liberation and cosmopolitan sexual mores. One argument to support the apparent difference between masculine and feminine archetypes is that women need the stability and security of a permanent relationship in order to raise and educate children. But men seem to have an equally strong need to raise and educate children. Studies of animals with their young suggest it is so for them too. Even among the Olympian deities the goddesses, including the mother goddess, Demeter, have as much need to be free and uncoupled as do the males. Unless we believe that Zeus entered into marriage with Hera only in order to satisfy his lust, we must assume that the great father god was equally committed to the *hieros gamos*.

Among mortals once the honeymoon is over, typically one spouse remains secure and content while the other begins to feel dissatisfied with bondage, unfree to pursue fantasies and desires (sexual and otherwise) which don't involve the spouse. Jung uses the metaphor of the container and the contained as a way of viewing this phenomenon. He sees one partner as having a more complex nature than the other. "The simpler nature works on the more complicated like a room that is too small, that does not allow him enough space. The complicated nature, on the other hand, gives the simpler one too many rooms with too much space, so that she never knows where she really belongs. So it comes about quite naturally that the more complicated contains the simpler."[1]

The notion of one person as more spiritually developed or psychologically complex than another is such fertile soil for moralistic judgments that I have not found it very helpful. When Jung says, "It is an almost regular occurrence for a woman to be wholly contained spiritually by her husband, and for a husband to be wholly contained, emotionally, by his wife," the concept grows ambiguous. Another objection I have to the container-contained model is that it implies that the simpler nature must become more psychologically aware and developed so the more complex partner will not feel so confined. I agree that a psychologically creative marriage requires the partners to pursue a path of psychological development, but I disagree that marriage or any relationship can contain the soul.

Hand in hand with the need to be coupled goes the need to be uncoupled, always there as soon as the coupling instinct moves us toward another person. Seen from this perspective, the freedom the soul needs is to be able to experience being *simultaneously coupled and uncoupled*. How is it possible to experience oneself bound and committed and at the same time separate, free and unattached? Is it possible to honor the traditional marriage vows and still feel free to behave as a single, unattached person?

In a monogamous culture, by definition, only one marriage at a time is allowed; if I desire to have an intimate relationship with another woman the coupling instinct soon enters and my marriage is immediately threatened. The soul-splitting tension this rather common situation creates can become unbearable and destructive. It results in a holding back in both relationships even if the tension is resolved in the traditional manner by maintaining a dayworld legitimate marriage and going underground with the other person. Even with this resolution the pressure to choose one or the other is always present. For a man this tension is experienced as a terrible pull between two women (internally between two polarized aspects of the feminine), and the fact that the split is *within the marriage archetype itself* gets lost. Instead of dealing with the soul's need to be free and unattached, the split is experienced as being between "wife-mother" and "adventurous, exciting, mysterious other woman." This tricks each woman into deeper indentification with her role, which becomes increasingly oppressive to all parties involved. The phenomenon is similar when it is a woman who takes a lover: husband becomes identified with "husband-father," the lover with "adventurous, exciting, other man." This soap-opera pattern has accompanied the marriage commitment for a long time.

What is missed in the Western love affair as well as in polygamous systems is the soul's need to be both married and unmarried. While the need to feel free and unattached within my marriage may lead me to seek an intimate involvement with another woman, won't I experience this polarity with the other woman? If so, won't it be more to the point if I focus on the split within my soul which has led me toward the other woman in the first place? I resist being coupled to the other woman as much as I resist being coupled to my wife, yet experience the desire to be coupled to both. If I can resolve this conflict in either relationship, it may lead me to a resolution in the other. If I can experience being bound and coupled, free and uncoupled with the other woman, perhaps I can achieve that state with the woman to whom I am literally married.

By maintaining the connection to both the desire to be coupled and the desire to be uncoupled, both poles can be experienced and lived as complementary rather than as divisive opposites. Connection implies separation. In this instance it means that one separates oneself from identifying with either the desire to be coupled or uncoupled while maintaining awareness of both needs.

At the moment of union, souls feel bound together in a sacred marriage. The desire to love, cherish, serve, protect and be sexually faithful to the beloved belongs to the total experience. Traditional rituals reflect these human sentiments. In spite of these basic emotions, these psychological truths, which support the traditional marriage vows, it seems essential that modern couples have the freedom to explore other intimate relationships, which may or may not involve sexual intimacy. Won't the soul feel sinful, guilty, if it transgresses the vow of sexual fidelity? I believe that as long as the Zeus-Hera structure of the marriage archetype remains the dominant image of marriage within the soul, the answer is yes. A new image and model is needed that will allow for the possibility of experiencing the *hieros gamos* with more than one person while still honoring the sentiment and psychological truth expressed in the traditional marriage vows.

NOTES

[1]Jung(1954).

Marriage as Transformative Work

J. G. Bennett

Sex energy plays an important part in producing out of the experiencings, actions, and sufferings of our physical existence, a finer or "spirit" body, free of the constraints of the earthly body. Through the sexual relationship, it is possible for there to come about a unification of the man and woman in their finer or inner bodies. When it is said in the Bible, "And they shall become one flesh," it was the flesh of the spirit body that was intended. This is a union of being and makes it possible for the man and woman to understand each other and share in the same perceptions.

But the man and woman remain separate spiritually, that is, in their wills, for they make decisions still each in his or her own way. Only when there is a union of will, do the two natures of man and woman become one. There is a fusion in which the distinction remains but is transcended, so that each has the other nature as well as his or her own. The fusion of natures is a new creation. It is the true soul of man through which he can fulfill his destiny.

The immortal soul of man, which Gurdjieff referred to in *All and Everything* as "the higher being body," is not male or female. It is quite different in kind from the sexually divided parts of our nature, and the normal formation of the soul in man is through the union of the sexes. Some great teachers, for example, Muhyiddin Ibn Arabi, say that it is through the union of man and woman that the soul is prepared for universal love, and that the love of God begins with the love of man and woman. But when he speaks thus, he makes it very clear that what he is referring to is a union of wills. This union is the one which is properly called "marriage," and it is a hard but true saying that real marriage is a very, very rare event in human life, which is provided for only in cases where there is a potential for a particular kind of service. It is only when one has entered into this union that the full significance of sex can really be seen and experienced. Then it can be seen as a total thing, which makes one whole, right from the physical, carnal act of the union of the bodies of man and woman through all the different stages. This is the real mystery of sex, that it has an energy which goes beyond nature and which is the means by which man can enter the spiritual world.

Probably the best terminology there is for the transcendental possibilities opened to us by sex is the Sufi one of the "abodes," though we must remember that here, any language has at best an indicative value, for our spiritual nature is inevitably beyond the reach of all of our ordinary faculties. Going back particularly to the teachings of the Khwagagan, the Masters of Wisdom, more than to any other branch of Sufism, the degrees of union are thought of as three abodes (*beit*) or dwellings in man. These can be said to be in the heart of man, in the depth of his own feeling nature, which is hidden from the reach of his ordinary emotions. The first abode is called the *Beit-ul-Muharem*. *Muharem* means private, interior, or hidden, and comes from the same root as *harem*, which is the hidden place in the house where strangers do not enter. As I have said, our nature is incomplete. To become complete we require union with the other sex. The true union, which is more than an event in the physical world— *marriage* in the real sense of the word—is an act of will, a decision which consists in the mutual acceptance by a man and woman of each other. The Beit-ul-Muharem is the place where man and woman come together in this union, which is the true goal of the sexual life.

It is only through the unconditional acceptance of the other that we come to the wholeness that is marriage. When one has any kind of reservation and bargaining, and one says that "I will put myself second in all except in this respect where I am better or I know better," then this acceptance is not possible. Complete acceptance does not mean subordination, nor does it mean blinding oneself to the weaknesses or defects of the other. If one did, it would not be acceptance: we must accept with our eyes open. This acceptance is a real discipline, and like the will of which it is a manifestation, it is only acquired gradually. When people ask me about marriage, I simply say that if they wish their marriage to become a spiritual union, they must set themselves always to put the other first and themselves second; unless this is constantly practiced they will not come to the Beit-ul-Muharem.

It is really very extraordinary that in the whole economy of human nature and in the process of human evolution such a spiritual union should be made possible by the same relationship of man and woman that is required for continuation of our race in time, because this spiritual union is quite different from the union of reproduction. It is possible for it to occur without the sexual act at all and though the normal thing is that it does occur through the sexual act, it is not even essential that the partner in this union should be a living being. There is something that is called the mystical union or mystical marriage which has the same effect, though it must be realized that such a mystical union is even rarer than real marriage itself, and that it can take place only in special circumstances and as the result of a particular need.

Despite the difference between the procreative union and the spiritual union, it can arise as a result of the procreative union that one recognizes that the other person is right for this deeper union. It is so arranged that, on the whole, such a recognition comes from the side of the woman rather than the man. There are reasons for this connected with the woman recognizing the appropriateness of the man to be the father of her children. If, however, this recognition is to lead to the deeper form of union, then it must be a reciprocal thing, must become the foundation of a shared undertaking, a joint commitment to achieve this mutual acceptance. Then, when every aspect of the relationship, great or small, is approached from the view of what is necessary to help realize this acceptance, there can begin to be realized, to emerge, a single will, despite the differences in the ordinary faculties of thought, feeling, and sensation.

For all this to come about, there has to be a subordination of egoism. To come to the state where there is such acceptance of one another is only possible if there is an appropriate third force present. I have heard this put very well by priests when a couple come to be married: "You come to be married as two, but now you are three because Christ is making the third, and now you are three with Christ, through Christ you can be one." But if we do not like to use this language—because we feel somehow that it has become debased—then, using our language we speak of the third force necessary for this union as "the Work."

This is difficult to understand. We can see the visible differences between a couple, the sorts of conflicts that arise in their external relationship. But more deeply still, and quite beyond anything we ourselves can experience, there are still conflicting forces at work between man and woman, which cannot be reconciled as long as they are not of one will. It is my conviction that it is virtually impossible to have marriage in the true sense without the Work, because only the Work can serve to reconcile these inmost conflicting forces. It is not that these conflicting forces disappear. Instead, they are reconciled in such a way that the three become one, such that the Work is really incarnated in them. When a complete acceptance of one another has been made possible in this way, there comes a certain moment in the evolution of the sexual life when this inner unity of will becomes unmistakable, and it is clear that there is no domination by the one over the other and their decisions are identical. They may become aware, for example, that their thought now is often the same, or that their perceptions have broadened to the point that when they look at something they recognize that they have seen the same thing. Most important, however, is the certainty that they can, and in fact, do accept the whole of the relationship, and, very simply, each is completely free while at the same time there is a complete union of the two as one. The awareness that there is no demand and no possessiveness and the recognition that there is an identity of will are all indications that the Beit-ul-Muharem has been opened.

A further stage in this inner evolution of the sexual life is reached when the man and woman, having created in themselves the required "ableness-to-be," go, in a further act of acceptance, from the Beit-ul-Muharem into the *Beit-ul-Mukades*. In this place, others may enter. It is more than a private dwelling place. The word *Mukades* means sacred and when a man and woman have entered in here they have become altogether different from anyone we can know ordinarily. In Buddhism, for example, one who has entered into this abode is described as the *bodhisattva*.

Having transcended themselves, the man and woman are able to enter into an acceptance of the human race which Gurdjieff described as "impartial love," in which *all* people are accepted inwardly as they accepted each other in the Beit-ul-Muharem.

In considering the union of men and women there is a single thread throughout. This is acceptance. We should not be timid in front of sex and think that the only reality that means anything is the ultimate union in which the truly sacred aspect of sex is realized. Even without what I call total acceptance, there can be a transient acceptance, a moment in which a man and a woman have no conscious reserve or withholding from one another. If it is only transient, it remains only as a memory; leading people to try to resume it again, which they cannot do, for the creative energy is not at our command.

There can be a very strong attraction between a man and a woman, even love; yet within, in their consciousness, they are aware that there is not a total and unreserved acceptance. Anything less than total acceptance will not realize the extraordinary potential of our human nature. It requires sacrifice, not the superficial sacrifice of one's interests or inclinations, but the sacrifice of oneself and a willingness not to be oneself but to be ourselves.

It is a great tragedy when people who are capable of the act of marriage miss the opportunity because they do not know what is required, what the secret is. Marriage is a great step in one's transformation, but if a man and woman are able to accept one another totally, they are very close to being able to accept all other people as well. That is why it is said that there cannot be such a thing as partial love: if anyone truly loves, they love everyone, love all. Those who enter into marriage by that act alone do great service for humanity.

On Intimacy and Death

Elizabeth K. Bugental

It seems strange at the age of forty-three to be writing about my first full experience of love and intimacy, and yet this is so. It isn't that I haven't loved before in my life and been loved in return. In fact, looking back over the years, I see face after face emerging from my memory. They are young and old, men and women; and their expressions are filled with such tenderness, sympathy, and understanding, I feel deeply grateful for all that love; receiving and returning it has kept me alive.

But now I am here today, in *our* house—Jim's and mine—knowing for the first time the experience of being in "my own place." When I say those words I mean my own internal place: the space I seem to have been searching out for so many years. I know I am "at home" chiefly because I do not feel as if I have to try to prove to myself or to anyone else why it is right and good and truly mine.

Sometimes I am tempted simply to hand myself over to that gentle, loving man who is my husband, to make him a kind of god whom I lovingly serve, instead of my equal and partner. Giving myself over to him would be, at least initially, so restful. I would never have to risk withstanding him, or confronting him, or seeking my own wants. I could be pleasing and adjusting and certain of tomorrow. Yet if I did that, I know I would soon become absorbed into him; then it would no longer be possible to be intimate, since we would be "one." There would be no "other" with whom to relate. In time, my repressed and tranquilized *I* would either die or erupt in a frantic revolt against its kind jailer and its own self-imprisonment.

At other times I am tempted to run away, to travel my own road in apparent emotional independence. In that case, the two of us might achieve a comfortable "living arrangement" of the kind considered ideal in so many sophisticated circles today. We would meet when we both wished—perhaps we would even arrange romantic interludes—each of us coming from our own separate worlds. There would be a certain investment, a certain excitement, and then we would separate again, even if we continued to occupy the same house. In that case, although I might have close, even warm, moments, I would live essentially alone. There would be fewer risks, but the price seems very high.

These are the pulls of the two extremes, and it seems to me that many people I know live somewhat uncertainly between the two; a few live at one extreme, a few live at the other. I know that neither the extremes nor the uncertain middle would be enough for me, that none of these alternatives offers me the real intimacy I am striving to live and which at the present moment I find so deeply satisfying.

My free choice to live intimately rests basically on sustaining my strong sense of life as a "process," rather than as a lived-out plan. This lifestyle means a constant "being inside of myself" while being together with the other. It assumes a very large "yes" to being seen and known and therefore some strong fundamental sense of my own worth. I find that on the days during which, for one reason or another, I am indulging in self-hate (I call them my "ugly days"), I am almost entirely unable to "be with" Jim. He often describes my investment in these feelings as his "only real rival," and he is right. At those moments I am afraid my "true self" will be discovered, and so I shut down in order to avoid detection. When those moments have passed, I realize that in shutting myself away from Jim, however subtly, I have chosen to wallow in my self-contempt and closed off my best means of confronting and vanquishing it. I am now learning to tell him when I feel these first murmurings of self-loathing, and together we try to hear and confront them.

I too have my rivals in Jim's fears, in his periods of anxiety when he tends to withdraw until he feels he can again present his controlled and "perfect" self for my admiration. Then I try to break through and stay with him as he has done with me. At these times especially, each of us needs to be aware of his own personal feelings, even if those feelings are confused or ambivalent or angry.

It seems to have taken me such a long time to arrive at enough acceptance of myself to allow another this close view of all my messiness and fears. Dropping my defenses without relinquishing my identity still requires continuous awareness. However, this task does not feel nearly as heavy as the struggle to support that thick impenetrable mask of perfection with poor little weak *I* cowering behind. Whereas the former task is a *process* that I can manage little by little, moving from one moment to the next, the latter is a stance (or at best a strict march) that I must maintain vigorously lest I be caught unawares with my perfection down.

So in my search for a way to live intimately, I find no "method" except to be with each moment as it arrives: open to the experience of self and the other in a continual balancing of the strongly centered and the freely open *I*. But there is a feeling of danger that accompanies this lovely life-giving movement. There is no way I can "take care" of my future. Because I *do* exist in this moment, and because I can feel that it is the only one I have, I do not know how long this inner peace will last. If I am truly *here* and *now*, I cannot know what will be. Now I experience a twinge of pain, and I am aware of the wrinkles on my hands and the clock above the oven. They speak to me of time and contingency, and I know that even as I cherish this moment it dies to make room for the next.

This is the paradox about which I write: only at the moment in which I allow myself fully to realize my joy and my communion with another do I touch that intensity of pain which bids me to let the moment go. I can only experience the joy when I do not clutch and freeze it; and yet when I do not imprison it, I must let it separate from me and die. And when I experience this moment as it moves through me, I see that I grow older, that the very vitality of the love between my husband and myself, the lovely easy sharing of the moment, must also move on. We must move where we must, and someday, finally, we too must separate and die. I have no morbid sense as I write this; I have only an acute awareness of the beauty of this moment and of the pain so deeply wedded to that joy. I cannot really have one without the other; and I, from inside my own place, know this as I have never allowed myself to know it before.

I'm looking through our bookshelf into our yard, where the late afternoon sun caresses the bark of the giant oak, and I am remembering that I was sitting here looking at that same tree when I wrote the following:

Yesterday, someone I love died. I hadn't known him for a very long time—less than a year. Maybe it's his wife that I really know, because we have talked together for longer periods of time, while he was sleeping. He had been dying since I met him, and that is important. There had never been time for pretending, for fake conversations, for stepping cautiously into private worlds.

I sat in his room in the green chair, looking at his wasted and frail body against the blue sheets. He sat on the edge of the bed in his red kimono, and he tried to tell me about the pain. We held each other across the space between us—he in his pain and I in my fear—and the brown wood of the walls and furniture cooled and soothed us, until a sharp spasm struck him and he asked, "What did I do just then?"

"You jumped suddenly. Was it a pain?"

"Yes, they come so suddenly. What shall I do, Liz?"

My fear held me by the throat, and nothing came out but my tears. He looked at me silently, without expression. "You are very beautiful. I don't know where you come from, but you are a very beautiful creature." When it was time for me to leave, he put his head back, and I leaned over and kissed him goodbye.

His wife and I sat on the green couch while he slept. She was a child-woman, romantic and tender in her black silk pajamas. She had only just begun to live with him. We spoke quietly and gently to one another but all the while, within myself, I was screaming at her:

How can you be in here with me? You must touch him every minute. You must keep your hand on his arm. You must look at him, hold him every minute. You have only now, right now. Death is waiting, and he will be gone, and you will be alone. Your body, your skin and his—this moment, this moment, this moment. Then what? Run in there where he sleeps and touch his cheek with your finger. Run your hand along his arm over his eyelids, his lips. Sit quietly on the floor near his bed, and watch him sleep.

Yesterday I put the clothes in the washer, and I thought about him. I was in the middle of making the bed, and I saw their faces in my mind. I sat down at the typewriter, and I felt their presence. I knew something was happening at their house, and as I gave way to the feelings, I found that I was frightened. I told Jim there was something ominous happening there.

I was fixing lunch and telling Jim this when I became aware of another kind of feeling. I said, "Do you remember when you were a child, and you were looking forward to some special event? You felt secretly excited inside all the time. Then you would go to sleep or get busy doing something and forget about it. Then, suddenly, like a surprise, you'd remember again, and all the excitement would come rushing back even bigger than before. That's the same way I feel now—as if something very special is going to happen, and I've just realized it again. Only I don't know what it is, and I feel afraid."

At 7:30 P.M., I telephoned my friend's wife and told her of my experience. Had anything happened that day? She said that for the first time her husband had talked to her about his dying. He knew it would come soon, but he found that he was not afraid. He told her, "My body is dying." Later, she understood that he felt he would somehow continue to live. He was sad about death, sad to leave her so soon. He wanted to stay, but he knew he couldn't, and he was not afraid. She told me how they had cried together, how close they had been; she told me of the deep sadness she felt, and yet how much it mattered to know that he wasn't afraid.

I heard her talking to me and I cried her tears as I am crying now. And inside myself I am saying, "No, it can't be true. I only just came to life. I am a child and I am in love with life." But then I began to understand that she knew that it was time, even as she had known enough to wait in the other room and allow him to sleep. And that night, last night, he let himself die; and she let him go.

Intimacy with another—the closeness of living the shared moments, each as it arises, the easy comfort of being known without the disguises of attempted "perfection," the willingness to be where I am without a blueprint or an image to be fulfilled—this particular joy is what is so new in my life. Each moment seems to contribute to and nourish the next so that at times I find it almost too much to allow; whatever the next moment holds cannot possibly live up to this one. And yet, if I stay with myself, in my own present—if I allow Jim in, if he allows me—I do not find myself falling into some abyss. Rather, I am constantly surprised by what I am feeling *now*, and *now*, and *now*.

Once, when I was suffering great pain in relinquishing, someone I love very much told me, "There are no endings, there are only new beginnings." My gradual discovery of this truth, in the way I have been describing, makes continual aliveness and intimacy possible; yet because that experience is so fulfilling, death seems all the more painful. Other contingencies are frightening, but they are not absolute, and I have some experience which will help me to meet them. But I have no experience of the *kind* of new beginning offered by physical death. It feels like only an ending from where I now stand.

At the same time, I have some dim but hopeful awareness which has not yet found its way from the back of my head to the pit of my stomach. Right now I can only attempt to *describe* it: I would like to feel that whenever death comes I will be able to let go—of the moment, of myself, of Jim, and of others whom I love. I want to *be* there then, to be *in* my own death, rather than simply watching it happen to me. I would like somehow *to see* that it is time, and *choose* to let go, even as I am now learning to love and relinquish my present moments.

IV. Sexuality:
The Meeting of Two Worlds

Introduction

Sexual exchange is the point of contact where men and women most vividly engage, where they can express the whole range of feeling between them, from friction to harmony, in all its shades and colors. It is literally where we are most exposed, and also, perhaps, where we are darkest and most opaque, even to ourselves. Although some people, particularly those of an orthodox religious persuasion, claim that the main function of sex is procreation, none of the writers here would agree. (Solovyov's chapter in Part I is an effective argument against that claim.) And yet, if the purpose of human sexuality is not primarily to perpetuate the species, what is the essential meaning of this energetic interchange? We can't simply answer "pleasure," because sexual activity often carries with it a full complement of pain as well, either during or soon afterward. Going along with Solovyov's thesis that human love has not yet reached conscious fruition, we might regard human sexuality as also still evolving—not yet having reached what Lawrence calls its "full conscious realization." Sexual experience invites us to discover a new consciousness, while at the same time rooting us in the ground of our most primal origins and awareness. Sexuality offers us the occasion to bring together two worlds—not only within us, but also between ourselves and another, wholly different being.

In the face of the great unknown that surrounds and permeates much of our sexual experience, perhaps the most common human response has been to make it safe and comfortable by fashioning an ideal image of "how it should be." Since these images and ideals have varied greatly from epoch to epoch as well as across different cultures, it is clear that there is simply no one way it "should" be. In fact, this very attempt to live up to some ideal has led to much of the unconsciousness and distortion in our sexual exchanges. Perhaps the great challenge for us today is to learn to bring a finer and deeper awareness to sexuality, so that we can discover it freshly, as a vibrant expression of the mysterious communion of the sexes.

This section opens with an amusing and revealing piece on how the modern search for pleasure in sex has been taken over by the puritan work ethic. Lewis and Brissett's study of sex play as a serious pursuit in the marriage manuals of the 1950s and 1960s provides classic examples of what Lawrence called "sex in the head." Of course, the sex manuals were themselves a reaction against the Victorian conspiracy of silence about sex. But they went to the other extreme, killing off spontaneity by emphasizing technique, strategy, and conscientiousness, so that a whole generation became afflicted with a new sexual problem—"performance anxiety."

In sharp contrast to the hygienic approach of the sex manuals, Alan Watts presents a vision of sexuality as a particularly vivid instance of the natural, sacred communion between body and world. In Watts' words, "As a means of initiation into the 'one body' of the universe, it requires a contemplative approach." Because it so literally "puts us in touch," sexuality—far from being at the opposite end of human experience from spirituality—actually requires a meditative awareness to be fully appreciated. Because it can so accurately reflect the grasping with which we approach our experience, sexuality can also provide opportunities to slow down, relax goal-directedness, reveal ourselves without pretense, and appreciate the richness of discovering another being in all his or her bodily, sensual immediacy.

Julius Evola, in an excerpt from his dense but illuminating treatise *The Metaphysics of Sex*, sees sexual attraction not as "animal magnetism" or projection of anima/animus, but rather as the magnetic resonance between men and women at a deeper level of consciousness, known in the esoteric traditions as the "energy body" or "subtle body." Evola's view that sex interrupts ordinary waking consciousness to provide an opening for the communion of larger energies beyond ego relegates modern views of sex as an animal instinct, a plaything, or a work performance to the dustbin of triviality.

Bernd Jager, in his phenomenology of passion, shows how sexual passion both heightens and heals the split between the polarities of our nature as human beings. The power of passion arises from the shock of polar energies meeting, which reveals another world of power and depth on the other side of our familiar daily routines. For this reason, Jager would agree with the other authors here that sex should not be robbed of its transformative power by treating it as another "wholesome practice," as a form of mutual gratification and stress-reduction, or as a performance to be worked at.

This section of the book is shorter than the rest, partly because there is not much great writing on sex—it is a hard subject to write about. Also, many aspects of sex have been touched on in other sections. To include a separate section on this subject could even be misleading if it makes sex seem like something that stands apart from the totality of the man/woman relationship. Depending on how fully we accept it as part of our whole being, sexual experience can be either strange and problematic, or an opportunity to heal the debilitating split between mind and body. These are points D. H. Lawrence clearly addressed when he wrote:

Today the full conscious realization of sex is even more important than the act itself. . . . In this one respect, sexual and physical, we have left the mind unevolved. Now we have to catch up, and make a balance between the consciousness of the body's sensations and experiences, and these sensations and experiences themselves. . . . It means having a proper reverence for sex, and a proper awe of the body's strange experience. . . . Life is only bearable when the mind and body are in harmony, and there is a natural balance between them, and each has a natural respect for the other.[1]

What is sex, after all, but the symbol of the relation of man to woman, woman to man? And the relation of man to woman is wide as all life. It consists in infinite different flows between the two beings, different, even apparently contrary. Chastity is part of the flow between man and woman, as is physical passion. And beyond these, an infinite range of subtle communication which we know nothing about. . . . For sex, to me, means the whole of the relationship between man and woman.[2]

NOTES

[1]Lawrence (1961), pp. 89–90.
[2]Lawrence (1936), p. 193, 194.

Sex as Work

Lionel S. Lewis and Dennis Brissett

It is commonly accepted that America is a society of leisure. The society is said to have shifted from one of production to one of consumption. The American of today spends little time working; he has a great deal of time to play. With this surfeit of leisure, Americans have been called upon to engage in forms of consumption quite unknown to their inner-directed predecessors. There exist extensive opportunities for play, but little knowledge of how to conduct oneself in this play. Knowing how to play has become problematic; it is something the individual must learn. Quite recently, Nelson Foote has observed that sex, since it is becoming increasingly dissociated from procreation, is becoming more and more a kind of play activity. The arena of consumption is extended to include the realm of man's sexual activity.

Concomitant with this increasing amount of leisure time, and the attendant problem of learning how to play, it has been observed that the play of most Americans has become a laborious kind of play. "Fun, in its rather unique American form, is grim resolve. . . . We are as determined about the pursuit of fun as a desert-wandering traveler is about the search for water."[1] Consumption, to most Americans, has become a job. Like work, play has become a duty to be performed. This interpretation is supported by the emergence of what Wolfenstein has labeled a "fun morality." Here "play tends to be measured by standards of achievement previously applicable only to work . . . at play, no less than at work, one asks: 'Am I doing as well as I should?'" Consumption very definitely has become production.

Marital sex, as depicted by the marriage manuals, is an activity permeated with qualities of work. One need not even read these books, but need only look at the titles or the chapter headings to draw this conclusion. Thus, we have books titled *The Sex Technique in Marriage* (9), *Modern Sex Techniques* (13), *Ideal Marriage: Its Physiology and Technique* (14). There are chapters titled "How to Manage the Sex Act" (2), "Principles and Techniques of Intercourse" (6), "The Fourth Key to Soundly Satisfying Sex: A Controlled Sexual Crescendo" (4).

From the outset, as we begin to read the books, we are warned not to treat sex frivolously, indeed not to play at sex:

An ardent spur-of-the-moment tumble sounds very romantic. . . . However, ineptly arranged intercourse leaves the clothes you had no chance to shed in a shambles, your plans for the evening shot, your birth control program incomplete, and your future sex play under considerable better-be-careful-or-we'll-wind-up-in-bed-again restraint (4, pp. 34–35).

In other words, marital sex should not be an impromptu performance.

Moreover, sex should not be approached with a casual mien. Rather, we are counseled, sexual relations, at least good sexual relations, are a goal to be laboriously achieved. It is agreed that "satisfactory intercourse is the basis for happy marriage." However, it is added, "it does not occur automatically but must be striven for" (11, p. 39). In the plain talk of the sex counselor, "Sexual relations are something to be worked at and developed" (6, p. 6).

This work and its development are portrayed as a taxing kind of endeavor; as behavior involving, indeed requiring, a good deal of effort. That sex involves effort is a pervasive theme in the manuals. From the start one is advised to direct his effort to satisfying his or her mate so that mutual climax is achieved, sexual activity is continual, and one's partner is not ignored after climax. Thus, we are told:

Remember, couple *effort for* couple *satisfaction! That's the key to well-paced, harmonious sex play (4, p. 62).*

The female is particularly cautioned to work at sex, for being naturally sexual seems a trait ascribed only to the male. The affinity of sex to her other work activities is here made clear: "Sex is too important for any wife to give it less call upon her energy than cooking, laundry, and a dozen other activities" (4, p. 36). To the housewife's burden is added yet another chore.

Even the one manual that takes great pains to depict sex as sport injects the work theme. It is pointed out that

You certainly can strive and strain at having a climax—just as you can . . . help yourself to focus on a complex musical symphony. . . . Just as you strive to enjoy a party, when you begin by having a dull time at it. Sex is often something to be worked and strained at—as an artist works and strains at his painting or sculpture (5, p. 122).

Sex, then, is considered a kind of work; moreover, a very essential form of labor. In the majestic functionalist traditions, "A happy, healthy sex life is vital to wholesome family life, which in turn is fundamental to the welfare of the community and of society" (1, p. xiii). Marital sex, most assuredly, is the cornerstone of humanity, but not any kind of marital sex—only that which leads to orgasm. "It is the orgasm that is so essential to the health and happiness of the couple . . ." (9, p. 80).

Indeed it is the orgasm which may be said to be the *product* of marital sexual relations. It is the *raison d'être* for sexual contact, and this orgasm is no mean achievement. In fact,

Orgasm occasionally may be the movement of ecstasy when two people together soar along a Milky Way among stars all their own. This moment is the high mountaintop of love of which the poets sing, on which the two together become a full orchestra playing a fortissimo of a glorious symphony (3, pp. 182–183).

In masculine, and somewhat more antiseptic, terms, "ejaculation is the aim, the summit, and the end of the sexual act" (14, p. 133). Woe be to the couple who fail to produce this state as there are dire consequences for the unsuccessful, particularly for the woman.

When the wife does not secure an orgasm, she is left at a high peak of sexual tension. If this failure to release tension becomes a regular thing, she may develop an aversion to starting any sex play that might lead to such frustrations. . . . Repeated disappointments may lead to headaches, nervousness, sleeplessness, and other unhappy symptoms of maladjustment (1, p. 65).

So important is it to reach orgasm, to have a product, that all the other sexual activities of marriage are seen as merely prosaic ingredients or decorative packaging of the product.

The central importance of experiencing orgasm has led many of the authors to de-emphasize the traditional organs of intercourse. The male penis (member) is particularly belittled. It is considered "only one of the instruments creating sensation in the female, and its greatest value lies as a mental stimulant and organ of reproduction, not as a necessary medium of her sexual pleasure." The same author adds, ". . . the disillusioning fact remains that the forefinger is a most useful asset in man's contact with the opposite sex . . ." (13, p. 71).

One must often deny himself immediate pleasure when manufacturing the orgasm. One author, in referring to an efficient technique to attain orgasm, states that: "Unfortunately, some men do not care for this position. This, however, should be of little importance to an adequate lover, since his emotions are the less important of the two" (13, p. 122). Likewise, the woman may have to force herself in order to reach orgasm, even though she may not desire the activity which precedes it. It is specified that "If you conscientiously work at being available, you may ultimately find the feminine role quite satisfying even in the absence of ardor or desire" (4, p. 38). The work ethic of the sexual side of marriage, then, is one resting quite elaborately on what has been referred to as the "cult of the orgasm."

Still, one cannot easily perform one's job; its intricacies must first be mastered. "Remember that complete development of couple skills and adaptations takes literally years" (4, p. 206). There is a great deal to be learned. One author talks of eight steps "in order to facilitate sexual arousal and lead, finally, to satisfactory orgasm" and of seven "techniques which she and her mate may employ to help her attain full climax" (5, pp. 124–126).

All of this requires a good deal of mastery, a mastery that is necessary if the sex relationship is not to undergo "job turnover." Marital sex is said to necessitate a good deal of preparation if it is to be efficiently performed. In one author's words: "This complete satisfaction cannot be achieved without study, practice, frank and open discussion . . ." (11, p.45). This overall preparation seems to involve both a passive and an active phase. The passive phase seems most related to an acquisition of information previous to engaging in sexual, at least marital sexual, relations. The active phase best refers to the training, one might say on-the-job training, that the married couple receive in the sexual conduct of wedlock.

The matter of passive preparation receives a great deal of attention from the manuals that call attention to the necessity of reading, studying, and discussing the various facets of sexual relationships. After listing a number of these activities, one author advises that "If the two of them have through reading acquired a decent vocabulary and a general understanding of the fundamental facts listed above, they will in all likelihood be able to find their way to happiness" (1, p. 20). Another counselor cites the extreme importance of reciprocal communication by noting that ". . . the vital problem . . . must be solved through intelligent, practical, codified, and instructive discussion . . ." (13, p. 7). The general purpose of all this learning is, of course, to dispel ignorance, as ignorance is said to lead to "mistakes at work," and such cannot be tolerated. The learning of the other partner's physiology is particularly emphasized, most counselors devoting at least one chapter and a profusion of illustrations to relieve the ignorance of the marriage partners. One author, however, quite obviously feels that words and pictures are insufficient. Presenting a sketch of the woman's genitals, he asserts that "It should be studied; on the bridal night . . . the husband should compare the diagram with his wife's genital region . . ." (13, p. 18).

Together with learning physiology, the various manuals also stress the critical importance of learning the methodology of marital sex. Sexual compatibility seems not a matter of following one's natural proclivities, but rather "The technique of the sexual relation has to be learned in order to develop a satisfactory sex life" (12, p. 172). One must know one's job if one is to be successful at it.

This learning process, according to most of the manuals, eventually becomes subject to the actual experience of matrimonial sex. The marriage bed here becomes a "training" and "proving" ground. In training, rigorous testing and practice are a must. In the words of one manual "experimentation will be required to learn the various responses within one's own body as well as to be expected from one's beloved . . ." (8, p. 7), and also, "After a variable time of practice, husband and wife may both reach climax, and may do so at the same time" (10, p. 10).

Both the husband and wife must engage in a kind of "muscular control" training if the sex act is to be efficiently performed. The woman's plight during intercourse is picturesquely portrayed with the following advice. "You can generally contract these muscles by trying to squeeze with the vagina itself . . . perhaps by pretending that you are trying to pick up marbles with it" (4, p. 97). Fortunately, the man is able to practice muscular control at times other than during intercourse. Indeed, the man, unlike the woman, is permitted to engage in activities not normally related to sexual behavior while he is training. It is advised that "You can snap the muscles at the base of the penile shaft a few times while you are driving your car or sitting in an office or any place you happen to think of it . . ." (4, p. 96).

In general, then, a careful learning and a studied training program are necessary conditions for the proper performance of marital sex. As seems abundantly true of all sectors of work, "'Nature' is not enough. . . .

Man must pay for a higher and more complex nervous system by study, training, and conscious effort . . ." (6, p. 34).

As in most work activities, the activity of marital sex is a highly scheduled kind of performance. There is first of all a specification of phases or stages in the actual conduct of the sex act. Although there is disagreement here, some authors indicating four or five distinct phases (14, p. 1), the consensus of the counselors seems to be that "Sexual intercourse, when satisfactorily performed, consists of three states, only one of which is the sex act proper" (10, p. 7).

The sexual act therefore is a scheduled act and the participants are instructed to follow this schedule. "All three stages have to be fitted into this time. None of them must be missed and none prolonged to the exclusion of others" (7, p. 155). Practice and study are said to insure the proper passage from one phase to another (11, p. 42). Moreover, to guarantee that none of the phases will be excluded, it is necessary to engage in relations only when the sexual partners have a sizable amount of time during which they will not be distracted: ". . . husbands and wives should rarely presume to begin love-play that may lead to coitus unless they can have an hour free from interruptions" (1, p. 51). Even then, however, the couple must be careful, for there is an optimal time to spend on each particular phase. For instance, "Foreplay should never last less than fifteen minutes even though a woman may be sufficiently aroused in five" (13, p. 43).

Given this schedule of activity, the marriage manuals take great pains to describe the various activities required at each particular phase. It is cautioned, for instance, that "all contact with the female genital region . . should be kept at an absolute minimum" (13, pp. 42–43) during foreplay. The man is warned further more to "refrain from any excessive activity involving the penis" (13, p. 77) if he wishes to sustain foreplay. Regarding afterplay, the advice is the same; the partners must not permit themselves "any further genital stimulation" (14, p. 25).

The "job specification" is most explicit, however, when describing the actual act of intercourse. It is particularly during this stage that the sexual partners must strain to maintain control over their emotions. Innumerable lists of "necessary activities" are found in the various manuals. The adequate lovers should not permit themselves to deviate from these activities.

The "labor of love" espoused by the marriage manuals is one whose culmination is importantly based on the proper use of sexual technique. In fact, ". . . *miserable failure results from ignorance of technique*" (7. p. 177). Many times the depiction of particular coital positions takes on a bizarre, almost geometric, aura. In one such position, "The woman lies

on her back, lifts her legs at right angles to her body from the hips. . . .
At the same time, the woman's spine in the lumbar region is flexed at
a sharp angle . . ." (14, p. 218). Often, however, the mastery of sexual
technique seems to involve little more than being able to keep one's legs
untangled. ". . . When the woman straightens her right leg the man,
leaving his right leg between both of hers, puts his left one outside her
right, and rolls over onto his left side facing her" (1, p. 58).

At times, in order to make love adequately, it is required of the participants that they supplement their technique with special equipment.
Some of this equipment, such as lubricating jellies, pillows, and birth
control paraphernalia, is simple and commonplace. Others are as simple
but not as common, such as chairs, foot-high stools, and beds with foot-
boards or footrails. Some, like aphrodisiacs, hot cushions, medicated
(carbonic acid) baths, and sitz baths, border on the exotic.

The kinds of impressions assembled here seem to support the notion
that play, at least sexual play in marriage, has indeed been permeated
with dimensions of a work ethic. This paradox, play as work, may be said
to be an almost logical outcome of the peculiar condition of American
society. The American must justify his play. It is our thesis that he has
done this by transforming his play into work. This is not to say that he
has disguised his play as work; it is instead to propose that his play has
become work.[2] To consume is, in most cases, to produce. Through this
transformation of play, the dignity of consumption is seemingly established; it is now work, and work is felt to carry with it a certain inherent
dignity. The individual now is morally free to consume, and moreover
free to seek out persons to teach him how to consume, for learning how
to play is simply learning how to do one's job is society.

This tranformation of play into work has been attended by another
phenomenon that is also quite unique to contemporary American society.
Given the fact that work has always been valued in American society, a
cult of efficiency has developed. Thus there seem to be two antagonistic
forces operating in American society. On the one hand, there is an emphasis on work and, on the other hand, there is an emphasis on attaining
maximum pleasure.

It is as if the sex counselors were trying to solve a dilemma for their
audience by reminding them to both "let themselves go" while cautioning
them that they should "work at this." If sex be play, it most assuredly is a
peculiar kind of play.

NOTES

[1] Henry (1963), p. 43
[2] Wolfenstein (1958), p. 93.

Numbers in parentheses in this article refer to the following marriage manuals:

1. Butterfield, O. *Sexual Harmony in Marriage* (New York: Emerson Books, 1964).
2. Chesser, E. *Love Without Fear* (New York: New American Library, 1947).
3. Davis, M. *Sexual Responsibility in Marriage* (New York: Dial Press, 1963).
4. Eichenlaud, J. *The Marriage Art* (New York: Dell, 1961).
5. Ellis, A., and Harper, R. *The Marriage Bed* (New York: Tower, 1961).
6. Greenblat, *A Doctor's Marital Guide for Patients* (Chicago: Budlong Press, 1964).
7. Griffith, E. *A Sex Guide to Happy Marriage* (New York: Emerson, 1956).
8. Hall, R. *Sex and Marriage* (New York: Planned Parenthood, 1965).
9. Hutton, I. *The Sex Technique in Marriage* (New York: Emerson, 1961).
10. Levine, L. *The Doctor Talks with the Bride and Groom* (New York: Planned Parenthood, 1964).
11. Lewin, S., and Gilmore, J. *Sex Without Fear* (New York, Medical Research Press, 1957).
12. Stone, H., and Stone, A. *A Marriage Manual* (New York: Simon and Schuster, 1953).
13. Street, R. *Modern Sex Techniques* (New York: Lancer Books, 1959).
14. Van de Velde, T. *Ideal Marriage: Its Physiology and Technique* (New York: Random House, 1961).

Sex as Contemplative Activity

Alan Watts

Love brings the real, and not just the ideal, vision of what others are because it is a glimpse of what we are bodily. The mysterious and unsought uprising of love is the experience of complete relationship with another, transforming our vision not only of the beloved but of the whole world. We need to recognize the physical reality of relationship between organisms as having as much "substance" as the organisms themselves, if not more. Thus however defective its doctrine of marriage in many respects, the Christian Church is perfectly correct in saying that husband and wife are one flesh.

   This makes it the more strange that conventional spirituality rejects the bodily union of man and woman as the most fleshly, animal, and degrading phase of human activity—a rejection showing the extent of its faulty perception and its misinterpretation of the natural world. It rejects the most concrete and creative form of man's relation to the world outside his organism, because it is through the love of a woman that he can say not only of her but also of all that is other, "This is my body."

   Despite the Christian intuition of the world as the Body of Christ, the natural universe has been considered apart from and even opposed to God because it has not been experienced as one body. This comes from the failure to see that individual bodies are only the terms, the end-points, of relationships—in short, that the world is a system of inseparable relationships and not a mere juxtaposition of things.

   In this light it will be clear that consciousness is no mere phosphorescent scum upon the foundations of fire and rock—a late addition to a world which is essentially unfeeling and mineral. Consciousness is rather the unfolding, the "evolution," of what has always been hidden in the heart of the primordial universe of stars. It is in the living organism that the whole world feels: it is only by virtue of eyes that the stars themselves are light. Relationship is a kind of identity. The stars and human eyes are not mutually alien objects brought into relation by mere confrontation. Suns, stars, and planets provide the conditions in which and from which organisms can arise. It is only the time lag and the immense complexity of the relations between stars and men which make it difficult to see that they imply one another just as much as man and woman, or the two poles of the earth.

The failure to realize the mutuality and bodily unity of man and the world underlies both the sensual and the ascetic attitudes. Trying to grasp the pleasure of the senses and make their enjoyment the goal of life is already an attitude in which man feels divided from his experience, and sees it as something to be exploited and pursued. But the pleasure so gained is always fragmentary and frustrating, so that by way of reaction the ascetic gives up the pursuit, but not the sense of division which is the real root of the difficulty. He accentuates dividedness by pitting his will against the flesh, by siding with the abstract against the concrete, and so aggravates the very feeling from which the pursuit of pleasure arose. Ascetic spirituality is a symptom of the very disease which it intends to cure.

Ascetic and sensualist alike confuse nature and "the body" with the abstract world of separate entities. Identifying themselves with the isolated individual, they feel inwardly incomplete. The sensualist tries to compensate for his insufficiency by extracting pleasure, or completeness, from the world which appears to stand apart from him as something lacking. The ascetic, with an attitude of "sour grapes," makes a virtue of the lack. Both have failed to distinguish between pleasure and the pursuit of pleasure, between appetite or desire and the exploitation of desire, and to see that pleasure grasped is no pleasure. For pleasure is a grace and is not obedient to the commands of the will. There is obviously nothing degrading in sensuous pleasure which comes "of itself," without craving. But in fact there is no other kind of pleasure, and the error of the sensualist is not so much that he is doing something evil as that he is attempting the impossible. Naturally, it is possible to exercise the muscles in pursuing something that may, or may not, give pleasure; but pleasure cannot be given unless the senses are in a state of accepting rather than taking, and for this reason they must not be, as it were, paralyzed and rigidified by the anxiety to get something out of the object.

All this is peculiarly true of love and of the sexual communion between man and woman. This is why it has such a strongly spiritual and mystical character when spontaneous, and why it is so degrading and frustrating when forced. It is for this reason that sexual love is so problematic in cultures where the human being is strongly identified with the abstract separate entity. The experience neither lives up to expectations nor fulfills the relationship between man and woman. At the same time it is, fragmentarily, gratifying enough to be pursued ever more relentlessly for the release it seems to promise. Sex is therefore the virtual religion of very many people, the end to which they accord more devotion than any other.

The problems of sexuality cannot be solved at their own level. The full splendor of sexual experience does not reveal itself without a new mode of attention to the world in general. On the other hand, the sexual relationship is a setting in which the full opening of attention may rather easily be realized because it is so immediately rewarding. It is the most common and dramatic instance of union between oneself and the other. But to serve as a means of initiation to the "one body" of the universe, it requires a contemplative approach. This is not love "without desire" in the sense of love without delight, but love which is not contrived or willfully provoked as an escape from the habitual empty feeling of an isolated ego.

It is not quite correct to say that such a relationship goes far beyond the "merely sexual," for it would be better to say that sexual contact irradiates every aspect of the encounter, spreading its warmth into work and conversation outside the bounds of actual "love-making." Sexuality is not a separate compartment of human life; it is a radiance pervading every human relationship, but assuming a particular intensity at certain points. Conversely, we might say that sexuality is a special mode or degree of the total intercourse of man and nature. Its delight is an intimation of the ordinarily repressed delight which inheres in life itself, in our fundamental but normally unrealized identity with the world.

A relationship of this kind cannot adequately be discussed, as in manuals of sexual hygiene, as a matter of techniques. It is true that in Taoism and Tantra there are what appear to be techniques or "practices" of sexual relationship, but these are, like sacraments, the "outward and visible signs of an inward and spiritual grace."

The general idea of Tantric *maithuna** is that sexual love may be transformed into a type of worship in which the partners are, for each

---

*A ritual of sexual yoga in the Hindu Tantric tradition (Ed.).

other, incarnations of the divine. The partners are therefore seated in the cross-legged posture of meditation, the woman clasping the man's waist with her thighs and her arms about his neck. Such a position is clearly unsuitable for motion, the point being that the partners should remain still and so prolong the embrace that the exchange between them would be passive and receptive rather than active. Nothing is *done* to excite the sexual energy; it is simply allowed to follow its own course without being "grasped" or exploited by the imagination and the will. In the meantime the mind and senses are not given up to fantasy, but remain simply open to "what is," without trying to make something of it.

The importance of these ancient ideas to us lies not so much in their technicalities as in their psychological intent. They express an attitude to sexuality which, if absorbed by us today, could contribute more than anything else to the healing of the confusion and frustration of our marital and sexual relations. It remains, then, to separate the underlying sexual philosophy of Tantra and Taoism from symbolic and ritual elements which have no meaning for us, and to see whether it can be applied in terms of our own culture.

To clarify the basic intent of sexual yoga we must study its practice in context with the underlying principles of Buddhist and Taoist philosophy. For Buddhism the basic principle is to have one's consciousness undisturbed by *trishna*, or grasping desire, in such a way that the senses do not receive a distorted and fragmentary vision of the world. For Taoism the principle differs only in terminology: it is *wu-wei*, or noninterference with the Tao or course of nature, which is the organic and spontaneous functioning of man-in-relation-to-his-environment. Both involve the contemplative or open-sensed attitude to experience. In their respective yogas, both practice "watching over the breath" because the rhythm of breathing determines the total disposition of the organism. Now, their attitude to breathing is one of the main keys to understanding their attitude to sexuality.

"Watching over the breath" consists in letting the breath come and go as it wants, without forcing it or clutching at it. In due course its rhythm automatically slows down, and it flows in and out so smoothly that all rasping and hissing ceases *as if* it had stopped. This is both a symbol of and a positive aid to letting one's whole life come and go without grasping, since the way a person breathes is indicative of the way he lives.

As contemplation of the breathing process automatically slows it down, sexual contemplation naturally delays the orgasm. For there is no value in prolonged and motionless intercourse as such; the point is to allow the sexual process to become spontaneous, and this cannot happen without the prior disappearance of the ego—of the forcing of sexual pleasure. Thus the orgasm is spontaneous when it happens of itself and in its own time, and when the rest of the body moves *in response* to it. Active or forced sexual intercourse is the deliberate imitation of movements which should ordinarily come about of themselves. Given the open attitude of mind and senses, sexual love in this spirit is a revelation. Long before the male orgasm begins, the sexual impulse manifests itself as what can only be described, psychologically, as a melting warmth between the partners so that they seem veritably to flow into each other. To put it in another way, "physical lust" transforms itself into the most considerate and tender form of love imaginable.

The point is so important that it can bear repetition: contemplative love—like contemplative meditation—is only quite secondarily a matter of technique. For it has no specific aim; there is nothing particular that has to be made to happen. It is simply that a man and a woman are together exploring their spontaneous feeling—without any preconceived idea of what it ought to be, since the sphere of contemplation is not what should be but what *is*. In a world of clocks and schedules the one really important technical item is the provision of adequate time. Yet this is not so much clock time as psychological time, the attitude of letting things happen in their own time, and of an ungrasping and unhurrying interchange of the senses with their objects. In default of this attitude the greater part of sexual experience in our culture falls far short of its possibilities. The encounter is brief, the female orgasm relatively rare, and the male orgasm precipitate or "forced" by premature motion. By contrast, the contemplative and inactive mode of intercourse makes it possible to prolong the interchange almost indefinitely, and to delay the male orgasm without discomfort or the necessity of diverting full attention from the situation. Furthermore, when the man has become accustomed to this approach, it is possible also for him to engage in active intercourse for a very much longer period, so affording the greatest possible stimulation for the woman.

One of the first phases of contemplative love is the discovery of the depth and satisfaction of very simple contacts which are ordinarily called "preliminaries" to sexual activity. But in a relationship which has no goal other than itself, nothing is merely preliminary. One finds out what it can mean simply to look at the other person, to touch hands, or to listen to the voice. If these contacts are not regarded as leading to something else, but rather allowed to come to one's consciousness as if the source of activity lay in them and not in the will, they become sensations of immense subtlety and richness. Received thus, the external world acquires a liveliness which one ordinarily associates with one's own bodily activity, and from this comes the sensation that one's body somehow includes the external world.

It was through the practice of *zazen* or "sitting meditation" in this particular attitude that Japanese Buddhists discovered the possibilities of such arts as the tea ceremony, wherein the most intense aesthetic delight is found in the simplest social association of drinking tea with a few friends. For the art developed into a contemplation of the unexpected beauty in the "primitive" and unpretentious utensils employed, and in the natural simplicity of the surroundings—the unchiselled mountain rocks in the garden, the texture of paper walls, and the grain of rough wooden beams. Obviously, the cultivation of this viewpoint can lead to an infinitely refined snobbery when it is done with an eye to oneself doing it— when, in other words, the point becomes not the objects of contemplation but the "exercise" of contemplating. For this reason, lovers who begin to relate themselves to each other in this way need not feel that they are practicing a skill in which there are certain standards of excellence which they *ought* to attain. It is simply absurd for them to sit down and *restrain* themselves just to looking at each other, while fighting off the intense desire to fall into each other's arms. The point is to discover the wonder of simple contacts, not the duty of it, for which reason it may be better at first to explore this type of relationship after intercourse than before.

The fact remains, however, that if they let themselves come gradually into contact, they create a situation in which their senses can really work, so that when they have discovered what it can mean just to touch hands, the intimacy of a kiss or even lips in near proximity regains the "electric" quality which it had at the first meeting. In other words, they find out what the kiss *really* involves, just as profound love reveals what other people really are: beings in relation, not in isolation.

If we say that from such contacts the movement toward sexual intercourse grows of itself, it may be supposed that this is no more than what ordinarily happens. Intimacy just leads to passion; it certainly does not have to be willed. But there is all the difference in the world between gobbling and actually tasting food when one is hungry. It is not merely that appetite needs restraint; it needs awareness—awareness of the total process of the organism-environment moving into action of itself. As the lead and response of good dancers appears to be almost simultaneous, as if they were a single entity, there comes a moment when more intimate sexual contact occurs with an extraordinary mutuality. The man does not lead and the woman follow; the man-and-woman relationship acts of itself. His "advance" and her "response" seems to be the *same* movement.

At a particular but unpredetermined moment they may, for example, take off their clothes as if the hands of each belonged to the other. The gesture is neither awkward nor bold; it is the simultaneous expression of a unity beneath the masks of social roles and proprieties by the revelation and contact of the intimate aspects of their bodies. Now, these aspects are ordinarily guarded because of their extreme sensitivity, or awareness of relationship. Only the eyes are as sensitive, and in ordinary social intercourse prolonged eye-contact is avoided because of its embarrassing intimacy—embarrassing because it creates a sense of relationship belying and overpassing the separative roles which we take so much trouble to maintain. For the sensitive organs of the body which we call most intimate and private are not, as might be supposed, the most central to the ego. On the contrary, they are those which most surpass the ego because their sensitivity brings the greatest contact with the outside world, the greatest intimacy with what is formally "other."

The psychic counterpart of this bodily and sensuous intimacy is a similar openness of attention to each other's thoughts—a form of communion which can be as sexually "charged" as physical contact. This is the feeling that one can express one's thoughts to the other just as they are, since there is not the slightest compulsion to assume a pretended character. This is perhaps the rarest and most difficult aspect of any human relationship, since in ordinary social converse the spontaneous arising of thought is more carefully hidden than anything else.

It is significant that we commonly say that those with whom we can express ourselves most spontaneously are those with whom we can most fully be ourselves. For this already implies that the full and real self is not the willing and deliberating function but the spontaneous. In the same way that our most sensitive organs are guarded because they transcend and break the bonds of ego, the flow of thought and feeling—though called one's "inner self"—is the most spontaneous and role-free activity of all. The more inward and central the form of activity, the less it partakes of the mask of the ego. To unveil the flow of thought can therefore be an even greater sexual intimacy than physical nakedness.

In contemplative love we do not speak of the sexual "act," since this puts intercourse into its own special dissociated compartment. Perhaps one of the subordinate reasons why sex is a matter for laughter is that there is something ridiculous in "doing" it with set purpose and deliberation—even when described with so picturesque a phrase as the Chinese "flowery combat." Without wanting to makes rules for this freest of all human associations, it is certainly best to approach it inactively. For when the couple are so close to each other that the sexual parts are touching, it is only necessary to remain quietly and unhurriedly still, so that in time the woman can absorb the man's member into herself without being actively penetrated.

It is at this juncture that simple waiting with open attention is most rewarding. If no attempt is made to induce the orgasm by bodily motion, the interpenetration of the sexual centers becomes a channel of the most vivid psychic interchange. While neither partner is working to make anything happen, both surrender themselves completely to whatever the process itself may feel like doing. The sense of identity with the other becomes peculiarly intense, though it is rather as if a new identity were formed between them with a life of its own. This life—one might say this Tao—lifts them out of themselves so that they feel carried together upon a stream of vitality which can only be called cosmic, because it is no longer what "you" and "I" are doing. Although the man does nothing either to excite or withhold the orgasm, it becomes possible to let this interchange continue for an hour or more, during which the female orgasm may occur several times with a very slight amount of active stimulation, depending upon the degree of her receptivity to the experience as a process taking charge of her.

In due course, both partners feel relieved of all anxiety as to whether orgasm will or will not happen, which makes it possible for them to give themselves up to whatever forms of sexual play may suggest themselves, however active or even violent. We say "suggest themselves" because this is a matter of immediate feeling rather than learned technique—a response to the marvellously overwhelming urge to turn themselves inside out for each other. Or it may happen that they prefer simply to remain still and let the process unfold itself at the level of pure feeling, which usually tends to be the deeper and more psychically satisfying way.

Feelings which at the height of intercourse are often taken for the extremity of lust are simply the *ananda*, the ecstasy of bliss, which accompanies the experience of relationship as distinct from isolated selfhood. "Abandon" expresses the mood better than "lust," because the two individuals give themselves up to the process or relationship between them, and this abandonment of wills can become so intense that it feels like the desire to give up life itself—to die into the other person. De Rougemont maintains—I think wrongly—that this "death wish" distinguishes mere passion or eros from divine love or agape. But the death wish in love is figurative, the giving up of life being a poetic image for the mystical, self-transcending quality of sexual transport. Death in the same figurative sense, as "dying to oneself," is commonly used in mystical literature for the process whereby the individual becomes divine.

The mood of intense sexual delight is not, however, always quite so overwhelming as a desire to "die." The sense of "abandon" or of being carried out of oneself may equally find its expression in gaiety, and this is peculiarly true when the experience brings a strong sense of fulfillment. This is above all true when the partners are not *working* at their love to be sure that they attain a "real experience." The grasping approach to sexuality destroys its gaiety before anything else, blocking up its deepest and most secret fountain. For there is really no other reason for creation than pure joy.

It is no matter for timing by the clock how long this play should continue. Let it be repeated again, its timeless quality is not attained by endurance or even duration, but by absence of purpose and hurry. The final release of orgasm, neither sought nor restrained, is simply allowed to "come," as even the popular expression suggests from our intuitive knowledge that it is not a deed but a gift and a grace. When this experience bursts in upon fully opened feelings it is no mere "sneeze in the loins" relieving physical tension: it is an explosion whose outermost sparks are the stars.

This may seem irreverent, or just claiming too much, to those who are unwilling to feel it completely, refusing to see anything mystical or divine in the moment of life's origin. Yet it is just in treating this moment as a bestial convulsion that we reveal our vast separation from life. It is just at this extreme point that we must find the physical and the spiritual to be one, for otherwise our mysticism is sentimental or sterile-pure and our sexuality just vulgar. Without—in its true sense—the lustiness of sex, religion is joyless and abstract; without the self-abandonment of religion, sex is a mechanical masturbation.

The height of sexual love, coming upon us of itself, is one of the most total experiences of relationship to the other of which we are capable, but prejudice and insensitivity have prevented us from seeing that in any other circumstances such delight would be called mystical ecstasy. For what lovers feel for each other in this moment is no other than adoration in its full religious sense, and its climax is almost literally the pouring of their lives into each other. Such adoration, which is due only to God, would indeed be idolatrous were it not that in that moment love takes away illusion and shows the beloved for what he or she in truth is—not the socially pretended person but the naturally divine.

Mystical vision, as has always been recognized, does not remain at the peak of ecstasy. As in love, its ecstasy leads into clarity and peace. The aftermath of love is an anticlimax only when the climax has been taken and not received. But when the whole experience was received the aftermath finds one in a marvellously changed and yet unchanged world, and here we are speaking of spirituality and sexuality in the same breath. For the mind and senses do not now have to open themselves; they find themselves naturally opened, and it appears that the divine world is no other than the everyday world.

Magnetic Attraction

Julius Evola

Except in cases of complete transcendence of the human condition, sex must be conceived as a "destiny," a basic fact of human nature. There is no existence except as men and women. This point of view is held against the belief that being a man or a woman is something accidental or secondary as compared with being human in general. Before and besides existing in the body, sex exists in the soul and, to a certain extent, in the spirit itself. We are man or woman inwardly before being so externally; the primordial male or female quality penetrates and saturates the whole of our being visibly and invisibly, just as color permeates a liquid. Eros must be considered as a state governed directly by the polarity of the sexes in the same way that the presence of positive and negative poles governs the phenomenon of magnetism and everything connected to a magnetic field.

This point of view corresponds to the knowledge of ancient traditions. For example, in the traditional teachings of the Far East, when a man and woman meet, even without any physical contact, a special energy or immaterial "fluid" called *tsing* is aroused in the deepest layers of their beings. This energy springs from the polarity of the yin and the yang, which we provisionally define as the pure principles of female and male sexuality. This energy, *tsing*, is a specification of the radical, vital force *tsri* and grows in proportion to the degree of yang and yin present in man and woman. This special magnetically induced force has as its psychological counterpart the state of diffused intoxication, vibration, and desire proper to human eros. The occurrence of this state causes the first displacement of the ordinary level of waking consciousness, which can be followed by other stages. The mere presence of the woman in front of the man arouses the elementary degree of *tsing* and its corresponding state. In societies where a sense of this elementary force of sex has been retained, strict conventions are formulated from this deep existential basis rather than a moralistic one. This applies to the rule "that no woman can visit a man except in the presence of another man, particularly if the first man is married." If a man and woman are alone before each other, even if no contact takes place, it is just the same as if it had. This is because the first level of *tsing*, the elementary magnetism, has been awakened. The second level, already more intense, happens with bodily contact (ranging from holding hands and touching each other to kissing). The third degree is reached when the man penetrates the woman and is embraced by her. This is the limit of the magnetic development for most modern lovers. However, it is not the true limit, for yet other stages are reached in the practice of sex in sacred and evocatory forms or in sexual magic. "Subtle" changes, particularly in the breathing and the blood, accompany these various degrees. The psychic correlative is essentially like a state of vibration and heightening, of exaltation in the true sense of the word.

Therefore, we may speak of a "natural magic of love" that occurs in the life of the most commonplace, materialistic, and primitive of humans. Even if the views we have just expressed are incompatible with modern psychology, they are confirmed by popular knowledge. It is generally recognized that an attraction between a man and a woman is born only when something "like a fluid"—a certain chemistry—is established between them. When this fluidic relationship is lacking, any exchange of feeling from the coarsest to the most spiritual is impossible. It is still customary to speak of the "fascination" of a woman, a term that brings us back to the magical definition of love; *fascinum* was, in fact, the technical term used in earlier times for a kind of enchantment or witchcraft.

This concept was part of the theory of love held in the West even into the Renaissance, and it was known in other civilizations as well, notably in Islam. Ficino said that the basis of love-fever consists of a *perturbatio* (disturbance) and of a kind of infection of the "blood" provoked under the same conditions as the so-called evil eye, for it was actuated by means of the eye and the glance. If this is understood as happening on a subtle rather than on a material plane, then it is strictly correct. The fluidic state, the *tsing* force of Chinese teaching, is aroused in the beginning by a look and then goes on to spread throughout the blood. From that moment on, the lover bears his beloved in a certain way in his blood, no matter what distance may separate them. Theories aside, this knowledge is present in the universal language of lovers: "I feel you in my blood," "I've got you under my skin." These widespread and stereotyped expressions describe a fact that is much more essential and real than those focused on by contemporary sexology. But we should bear in mind that when ancient traditions spoke of blood, they almost always referred to a transphysiological doctrine. The traditional concept is well enough expressed in the following terms, which may perhaps seem rather sybilline to the ordinary reader: "Blood is the great sympathetic agent of life; it is the motor of the imagination; it is the animated foundation of the magnetic or astral light polarized in living beings; it is the first incarnation of the universal fluid; it is vital light materialized."[1]

In our own times a "magnetic" theory of love was roughly sketched by Mauclair. His theory helped to overcome the dichotomy between body and spirit, flesh and soul, a contrast that is really nonexistent in erotic experience. Everything takes place on an intermediate plane on which the two elements are fused and aroused by each other. (Whether the senses arouse the soul or the soul arouses the senses is a matter that depends on the particular constitution of the individuals, but in both cases the end state contains within itself both elements fused together, transcending them at the same time.) In this intermediate condition we can speak legitimately of a "magnetic" state observed directly. Mauclair's magnetic hypothesis explains best the unusual state of a couple transported with love and confirms "our daily experience that the state of love is neither spiritual nor carnal and escapes all categories of current moral philosophy." He adds: "The magnetic reasons are the only true ones and remain secret from and sometimes ignored by those who are themselves in love; for they cannot give precise motives for their love and, if they are questioned, bring forth a set of allegations . . . which are nothing other than reasons close to the essential reason, which cannot be articulated. A man does not love a woman because she is beautiful, pleasing, intelligent, or charming, nor because she is likely to produce an exceptionally strong sensual feeling. All these explanations are only given to satisfy ordinary logic. . . . He loves because he loves, quite apart from all logic, and it is precisely this enigma that reveals the magnetism of love."[2] Lolli had already distinguished three kinds of love—"platonic" love, sensual and physical love, and magnetic love—when he said that magnetic love is a mixture of the other two and is tremendously strong, spreading throughout every single part of man but having its main seat in the breath. But in reality, it is not a particular kind of love but is the ultimate basis of all love.

These ideas can be readily integrated with the traditional teachings mentioned just now. They give prominence to a fact that is elementary or primary, namely the "magnetic" structure of eros. And just as there is no attraction between man and woman when a special "fluid" has not been established between them either actually or potentially, so in the same way sexual love dies away when the magnetism wanes. In such a case all efforts to keep alive an amorous relationship will be doomed to failure, just like trying to keep a machine running when energy is lacking or like trying to keep a metal joined to an electromagnet when there is no longer any current to create a magnetic field. External conditions may even remain unchanged: youth, handsome bodies, liking, intellectual affinity, and so on; but when the state of magnetism comes to an end, eros and desire also fade away inevitably. And if everything does not end, if every interest of the one in the other does not die away, yet there will be a change from love in its full and proper meaning to a relationship based on affection, custom, social factors, and so forth. This represents not a sublimation but a substitute, a last resource and basically *another* thing as compared with that which is conditioned by the elementary polarity of the sexes.

It is important to observe that although the magnetic or magic fact or fascination—whatever we wish to call it—takes place spontaneously between lovers, they also find it useful to nourish and develop this magic intentionally. Stendhal's concept of crystallization in love is very well known: Just as the naked boughs of a tree are sometimes clad with crystals in the salty atmosphere of Salzburg, so the desire of a lover, when concentrated on the image of his beloved, crystallizes, as it were, an aura composed of every kind of psychic content.[3] That which is called magnetic fascination from an objective viewpoint can be rendered in psychological terms with the word "crystallization." This is a very essential element in every amorous relationship; the thoughts of the one are held more or less obsessively by the other in a form of partial schizophrenia (expressed in such phrases as "to be madly in love" and "I'm crazy about you"). This phenomenon of mental concentration "is an almost automatic fact, completely independent of the personality and will. Anyone who, whether lacking in will power or energetic, lazy or busy, knowledgeable or ignorant, poor or rich, falls in love, feels that at a certain moment his thoughts are literally chained to a given person without any possibility of escape."[4] For lovers, this concentration is a kind of barometer of love, and they take constant readings through such questions as "Do you think about me?" and "Will you always think of me?" They consciously nourish and strengthen this concentration as it gives the measure of their love, making use of all sorts of expedients to make it as continuous as possible. The phrase "You are always in my thoughts" is the correlative of "You are in my blood." Thus, unconsciously, lovers activate an authentic magical technique, which is grafted onto the primary magical magnetic fact and causes a further development of Stendhal's crystallization as an outcome. In his *Art of Courtly Love*, Andreas Cappellanus defined love as a kind of agony due to extreme meditation upon a person of the opposite sex.[5]

Eliphas Lévi, a writer who, unlike those already mentioned, professes to be a believer in occult sciences and in the Kabbalah, says that the meeting of the magnetic atmospheres of a man and woman leads to a complete intoxication of "astral light," the signs of which are love and passion. The special elation caused by the congestion of "astral light" should constitute the basis of amorous fascination. However, the terminology used by Lévi will remain obscure for the ordinary reader unless we add some clarification.

The congestion of astral light is the objective correlative of what we called "exaltation." "Astral light" is synonymous with *lux naturae* (a term used in particular by Paracelsus), with the *akasha* of Hindu tradition, the *or* of Kabbalism, and the *ch'i* of Chinese philosophy. Many other expressions of esoteric teachings have the same meaning and refer to the supraphysical foundation of life and of nature itself, to a "vital ether" understood as the "life of life." Regarding the term *lux naturae*, it can be noted that the association between light and life recurs in the traditional teachings of widely varying cultures and is echoed in the first words of the Gospel of John. This light can become an object of experience, but only in a state of consciousness different from the normal waking state, in which the imagination acts freely. Any displacement of consciousness provoked by a congestion or intoxication of "astral light" involves a form of imagination that in its way is magical.

In speaking of the teachings of the Far East, we said that the state of eros springs potentially from the relationship between the yang and yin qualities of two human beings. Eliphas Lévi was referring to the same phenomenon when he identified the cause of that state as the coming into contact of the magnetic atmospheres of two individuals of the opposite sex. It is best to go into this point more deeply, and that will lead us to the problem of sexual choice as well.

The current concepts of man and woman are little better than approximations. Indeed, the process of sexual development consists of multiple degrees, for we are not all men or women to the same degree. From a biological point of view it is known that during the earliest embryonic phases, hermaphroditism or bisexuality is encountered. In the formation of a new being, the action of the force that causes sexual differentiation becomes increasingly precise. By means of this force, the capabilities relating to one sex are developed, whereas those of the opposite sex are eliminated or stay in the embryonic or latent state. (One aspect of this is a latent bisexuality in every individual.)

In biology, the vitalism of Driesch and other authors has by now won acceptance, and so it is no longer heretical to look into forces [such as] entelechy. Entelechy is precisely the force that molds from within; it is the "life of life." In ancient times it was deemed to be the soul or "form" of the body; considered in this way, it has a supraphysical, nonmaterial character. It seems clear that this shaping force is at the root of sexual development. Since the basis of sex is supraphysical, it must lie in what the ancients have termed the "subtle body,"[6] intermediate between the material and the immaterial. If there is a difference between the plasma of man and woman, it must be something comparable to a "fluid" that surrounds, saturates, and qualifies the bodies of man and woman—not only giving each organ, each function, each tissue a sexual imprint, but also determining their inner natures. Thus, Weininger said that sex is present in every part of the body, that *every* part of the body of one sex produces erotic excitement in the body of the other sex. To explain this, it is necessary to bring in a supraphysical factor. In Eastern terms, this is a question of the yang and yin principles, which penetrate both the inner being and the material body of man and woman in the form of a "fluid" or an elementary molding energy.

One of the names given to this subtle body is "aromal body." The relationship with smell is not without sexological importance. The special part played by sweat in certain popular enchantments is well known. Smell plays an important part in the magnetism of physical love and in the "fluidic intoxication" of lovers. It was believed in olden times and is still believed among certain primitive peoples today that the fluid of a being penetrates to such an extent that it impregnates not only the body but also the clothing. Hence arise practices that are often continued in the customs of both lovers and primitive peoples. To breathe in the smell and to always carry a piece of the lover's clothing is believed to enforce the relationship and mutual faithfulness (a custom followed in the Philippines). The extreme case is that of an erotic intoxication that is liable to be aroused not only by a glance but even by a smell ("He looked at her and inhaled her, she looked at him and inhaled him"—W. Somerset Maugham). It is possible to see the basis of the ancient Mexican belief that reproduction is the outcome of the mingling of the breath of man and woman.

In every person both male and female qualities are present in different degrees, even if the vital force or "fluid" of the person is fundamentally yang or yin. This law was first expounded by Plato when he set as the basis of attraction the need for a complement; for this he used the image of the *symbolon*, an object broken into two parts, as used in ancient times by two persons to identify each other: The part shown by one person had to match perfectly the part kept by the other person. In the same way, said Plato, every human being bears within himself a distinctive sign and seeks instinctively and unendingly "the corresponding half of himself which bears the same distinctive sign," the complementary signs that make the two parts mate together.[7] The same idea, more closely specified, was developed by Schopenhauer, who said that the right conditions for a strong passion arise when two persons neutralize each other in turn, just as an acid and a base do when forming a salt. Such a situation arises when a given degree of virility finds its counterpart in a corresponding degree of femininity in the other being.

Weininger emphasized a corresponding formula for the first basis of sexual attraction.[8] When the absolute man and the absolute woman are taken as criteria, there is generally something of man in a woman and of woman in a man. He believed that the greatest attraction is aroused between a man and a woman when the masculine and feminine parts in both are added together and the totals obtained are the absolute man and the absolute woman. For instance, a man who is three-quarters man (yang) and one-quarter woman (yin) will be irresistibly attracted and develop the strongest magnetism with his female complement, a woman who is one-quarter man and three-quarters woman; this will be so because the sums of the fractions will reestablish the whole absolute man and absolute woman. In fact, it is the absolute man and absolute woman who form the true basis of the primordial polarity of the sexes and therefore provoke the first spark of eros. We can affirm that they are the ones who love each other and seek to be united with each other through the persons of every man and every woman; and so the saying is true that all women love only one man and all men love only one woman. . . .

Sex is the "greatest magical force in nature"; an impulse acts in it which suggests the mystery of the One, even when the relationship between man and woman deteriorates into animal embraces and is exhausted and dispersed in idealizing sentimentality or habitual routine. The metaphysics of sex survives in the very cases where, in looking at the vulgarity of infinite lovers of infinite races—endless masks of the absolute man seeking the abolute woman in a turn of the circle of animal generation—it is hard to overcome the temptation to accept the biological theory which says that human sexuality springs from the life of instincts and mere animality.

But for ordinary mankind it is sex alone which, even if only in the rapture of an instant, leads to some opening through and beyond the conditionalities of merely individual existence. This is the true foundation of the importance that love and sex have and will always have in human life, an importance unmatched by any other impulse.

NOTES

[1] E. Levi, *La Science des spirits*, Paris, 1865.
[2] C. Mauclair, *La Magie de l'amour*.
[3] Stendhal (1957).
[4] L. Pin, *Psicologia dell'amore*, Milan, 1944.
[5] Andreas (1941).
[6] The "subtle body" is considered by many esoteric teachings to be an "energy body" which connects the gross physical body and the "causal body" of pure consciousness or spirit. In Hinduism it is called the *sukshma-sarira*; in Buddhism it corresponds to the *sambhogakaya*; in the Western esoteric traditions, Paracelsus called it the sidereal body. Evola's point is that the magnetic attraction between men and women happens on this level, and cannot be explained either as a purely spiritual connection or as an instinctual drive (Ed.).
[7] Plato, *The Symposium* (1928).
[8] O. Weininger, *Geschlecht und Charakter*, Vienna, 1918.

Passion and Transformation

Bernd Jager

Passion alters the pleasant flow of the ordinary world of expressive inter-changes. Passion quickens that flow, or interrupts it. The face of passion announces a radical discontinuity in the light-dominated world of seeing, understanding, doing. It refuses to be domesticated by the light of reason, it will not passively fit itself to the measure of tasks and the orderly ar-rangement of daily affairs. Passion inaugurates the breakthrough of an-other side to things. Passion emerges from the depth, from the realm beyond the eye and below the light.

Passion is the insurrection of the flesh, of the depth, of the anony-mous. It reverses the relationship which obtains in the world of expressive interchange, that is, in the world of light. There the surface dominates the depth, speaks for the depth; there the face dominates the body and the light of the eye rules the flesh. There the face *heads* the body as the surface triumphs over the depth. But in the world of passion the depth no longer remains mere support for a brilliant surface; it wells up and de-stroys the charming play of light, the brilliant outer covering of things and beings.

This strange upheaval affects things as well as beings. We feel the texture of our clothing, the grain of wood, the feline seduction of silk. From outside the window comes the dark rustling sound of masses of agitated leaves. Everything unfolds a dark substantiality with which we are secretly linked. And we ourselves commune with all these things no longer merely by sight, through inspection or deduction, but rather by means of a deeper kinship, through our flesh.

In the world of passion the body is a vessel, a sounding board through which reverberates the turmoil from the depth and the surrounding. We feel the turmoil of all flesh in our flesh. The bounce of breasts reverberates in the pit of the stomach, the fullness of buttocks is experienced as a slight panic spreading through the entire body. In the world of passion we are communing vessels in which the upheaval collects itself, by which it sounds itself out and thereby slowly acquires definition. All the life here spreads in succeeding waves from the depth and the center. The surfaces here are the tight skins of drums or the blank tense steel of railroad tracks to which we press the ear to hear the rumble of an approaching event.

Passion is always an upwelling. The world of passion is structured around the advent of an apocalypse, it awaits the reversal of depth and surface, it anticipates a creative destruction which will sweep away the concealing surfaces to reveal the ground and the flesh of all things and all beings. Those in the grip of sexual passion await to be overpowered and flooded by the sweet oblivion of orgasm. Like sleep or anger, orgasmic excitation slowly gains strength as it erupts from its unknown depth to wash over all surfaces. A forceful current takes hold of the limbs, it floods over the skin, it takes possession of the face and removes from it the powers of light and reflection. The eyes grow vacant and turn upward. The mouth becomes drawn and the muscles are taut. The entire body stiffens as it cooperates through resisting. After passing through a peak of agitation the body relaxes and reawakens to the light. All passions repeat the crisis of our sexual life, all move toward their own moment of culmination and reversal. Sexuality has its orgasm as dying has its death; sleeping has its point of no return as pain has its collapse or as fury has its transfiguration.

All these passionate transformations are both radical and discontinuous. There always exists a gap between the first slow growth of passion and its culminating transformation. The life of passion demands leaps, discontinuous progress, transformations. If we were to envision the course of passion as a journey across the plains we would need to imagine the crossing of a broad river. If, on the other hand, we would see it as a journey across mountains we would need to imagine an abyss, or, if we were to think of a journey down a river we would have to think of rapids or of narrow straits.

To move from sexual excitation to orgasm means to move through a *crisis of passage*. This discontinuity in the road, this crisis, is frequently attended by anxiety. The Latin *angustiae* literally refers to narrow straits, to difficult passages. We can think of orgasm as the passing through narrow straits on the way to the calm of the open sea.

If we remind ourselves at this point of the foreshadowing of "passion" in the Latin *patior* for suffering and enduring, we can come to understand passion as a particular aspect of a journey when the determination of will or the foresight of reason no longer can make their contribution. It would refer us to that aspect of the journey when the channel through which we must pass becomes too turbulent and too swift for deliberate and premeditated action and when the good helmsman, after having done all he can, ties himself to the wheel and entrusts himself to the waves to carry him. Passion can be envisioned as a journey through narrow straits connecting otherwise uncommunicable realms. At the height of passion the water steers the ship.

Passion both evolves and overcomes a discontinuity in life, it separates and heals, it invokes death and brings new life. Freud may have been partly guided on his way by the original meaning context of the word sexuality, which refers us to what has been cut (*sectum*). Sexuality announces itself both as a loss and as a gain, as new life and as death within life. The world of sexuality cannot be described without reference to wounding, cleaving, or cutting (*secare*). To be a sexual being means both to be wounded and to be healed.

Genesis makes reference both to Adam's wounds and to his healing as the first step in his emancipation from a virginal, timeless, unblemished creature to the full status of a mortal, wounded sexual man living a life of conflict and redemption together with Eve, his opposite. This wounding of Adam is repeated in all men when they leave their mothers and in all women as they turn from their father's love. Sexuality requires a leave-taking or a wounding. Fertile sexuality requires the touch of mortality. Immediately after their expulsion from paradise Adam and Eve make love together. Their lovemaking impregnates Eve and she gives birth to their first son, Cain. It is in a very similar manner that Cain impregnates his wife immediately following his expulsion from the land of his father. Expulsion becomes the ground for a new kind of gain, and mutilation opens the door to a new integrity.

There exists still in countless non-Western societies an unvarying relationship between ritual cutting and admission to the status of an adult manhood or womanhood. The anthropologist van Gennep cites countless forms of such mutilations which, once healed, are the marks of sexual maturity. He mentions, among others, the cutting of the foreskin of the penis, the pulling of a tooth, the cutting of the little finger above the last joint, the perforation of the hymen, the sectioning of the perineum, the excision of the clitoris, the scarifying and tattooing of the face or of any other part of the body, and the cutting of hair in a particular fashion.[1] The first concern in the integration of mature sexuality is the acceptance of separation. The power of sexuality flows from a cut and a division. The great and nearly universal symbol of sexuality is that of a healed wound. Sexual intimacy becomes possible upon the basis of an *accepted* separation; only those who have accepted the wound can cultivate the healing. Only those who risk disturbing the earth may sow; only those who build a trench and a wall between themselves and others can be neighbors.

Aphrodite, the great goddess of love, emerged from the wound which Kronos cut when he castrated the oppressive sky god. At the beginning of human love and at its end stands "the huge sickle with its long jagged teeth." The love goddess of the Greeks was always closely associated with knives and swords and other instruments of war that could wound or kill. She married Hephaestus, the smith who made the armor of Achilles, and she betrayed him with her love for Ares, the fair god of the sword.

The cutting and scarring of adolescents at the time of their admission to full manhood and womanhood forms an instance of the ritualization of the discontinuity inherent in all passionate experiencing. Passion always moves between points in life which cannot be connected by means of industry or willpower, or logic. Passion always leads us outside the ordinary daily existence of activity and expression, of tasks and conversation. It moves us beyond this world of *continuity* towards a world made both generative and miraculous through our mortality, that is, our discontinuity.

We might ask how this discontinuity might be embodied in the organs of sex. A muscular organ such as a hand, with its responsive coordinated movements, overcomes difficulties, solves problems, unifies, and connects. Hands build a world, bring a world together. Hands explore and lose themselves in work. Sexual organs are inwardly turned, brooding organs, both inept and unresponsive to a daytime world of tasks. The rise and the fall of the penis is not a feat of strength, or even of agility or dexterity. Sexual activity is not a making or fashioning; it is not work. If certain expressions such as "tool" for "penis," and "making someone" for "sexual intercourse" persist, it is only because the anxieties inherent in the world of passion make us wish to escape to the world of work.

The world of passion offers a crisis of passing. The sweet heaviness of the body finds its clearest expression in the fullness and swelling of the sexual organs. It is only after a long and vulnerable period of filling and stiffening that the crisis is reached, that the *passing* to the other shore can take place with sudden miraculous swiftness. Like babies gorged with milk to the term of satiation, we drift to the point of crisis only then to cross over to the other side.

Wherever we look in the world of passion we find a thickening, a stiffening, a growing, an increasing fullness and mounting pressure, which lasts until the term is full and the limits are touched. This protracted phase of absorption which precedes the passionate response leaves the genitals and the entire sexual body in an odd position of exposure.

And it is precisely this vulnerable permeability which renders possible both sexuality and shame. It is only gradually and with the growth of sexual initiation that the first awkwardness is overcome and that the fearful undergoing and furtive doing is transformed into a positive offering, into a giving and receiving of hospitality. But the awkwardness, or at least the feeling of shame and reserve about sexual activity never is entirely lost. The reticence or guardedness which keeps sexual activity outside the routines of the workaday world doubtless owes something to the fact that the sexual organs in their mature transformations are but relatively late acquisitions of the body. To the genitals clings forever a feeling of strangeness, of power, of divine or diabolic magic. The penis, the breasts, the vagina seldom, if ever, acquire the absolute unself-consciousness or the complete self-evidence of the hand or the shoulder.

Sexuality not only opens an abyss within the body, between the sexes and within the sexes, it also throws a bridge across divided parts which make possible new alliances and unities. The rise of sexual desires in a friendship destroys the comfortable feeling of a prior unity, of being a brother to a brother, a sister to a sister. Sexual ardour between the sexes creates the battle of the sexes, a kind of constant tension or even open warfare which menaces ease and destroys comfort. Sexuality, as all passion, appears at first as a sower of discord, only subsequently to become a power of reconciliation.

To sexuality still clings the dread and awe, the guilt and exaltation which at one time belonged to the realm of the sacred. A thoroughly rationalized, efficiently managed sexuality, without flashes of terror and of benediction, becomes another consumer-good, another recompense for day's work at the office or in the factory. Sexuality as a "wholesome prac- tice," as a mere process of mutual gratification and ease of tensions, no longer can fulfill its ancient role of manifesting the depth and the other side of things and beings. Civil, cosmeticized sexuality, with blunted arrows, neutered, becomes the solid inhabitant of the middle, and the noon of life, cut off from dawn and dusk, from the beginning and the end, removed from the empire of passion, incapable of movement, blind to the beckoning and threatening horizons of the world. Such a sexuality, removed from pain and divisiveness, from suffering, from death and from the gods, ignorant of height and depth, becomes a harmless "feel-good," the itching of a scratch, a sucker in the hand of an idiot. Fertile sexuality, whatever its form, must live in the awareness of the beginning and the end, the source and the depth. Only from that perspective, only within that possession can it give birth to the other side of things and beings.

In passionate expressiveness it becomes possible for the first time to live in the full awareness of birth and death. And it is in the last instance this awareness of birth and death, of which all passion speaks.

NOTES

[1]Van Gennep (1969), p. 71.

V. Larger Visions of Relationship

Introduction

Throughout history, in all cultures, the relation of man and woman has been regarded as sacred, not just something pleasurable or exciting, but a microcosm of the dynamic interplay of larger energies in the cosmos. The ultimate context that gives intimate relationships meaning, beyond just "stirring the oatmeal," is the larger cyclical rhythm of life as a whole. Marriage has always been surrounded by sacred rituals designed to portray this union as an opening into some larger mystery that lies beyond our understanding. This section focuses particularly on the challenge of love as an invitation to surrender all our masks and pretenses and to wake up to our own innate wisdom.

The French feminist writer Suzanne Lilar opens this section with a spirited description of the sacred dimension of love. The sacred is characterized by the reconciling of opposites; for instance, while dissolving individual boundaries, love also heightens our appreciation of another's separate individuality. Lilar emphasizes the refining character of sacral love, sifting and scouring until it brings out the best qualities in the beloved and reveals the natural sacredness inherent in ordinary life.

In the next chapter, Orage explores the rare phenomenon of conscious love—willing the good of the other and acting in behalf of the full unfolding of the beloved, regardless of the consequences to oneself. Of course, such a service in behalf of love is not easy; it requires the development of wisdom, power, patience, and discipline. Orage compares this service to Bushido, the martial art of the warriors of ancient Japan, in which one must undergo long apprenticeship before one day attaining to mastery. One of the most important ingredients in conscious love is the ability and readiness to let go, when necessary, in order to allow the beloved to follow his or her true path, even if it leads in a different direction from one's own.

Drawing upon the ancient Chinese book of wisdom, the *I Ching*, Carol Anthony describes in greater detail certain principles of conscious love alluded to by Orage. Specifically, she discusses what is involved in letting go and helping to nurture someone else's growth without clinging to a particular outcome. An important aid in this process is modesty—the sword and shield of the "warrior of the heart." In essence, modesty means letting go of preconceptions, tuning in to what is appropriate in given situations, and allowing people to unfold in their own way, without control or manipulation. This requires patience and perseverance, as well as some basic trust in the creative powers of the universe.

In the next chapter, Chögyam Trungpa emphasizes that true warriors must renounce everything that keeps them from being available to others. The path of conscious love requires giving up our private hiding places and exposing the most tender and vulnerable parts of ourselves. This leaves us feeling alone, yet full, with a vibrant sense of connection with the world around us.

Just as the *I Ching* provides a valuable guide for helping us become more aware of the rhythm and flow of relationships, meditation can provide experiential practice in working with the polarities inside us and developing the qualities of character necessary for conscious love. My chapter makes a small beginning in exploring this topic.

The final selection of this book, from the letters of Rainer Maria Rilke, was the first writing that ever spoke to me about the real challenges of loving another person. Like Solovyov, Rilke has a vision of love evolving. Yet perhaps his most important point here is the need to cultivate and deepen our solitude as the most fertile ground for being able to give of ourselves to another human being. Perhaps we can only fully appreciate the tenderness of human love when we keep in mind that we are born alone, we die alone, and this aloneness is the larger, ever-present background or space in which all our relationships unfold. Rilke's eloquent description of the difficulties of intimate relationships, along with all their potential for initiating self-transformation, is a fitting conclusion to this book.

The Sacred Dimension

Suzanne Lilar

Hardly anyone dares to face with open eyes the great delight of love.
—Andre Breton

To some people, the sexual act is essentially and irremediably vile, shameful, degrading, and nothing can raise it from this indignity. To others, it requires to be sanctified by a sacrament. To others again, it is naturally sacred, without the help of any sacrament; is indeed itself a sacrament—not only sacred, but able to communicate the sacred: this is what I mean by *sacral*.

To what are such differences due? Both to doctrines and to individual temperaments. It goes without saying that those religions, metaphysical systems and doctrines of morality which teach the radical separation of body and spirit are not exactly favorable to sublimation through love. People whose natures are poor, inert, lacking in volatility, are no better placed. It is hard to see how souls deprived of a fundamental grace of connecting and harmonizing could be raised from their degradation; the real inability to love is an inability to connect.

The real lovers need no argument to convince them that love sanctifies. They know it: in love everything is possible, everything is permitted, everything is sacred, provided that sexuality is adopted in all its mystery, its gravity, its totality. The first gift lavished by love is this sense of infallible certainty. There is no better gauge of the greatness of a couple than its consciousness of its *sacrality*.

But this sacrality is not the product of affection, tenderness, esteem or other such edifying sentiments: it is by reference to sexuality that it will be decided whether a given conjugal union is sacred or profane. When, for instance, we read in de Beauvoir's *Les Mandarins*: "We were too closely united for it to be possible for the union of our bodies to have great importance, in renouncing it we lost practically nothing," it is at once obvious that the Anne-Dubreuilh *ménage* will turn out to be an association, a collaboration, a pact, anything but a couple adopting its sacral significance. But neither would this be adopted by a couple that relied on sexuality without love. In the couple the division of the sexes must be both felt and resolved.

Nothing is easier than to exhibit in sexuality the essential features of the sacred—its absolute otherness, its ambiguity, its ambivalence, its polarity, its twofold character of positivity and negativity. Here, unquestionably, we are in that zone of extremes which is also a zone of communication, "because the sacred dissolves the determinations of individual beings and makes possible a fusion that is like a kind of liquid condition where there is no longer separate existence." Comparisons of this sort have already been used as images of love. The same words, the same images occur to those who would describe both eros and the powerful mystical experiences—their "characteristics of excess, outgoing and fusion." Even that tendency to lose oneself, to annihilate oneself finds an amazing analogue in the consummation of the sexual act. Indeed, one cannot help agreeing with Paul Ricoeur: "It is not possible, in point of fact, to understand the adventurous history of sexuality apart from that of the sacred among men."

It might seem that, once this point is made, all that remains is to arrange couples in two classes, those who attach great importance to sexual love and those who grant it only the indispensable minimum—the former being promoted to the dignity of that model Couple whose condition we have now to define. Nothing could be more false. There is a germ of the sacred in any and every physical love, and in this context it is unquestionable that even the brute is susceptible to a kind of cosmic *participation*—perhaps more so than the intellectual, who has too often succeeded in stifling his subconscious under bookish rubbish (D. H. Lawrence would certainly have thought so). But, in spite of this, the highest, most perfect, fully worked out love, the love that has gone furthest, is certainly the one that assumes the sacral quality; and assumption presupposes awareness. If it is true that "the Spirit feels nothing except with the help of the body," it is also true that the body is called upon, is appointed to bring the spirit into the world, to be *delivered* of it. There

can be no great couple without strong sexuality, nor can there be one that
has not learned to fetch it in and master it.

Nothing is rarer than a love completely adopted. Camus thought
that there are only two or three great loves per century. Nonetheless, the
thing exists, it has been lived; and, if one cannot carry it through to the
end, one can and should bear witness that there is a true greatness and
dignity even in striving towards it.

We are concerned here with the kind of love that is able to resacralize
the couple. This can only be the love that consecrates, instead of *abstract-
ing*, the individuals—the "love that takes absolute power, claims the whole
length of life and of course only consents to recognize its object in a
single being." *L'amour fou* ("crazy love"), Breton called it, and Benjamin
Peret described it as sublime love, the hermetic philosophers as perfect
love. It was Plato's divinizing love, a total and unreasonable love. It is in
fact simply love, the only kind that needs no qualification or description
because those who come upon it recognize it without a second's hesitation. Why do they? Because it is like nothing else. Because it is a "thing
apart" and makes its appearance as an incredible privilege. It is with the
feeling, so often described, of a privileged moment, of an instant set apart
that the consciousness of the *sacral* of which I have spoken begins.

Anyone who is living through a privileged experience naturally desires to go on with it. Hence that fear of ceasing to love, of falling back
into the common condition. There is no example of a man or woman
truly in love having sincerely desired to stop being so. We are so familiar
with the irritation of people in love when someone tries to "cure" them:
these sick, mad, schizophrenic people do not envy the world of the
healthy in the least. Is this stupidity, obstinacy, masochism, or play-acting?
Or is it, on the contrary, an awareness of having been singled out for a
noble and prodigious fate?

What do we mean by lower and higher accomplishments of love? In
the first part of life the aim of love is often physical union, and procreation, while in the second "it is more a question of a *spiritual* union with
the partner of the other sex in order to bear fruit—the spiritual offspring
which confer the lasting quality to the whole spiritual existence of the
united partners."[1]

Both psychology and biology invite us not to reduce the object and
meaning of love to proceation. To create a family is only the first of the
couple's accomplishments—the first starting from below. Even then it
must not serve as a pretext for the partners to close up, to shut themselves
away more narrowly instead of opening out, expanding, renouncing
their preconceptions of themselves. Every love must be *gone through*, even

that of parents: it is from unwillingness to do this that voracious mothers (often in search of a compensation for their disappointments with sex and love) have weighed down the destinies of their sons. Browning's mother, for instance, would not allow the communicating door between their rooms to be closed at night, and "so closely mixed up were their lives," says André Maurois, "that when she fell ill, he at once sickened, then recovered as soon as Mrs. Browning was better again." D. H. Lawrence became aware that to his mother he was both a son and the husband that she did not love, and in due course he said of motherly love that it was a monstrous manifestation of egoism. The mother's instinct takes its right place and its true dimension within the deep and total love of a real couple.

But if procreation is only the first of the accomplishments of the couple, what are the others? According to whether a person is drawn to the lower or to the higher accomplishments of love, he or she is also drawn to the choice of a partner answering this ambition. The choice of a partner in love depends on the meaning and range that one is unconsciously preparing to accord to love. Just as there are men, usually young, simple and healthy, who merely seek to have children and instinctively look for *une bonne pondeuse* ("a good layer"), others, whose yearning is for a passionate love, will be caught by a fine face or gaze, by a woman "who has an air of destiny about her."

In both cases the desire settles on a person with whom the chooser has a presentiment that love will take on its full sense and all its savor, on the being who will engage us the most compellingly in her (or his) movement—a movement of which, of course, one will often lose control. The sister soul is the one that will make us live—and die—most intensely. Sister souls recognize each other. But this idea of predestination in love must not be taken too literally: one thinks one recognizes a face—what one is recognizing is only one's own dream, which one *projects*, and could, no doubt, project on several other persons.

Sometimes this appeal is so strong that it works like a stream of energy, forcing the defenses of a human being who fights against it and is, as it were, sucked by it out of his or her self. In such a case he or she is chosen rather than chooses. Sometimes hatred and repulsion are the advance signs of a great passion, the febrile symptoms of a violent but vain psychical defense. Alessandra di Rudini Carlotti detested d'Annunzio; though he was a friend of her brother's, she obstinately refused to meet him; she considered him ugly, vain and ridiculous; she made fun of his small stature, his baldness, his histrionic performance in the part of a man of letters, his scandalous reputation—until the day when they met face to face at a wedding. Immediately she felt her prejudices melt away. Less than a month afterwards she followed him.

Nothing could be more incomprehensible, absurd, and disappointing than such choice, if love were not at the same time love for something else. Love is, precisely, the miracle of a person, a human body, that has become wholly meaningful, and of a desire that branches out beyond all limits. For, whether it be kept down or flattered, desire remains the motive power of love: it is always the being who is most desired who will be the most illuminating. When a woman who seems to have all the gifts—beauty, sensibility, ardor—proves incapable of inspiring a strong passion in a man who seems cut out to appreciate these merits, and he then falls in love stupidly with the first green girl that comes along, the world simply cannot understand: "after all, she had everything required to make him happy." But what if he was seeking not to be happy but to love (for people make over and over again the Platonic discovery that to love is more divine than to be loved)? To give himself up to an activity of loving one person who is yearned for, singled out from all others, isolated in her shocking uniqueness?

The attractive but factitious image of crystallization has created confusion on this subject. Crystallization is an image of addition, of accretion. Placed in a mother-liquid a crystal fattens; but all who have thought at all deeply about the working passion realize that, far from adding to the loved one, love digs out, scours, clears. If the result is to bring together something like a mountain, it can only be a mountain of debris, like the slag-heaps in the neighborhood of mines. To lovers everything is an occasion for bringing them face to face: a town that comes up in conversation, a season whose advance signs they notice, a piece of music to which they listen—the imagination seizes hold of many things to test love and to derive from them fresh perceptions of it. But these occasions do not cling to love—they do not accumulate, any more than do the acids or other agents used on a substance that contains a precious metal. In any case love disengages, strips, and discovers: it separates what is worthy to be loved from what is not.

Alessandra di Rudini Carlotti was not mistaken in seeing d'Annunzio as short, rather ugly, and in some ways absurd: she had succeeded perfectly in distinguishing what she loved from what she did not love. But from the moment of crossing a certain threshold her attention, letting drop the negative elements in order to concentrate on the rest, literally *dis-covered* in d'Annunzio what was truly beautiful, great, and worthy of being loved, sympathized with, and consoled—perhaps the look in his eyes, perhaps his forehead, perhaps his voice or speech, his infinite love of beauty, or the gift he had of converting the humblest thing into magnificence.

Far from producing illusion (as is so often believed) love has a pitiless lucidity. "The passion of love is not blind," writes a great enemy of love, Robert Poulet. "It sees in its object, with perfect clearness, two or three points, two or three signs which could, it is true, be seen just as well in a hundred thousand other people. *It refuses to see the rest.*" And another great enemy of love, Ludwig Klages, maintains that, far from loving the exemplary, we love only the singular—often an irregularity, a defect: how indeed, he asks, could we love in anyone what this person has in common with the others: Is not the beloved person irreplaceable to us because of his particularity? "To Kriemhilde there is only one Siegfried, to Tristan one Isolde, to Ophelia one Hamlet, to Dante one Beatrice, to Romeo one Juliet." And so on. Is there a contradiction here? No; for what love seeks is the *coincidence of the exemplary with the specific*, the meeting of existence and essence.

Yes, it is possible to adore a pout, a frown, a wrinkle or a slight squint in a face otherwise incomparable (a lover, as Molière said, loves even the faults of those he loves), it is possible to love an element of ungrace in grace (though it is rare for a wholly graceless creature to be loved), and it is indeed at this meeting-point of the singular and the universal that love makes itself most sharply felt: this is the *daemonic paradox*. On what should a unitive activity exercise itself, if not on multiplicity and detail? Religious mysticism sets to work in the same way. Most deeply spiritual people take some concrete detail as a starting-point for their prayer. St. François de Sales teaches that the soul in love with God seeks out and chooses for herself motives for love; *she draws them to her* and then savors them. To seek out, to choose and to draw to oneself is to let the rest drop; it is to submit the object of one's love to a real critical activity. Yet love chooses only in order to adore better. All that is of God is by definition adorable and sacred; only human love consecrates, makes divine.

And so a relationship has to be established between the person and the divine, between the profane and the sacred. By holding back in its sieve some characteristics because they are exemplary and others because they are singular, love is merely bringing out clearly the two terms of this relationship. Probably, side by side with what was unquestionably *adorable* in d'Annunzio, Allesandra di Rudini Carlotti chose to adore also some detail of his tone of voice or bearing, the way he had of carrying his right shoulder lower than the left, or the scar on his eyelid, or the smell of the toilet water he used, or some other incredibly profane and personal thing whose function was to represent the poet's singularity as clearly (though symbolically) as a badge or a flag: so that, by steering for this characteristic, the divinizing activity could always reassure itself as to the *integration of the person*. The real object of such loving consecration is to lay bare the divine kinship and to savor it in the mystical sense.

The unburying—rarely completed—seems to be one of the most admirable of the tasks of love. When it is achieved, there are no more "illusions of love," there is no longer any deception about the beloved object. The person is really sacred, to the extent that it lets the sacred shine through.

In all this there is no dishonesty unless the lover stays stuck in a complacent adulation of the beloved—instead of venerating in him or her the "divine spark" which attests the true allegiance. This is the whole difference between a closed and an open love. Nor is there any objection to that work of sifting to which love proceeds, to that decision to keep one thing and forget another. Its aim is to restore the beloved to his or her original dignity. And so what we have here is not deception or abuse, but the generosity of love doing justice: not blindness, but the partiality of love cutting through appearance.

The truth is that every human being deserves to be looked at in this way at least once in a lifetime—loved and venerated for what is authentically divine in him or her. And every human being is called to this. It does seem, in fact, that where this perception prevails it is not the most beautiful people, nor even the youngest, who offer the finest material to love, but rather those whose nature is rich, who have "temperament," whose body and soul are gifted with a fine vitality. Perfect beauties can be discouraging, like souls dedicated to calm: they offer little purchase to the activity of loving, they leave it little to do. Graceless bodies and souls, which give it too much to do, are also discouraging. Plato—in spite of Greek fanaticism for bodily beauty—regarded the love of a beautiful body as a stage lower than the love for a "gentle soul in a body whose flowering is not brilliant." Fortunately it takes less marked physical advantages to give profound delight to one person only, awakening in him or her a passionate attention, than it does to please many superficially. Our ideas distorted by eroticism have overvalued the importance of physiological factors and of techniques of seduction: this is a regression of man towards sexual mechanics and animal eroticism. The only way in which the art of love in human beings can genuinely progress is towards an always greater awareness: it is a long elucidation of spirit. But such a *purification* does not fit in with the brevity of desire; it demands the long, infinite patience of true love. All the wiles of modern eroticism—which is, to my mind, already dated—remain inefficient at satisfying our real thirst, which is spiritual. And without a little of that love at which our world snaps its fingers, the most beautiful, seductive and desired of women may die as lonely as a masterless dog.

This approach is, of course, rarely carried to completion. People allow themselves to be fascinated by mirages, such as happiness, which melt away as they try to lay hold on them, and by diversions, such as pleasure pursued as an end in itself. Love is abortive as soon as it becomes self-interested.

The profound sacredness of love means that the couple, which decides to adopt this *sacrality*, feels bound by it from then onwards—and by the promotion which it confers on the humblest thing. It is altogether consistent with the economy of eros to hold that everything that is, has a share in the sacred, and that one of the essential tasks of love is to bring this out. Every woman in love knows instinctively that love extracts something authentically and primordially sacred from the humblest tasks—for instance, preparing a meal. But if the sacramental effect of love extends to that, how much more so to the husband or the wife in person.

If a couple succeeds, by force of lucidity, in outwitting all the snares and complacencies of self-deception and self-interest, then it will surely be guided to its aim by the critical and mystical activity of love. This will either reveal to the lover the true kinship of the beloved; or it will lay bare his or her own loving activity—an activity that converts to unity, producing the conviction of being *governed by Law*. In both cases we are shown a world of continuity, of coherence, and are led back to unity. This is the supreme accomplishment of daemonic eros. It is a method of knowledge as well as of salvation, and wisdom as well as of holiness.

Conscious Love

A. R. Orage

Conscious love rarely obtains between humans; but it can be illustrated in the relations of man to his favorites in the animal and vegetable kingdoms. The development of the horse and the dog from their original state of nature; the cultivation of flowers and fruit—these are examples of a *primitive* form of conscious love, primitive because the motive is still egoistic and utilitarian. In short, man has a personal use for the domesticated horse and the cultivated fruit; and his labor upon them cannot be said to be for love alone. The conscious love motive, in its developed state, is the wish that the object should arrive at its own native perfection, regardless of the consequences to the lover. "So she become perfectly herself, what matter I?" says the conscious lover. "I will go to hell if only she may go to heaven." And the paradox of the attitude is that such love always evokes a similar attitude in its object. Conscious love begets conscious love. It is rare among humans because, in the first place, the vast majority are children who look to be loved but not to love; secondly, because perfection is seldom conceived as the proper end of human love— though it alone distinguishes adult human from infantile and animal love; thirdly, because humans do not know, even if they wish, what is good for those they love; and fourthly, because it never occurs by chance, but must be the subject of resolve, effort, self-conscious choice. As little as Bushido or the Order of Chivalry grew up accidentally does conscious love arise by nature. As these were works of art, so must conscious love be a work of art. Such a lover enrolls himself, goes through his appren-

ticeship, and perhaps one day attains to mastery. He perfects himself
in order that he may purely wish and aid the perfection of his beloved.

Would one enroll in this service of conscious love? Let him foreswear
personal desire and preconception. He contemplates his beloved. What
manner of woman (or man) is she (or he)? A mystery is here: a scent
of perfection the nascent air of which is adorable. How may this perfection be actualized—to the glory of the beloved and of God her Creator?
Let him think, is he fit? He can only conclude that he is not. Who cannot
cultivate flowers, or properly treat dogs and horses, how shall he learn to
reveal the perfection still seedling in the beloved? Humility is necessary,
and then deliberate tolerance. If I am not sure what is proper to her
perfection, let her at least have free way to follow her own bent. Mean-
while to study—what she is, and may become; what she needs, what her
soul craves and cannot find a name, still less a thing, for. To anticipate
today her needs of tomorrow. And without a thought all the while of
what her needs may mean to me. You will see what self-discipline and self-
education are demanded here. Enter these enchanted woods, ye who
dare. The gods love each other consciously. Conscious lovers become
gods.

Without shame people will boast that they have loved, do love or
hope to love. As if love were enough, or could cover any multitude of
sins. But love, as we have seen, when it is not conscious love—that is to
say, love that aims to be both wise and able in the service of its object—is
either an affinity or a dis-affinity, and in both cases equally unconscious,
that is, uncontrolled. To be in such a state of love is to be dangerous
either to oneself or to the other or to both. We are then polarized to a
natural force (which has its own objects to serve regardless of ours) and
charged with its force; and events are fortunate if we do not damage
somebody in consequence of carrying dynamite carelessly. Love without
knowledge and power is demoniac. Without knowledge it may destroy
the beloved. Who has not seen many a beloved made wretched and ill by
her or his "lover"? Without power the lover must become wretched, since
he cannot do for his beloved what he wishes and knows to be for her
delight. Men should pray to be spared the experience of love without
wisdom and strength. Or, finding themselves in love, they should pray
for knowledge and power to guide their love. Love is *not* enough.

"I love you," said the man. "Strange that I feel none the better for it,"
said the woman.

Until you have wisdom and power equal to your love, be ashamed to
avow that you are in love. Or, since you cannot conceal it, love humbly
and study to be wise and strong. Aim to be worthy to be in love.

There is no necessary relation between love and children; but there is a necessary relation between love and creation. Love is for creation; and if creation is not possible, then for procreation; and if even that is not possible, then for creations of which, perhaps fortunately, we are unconscious. Take it, however, as the fundamental truth about love: that it always creates. Love created the world: and not all its works are beautiful! The procreation of children is the particular function of instinctive love: that is its plane. But above and below this plane, other kinds of love have other functions. The higher forms of love either exclude procreation, not artificially but naturally, or include it only as a by-product. Neither the purpose nor the function of conscious love is children; unless we take the word in the mystic sense of becoming as little children. For briefly, the aim of conscious love is to bring about rebirth, or spiritual childhood. Everybody with perceptions beyond those of male and female must be aware of the change that comes over the man or woman, however old in years, who loves. It is usually instinctive; yet it symbolizes the still more marvellous change occurring when a man or woman loves consciously or is aware of being consciously loved. The youth in such cases has all the air of eternity; and it is, indeed, the divine youth. The creations of such a spiritual child in each of the two lovers is the peculiar function of conscious love; and it depends neither upon marriage nor upon children. There are other creations proper to still higher degrees of love; but they must remain until we have become as little children.

Love without divination is elementary. To be in love demands that the lover shall divine the wishes of the beloved long before they have come into the beloved's own consciousness. He knows her better than she knows herself; and loves her more than she loves herself; so that she becomes her perfect self without her own conscious effort. *Her* conscious effort, when the love is mutual, is for him. Thus each delightfully works perfection in the other.

But this state is not ordinarily attained in nature: it is the fruit of art, of self-training. All people desire it, even the most cynical; but since it seldom occurs by chance, and nobody has published the key to its creation, the vast majority doubt even its possibility. Nevertheless it is possible, provided that the parties can learn and teach humbly. How to begin? Let the lover when he is about to see his beloved think what he should take, do or say so as to give her a delightful surprise. At first it will probably be a surprise that is not a complete surprise: that is to say, she will have been aware of her wish, and only delighted that her lover had guessed it. Later the delightful surprise may really surprise her; and her remark will be: "How did you know I should be pleased, since I should never have guessed it myself?" Constant efforts to anticipate the nascent wishes of the beloved while they are still unconscious are the means to conscious love.

Take hold tightly; let go lightly. This is one of the great secrets of felicity in love. For every Romeo and Juliet tragedy arising from the external circumstances of the two parties, a thousand tragedies arise from the circumstances created by the lovers themselves. As they seldom know the moment or the way to "take hold" of each other, so they even more rarely know the way or the moment to let go. The ravines of Mount Meru (i.e., Venusberg) are filled with lovers who cannot leave each other. Each wishes to let go, but the other will not permit it. There are various explanations of this unhappy state of affairs. In most instances the approach has been wrong: that is to say, the parties have leapt into union without thought of the way out. Often the first five minutes of the lovers' *first* meeting are decisive of the whole future of the relations. In some instances the original relation has been responsible for the subsequent difficulty of "letting go": it should never have been; or not have been in the precise circumstances of its occurrence. Mistimed relations always cause trouble. In other cases the difficulty is due to difference in age, education, or "past." One is afraid to "let go" because it appears to be the last hope, or because too much time has already been spent on it, or because it has been the best up to date, or because his "ideal," created by education, demands eternal fidelity even where it is not possible, because it is not desired by both; or because one is oversensitive from past experience and cannot face another failure, or because the flesh being willing the spirit is weak, i.e., neither party can use a knife; or because circumstances are unfavorable, i.e., the parties must continue to see each other; or because of imagination, as when one or the other pictures the happiness of the other without him or her. There are a thousand explanations, and every one of them, while sufficient as a cause, is quite inadequate as reason, the fact being that when one of the parties desires to separate, the other's love-duty is to "let go." Great love can both let go and take hold.

Jealousy is the dragon in paradise; the hell of heaven; and the most bitter of the emotions because associated with the sweetest. There is a specific against jealousy, namely, conscious love; but this remedy is harder to find than the disease is to endure. But there are palliatives of which the first therapeutic condition is the recognition of the disease and the second the wish to cure oneself. In these circumstances let the sufferer deliberately experiment. Much may be forgiven him or her during this process. He may, for instance, try to forward the new plans of his former beloved—but this is difficult without obvious hypocrisy. Or he may plunge into new society. Or he may engage himself in a new work that demands all his energy. Or he may cast a spell on his memory and regard his former beloved as dead; or as having become his sister; or as having gone away on a long journey; or as having become enchanted. Best, however, if he "let go" completely with no lingering hope of ever meeting her again.

Be comforted. Our life is but one day of our Life. If not today, tomorrow! Let go!

Coming to Meet:
Advice from the *I Ching*

Carol Anthony

Anyone who works with the *I Ching*, whether for purposes of self-development or for the most mundane-seeming things, is being taught "the way of the Sage,"[1] for no matter what our concern, to achieve progress requires a realignment in our attitude to the cosmic point of view. This realignment moves us toward understanding the higher realities. Ultimately we are working on our spiritual nature.

If we are already involved in defective relationships, these become the means by which we learn the "way of the Sage." In correcting them we learn the true power of modesty as a shield and sword. Modesty alone arouses the Creative Power.[2] Through modesty, that is, through doing nothing at all, we achieve everything.

In using the *I Ching* for guidance in difficult situations over a period of years, we come to understand not only how modesty brings about our defense and furtherance, but how it also acts as a tool for rectifying our relationships.

Modesty in the *I Ching* has several meanings. First, it is the humility of knowing we need help from the Sage, and asking for it. Second, it is will-power as reticence, restraining our clamoring inferiors.[3] Third, it is patience, holding firm when the pressures of the moment are intense, and when yielding to them in the slightest degree would cause us to lose our path. Fourth, it is conscientiousness, reflecting to see if we have overlooked any evil in ourselves, and keeping on guard against the entrance of any doubt. This conscientiousness amounts to an unflagging awareness so that one is not deceived by self-flattery or false enthusiasm brought on by the pressure to find "solutions." Fifth, modesty is enduring firmly through perseverance. Sixth, it is the will to accept things as they come, ever seeking clarity through acceptance and docility, for one realizes that clarity gives one the strength to see things through to completion. Finally, modesty is expressed as devotion to the path of the good for its own sake, for one sees clearly that staying on the path is the goal, and that everything good comes out of that. For a long time we must be content to wait and work without expectation. Then support comes. We need to realize that it can come only when we prove reliable—devoted to being led. Much of the work of self-development is to correct our relationship with the Sage by allowing ourselves to be led.

"Coming to Meet" (Hexagram 44) describes a correct relationship as one in which two people come to meet each other halfway. Halfway means that both are open and receptive to each other. Coming to meet halfway also must be mutually voluntary, based on the principle of spontaneous attraction described in "The Marrying Maiden" (54) as the "essential principle of relatedness." We must maintain reserve in our relationships until the coming to meet is mutual. Maintaining reserve is the correct action (or nonaction). Coming to meet halfway is possible only between people who are mutually honest and sincere in their way of life. It is the great joy of such relationships that they are full of mutual trust and sensitivity.

We understand "coming to meet" better if we compare it to a contract made between two people. If one is indolent in performing his part, or has mental reservations about what he is willing to do, the contract may fail. Although such a person may have entered the contract without any immediate objections, his attitude may contain objections which arise only at the time his obligations are to be performed. Such a person may secretly feel that contracts are not to be taken seriously, or, on seeing how difficult it is to fulfill his part, he may hedge on doing it because of some idea that all contracts are subject to fitting into his concept of what is "reasonable." In any case, it is impossible to come to meet such a person halfway, and the I Ching repeatedly advises us that it is better for us to go on our way alone and to wait until the fundamentals of unity are firmly established before we commit ourselves to other people. When we cater to another person's ego because it is uncomfortable to go on our way alone, we choose the high road of comfort rather than the low road of modesty and loneliness. Withdrawal from the high road is the action often counseled by the I Ching.

If a person is treating us presumptuously, and if we remind him of this, he may correct his habits for a few days, but gradually revert to the same pattern of neglect. This he does from egotistical indolence—something in his point of view makes him feel he has the right to be indifferent. Likewise, we must withdraw from the indolent person, "cutting our inner strings" of attachment to him, and no longer look at his wrong-doings with our inner eye. This enables the person to see what he is doing in the mirror created by the void. By dispersing any alienation we may feel, we also lend strength to his superior self. Momentarily, his ego is overcome. We need to realize that this change is short-lived, but it is an essential beginning. The change does not last because it is only founded on his response to feeling the void. It becomes a permanent change when he sees clearly that unity with others depends upon his devoting himself to correcting his mistakes. Only then can we abandon a more formal way of relating to him.

The sense of loss, loneliness, or poverty of self a person feels on our withdrawing from him is what, in "Biting Through" (21), is called "punishment." The punishment works only if it is applied in the way described in the lines of this hexagram. These lines make clear that on encountering the ego of another person, we must consistently and immediately withdraw, neither contending with him nor trying to force progress by leverage. We withdraw, accepting his state of mind, letting him go. We must take care not to withdraw with any other attitude than that required to maintain inner serenity, and to keep from giving up on him. If we withdraw with feelings of alienation, or of self-righteousness, our ego is involved as the punisher. The ego, as the third line of this hexagram says, "lacks the power and authority" to punish. The culprits not only do not submit, but "by taking up the problem the punisher arouses poisonous hatred against himself." One person's ego may not punish another person's ego.

When a person returns to the path of responding correctly, we likewise go to meet him halfway, rather than tell him he is doing things correctly. In this way he comes to relating correctly from his own need to relate correctly and we do not force it on him. Our consistency and discipline in feeling out each moment and responding to it does the work. It is unnecessary to watch a person's behavior to see if he is becoming worse or better; we need only be in tune with ourselves. Our inner voice warns us precisely when to withdraw and when to relate. We need only listen within.

It is an important *I Ching* principle to work with a situation only so long as the other person is receptive and open, and to retreat the instant this receptivity wanes. When we understand that this represents a natural cycle of influence, we learn to "let go" when the moment of influence passes, and not to press our views. This gives other people the space they need to move away from us and return of their own accord. The Sage relates to us in precisely this manner, and the hexagram comments that the Sage is never sad, in view of our coming and going, but is always like the sun at midday. In the same way we must avoid egotistical enthusiasm when we think we are making progress, or discouragement when the dark period ensues. Throughout the cycle we learn to remain detached, holding steadily to the light within us and within others. The instant we strive to influence, we "push upward blindly." If we insist on accomplishing the goal at all costs, our inner light is darkened and our will to see things through is damaged.

The strength of a person's ego corresponds to the amount of attention it can attract. On the most simple level this recognition is by eye-to-eye contact; on the more basic inner level we strengthen other people's egos by watching them with our inner eye. If we are annoyed with someone, we are watching him with our inner eye. Only when we withdraw both our eye-to-eye contact and our inner gaze do we deprive his ego of its power. An *I Ching* line says, "We cannot lead those whom we follow." By following others with our inner eye we do not walk our own path but attend to theirs. This gratifies their ego. It is as if we are attached to them by hidden underground cables which must be cut. It is as if we are acting as a lifeguard who is watching to save them from themselves. As long as they recognize that someone is going to save them, they carelessly begin to swim with the sharks. They do this not only because they feel a false sense of security, but because it guarantees that we pay attention to them. As long as we play the role of lifeguard, the others we care about will not save themselves; for their own good it is necessary to withdraw, cut our inner strings and leave matters up to them; this is also to cease doubting them.

Inner withdrawal is an action of perseverance that has its own reward, but only when it is modest perseverance, not an attempt to impress others by getting them to notice our withdrawal. In many situations the problem is resolved, not through any external action that arises spontaneously on our part, but by simply "letting it happen," through letting go of the problem. Our "action" is to "let go."

In practicing disengagement from negative images and their offspring emotions, we train ourselves not to brand adverse situations as "bad." By not deciding the situation is "unfavorable," we remain open to learning something from it, and allow the hidden force to resolve the difficulties in a favorable way. From the *I Ching* point of view, adversity provides the opportunity for inner growth and development as we overcome the doubts, anxieties and judgments that block our access to the Creative Power. It is also its view that all evil, either in us or in other people, arises from doubts and misunderstandings. Doubting that we, in and of ourselves, are sufficiently equipped to succeed in life, we develop a false self-image, or ego. Doubting that we have help from the Creative, we fear what life has to offer, therefore build defenses against the unknown. All these doubts and misunderstandings are at the root of how people relate incorrectly to each other.

In the foregoing examples we have seen that action tends to be expressed in terms of applying limits to our thoughts and actions. Accepting such self-imposed limits is the message of "Limitation" (60). One necessary limitation we must place on ourselves is that of restraining ourselves, through self-discipline, from expecting quick results. Our inferiors impatiently measure the other person's behavior to see if we are having an effect. The *I Ching* explains that we must learn to work with time as the vehicle of the Creative Force. Working with time, adapting to the fact that slow progress is the only progress that endures, is part of the process of nonaction. We need to withdraw from impatience and "flow," as with water that only runs downhill. We need to prohibit our inferiors from "watching the team horse," and from putting images of gloom and doom before our inner eye. Sometimes doing these things requires what can only be called "galling limitation," and "sublime perseverance," but it is only by such means that we can gain superiority over our recalcitrant inferiors. We also find that during such times we can overcome the assaults of our inferiors if we mount a resolute determination to withstand them. It is important to remember that they are but paper dragons and they do not have the invincible power they make us think they have. It is also important to remember that when we cling steadfastly to our path, we also get help from the Creative, but even more readily if we remember to ask for help.

Perfecting our inner nature in the ways described develops the power of inner truth. The hexagram "Revolution" (49) stresses that what we ask of people must "correspond with a higher truth and not spring from arbitrary or petty motives." What we think of as justice may not be so from the cosmic point of view. We may have imagined, for example, that a person who has been unfair with us ought to go through a series of steps to re-establish their credibility and good will. In effect, we are saying that we require them to meet conditions of our specifications, otherwise the injustice cannot be erased. Such demands are the work of our self-righteous pride and ego. The way in which a person returns to the path is not properly our business; furthermore, when they have returned, we must meet them halfway. We also need to avoid using the moment to gain the recognition that we were "right."

The action described thus far—that of nonaction, of keeping our inner attitude correct, works through the power of inner truth. Inner truth has to mount to great strength before it can break through obdurate situations. It mounts in strength in direct proportion to our inner perseverance to hold to the correct path, and it acts on the principle of gentle penetration described in "The Gentle" ("The Penetrating," Wind) (57). Just as roots penetrate rocks and break them apart, perseverance in the correct attitude breaks through closed minds.

A second type of action arises spontaneously out of a correct attitude. This action manifests as a response to what is happening. Although we realize we are acting, we do so with such detachment that the action happens through, rather than by us. We are conduits for what arises in the hidden world. Sometimes this action is very forceful and abrupt, and takes us completely by surprise. It had the correct effect and was appropriate, and we could not have planned it. Sometimes the action taken is a very quiet, calming action, but again, we are detached. Such moments do not come often, but usually happen in difficult situations in which the help of the Creative is greatly needed.

Such spontaneous action can only occur when we are in a receptive and open state of mind. It may take place after we have been misunderstood and challenged by other people's inferiors, and have strictly held to our limits. Suddenly we say or do the correct thing. Steadfastness has aroused the Creative Power to act through us. The state of mind in which such action can take place is that of emptiness. We have mentally disengaged from any intentions or plans, any feelings of urgency or alienation, of wanting to do or dreading to do anything about the situation at hand. We have also become free of any discouraging feelings of helplessness, and have allowed ourselves to rely on the cosmos to let things work out as they will. In arriving at this "empty place," the place of no thought, or what in Zen is called "no mind," we are in tune with the Creative.

Inner correctness also activates what the *I Ching* calls "the helpers"— those hidden and often suppressed great and good elements in other people that, once aroused, provide the necessary inner assent to accomplish needed changes. The lines in the *I Ching* that call for "seeing the great man"[4] and "holding to the great man" mean that we need to hold to the possibility of these elements in others, even though the most unpleasant elements are visible. If it is impossible to conceive of the great man in others, it is sufficient to disengage from our negative feelings about them: to be neutral in attitude is to automatically remain open to their potential goodness.

Similar to this spontaneous action is a slow-building action that steadily mounts in intensity to a denouement that just happens by itself. Complex, unseen movements are taking place. During this time the external situation seems to demand our taking some action, but we don't know what action. As "Preponderance of the Small" (62) tells us, it is necessary to wait in the "ambiguous spot," doing nothing. Doing nothing and waiting in the correct attitude results in a build-up of inner power. The taming and holding onto this power is the subject of "The Taming Power of the Great" (26), which speaks of daily self-renewal through keeping still as the only means of remaining at the peak of our inner powers. In "taming" this power by resisting the urge to act, we experience a sense of discomfort. Waiting in the ambiguous spot is galling to our inferiors who point to the "threatening dangers of nonaction." The rush of desire to do something, pictured as a bull's horns and a rhinoceros's tusk, may be controlled through seeing with clarity that it is not yet time to act. Finally, with our being hardly aware of it, the inner power has its effect and the obstacles are overcome. When this happens we get the top line, which says, "He attains the way of heaven, success." Through waiting and controlling our energy, inner power grew and the victory was won. It was as if the root inside the boulder swelled and split the boulder apart. At this final moment those who were hostile or unreceptive change and become open to us. This change is dramatic and inexplicable, outside the boundaries of any logical process.

Waiting in the ambiguous spot involves risks and dangers which must be overcome if we are to succeed. This sort of patience described in the *I Ching* is a unique focusing of will to hold to what is good in ourselves, in other people, and in the life process, so that the inferior man, wherever he exists, is overthrown. First we retreat from any inferior impulses we have; then we disengage our attention from the other person, leaving it truly up to him to do or not do the right thing. This kind of humble acceptance, in which we "cling to the power of truth," arouses the Creative Power. We do not need to like the person, or to believe in him, or to believe in our own power. Quite the opposite: truly, we are powerless. Without going from the extreme of disbelief to the extreme of belief, we simply relinquish, or sacrifice, our disbelief. In sacrificing it, we return to the empty place, the neutral place, the place of the Creative. In so doing we retain our inner dignity and we preserve his; by recognizing and accepting our own powerlessness we give him the space to find himself. This space acts as a kind of cosmic mirror in which the other person perceives and apprehends his inferior man. In this manner we make it possible for another person's superior man to regain control.

The build-up of inner power depends upon the self-limitation described. Inner power is maintained through daily self-renewal—letting go of everything and keeping still every day. At the same time, it is impossible to free ourselves from entrenched habits of mind all at once. We need to forgive ourselves for not always living up to our standards, and for frequently failing. It is unreasonable to expect too much, too soon, therefore the *I Ching* says we must put "limitation, even upon limitation."

NOTES

[1]"The Sage" refers to the unnamed universal teacher whose wisdom is expressed in the *I Ching*. This term could also be understood here as referring to our own native intelligence or place of inner wisdom.

[2]The Creative Power is the subject of the first hexagram of the *I Ching*, and is associated with the light, regenerative, centrifugal power of yang. This creative power of the universe is activated by its opposite, the dark, womb-like, cohesive power of yin. Being receptive to the needs of the moment allows the creative power of the universe to act through us.

[3]"The inferiors" is a term referring to lesser elements in our character which often clamor to take over and guide our acts. They often want short-term, immediate results, and lack the patience to persevere through difficult times. These are the parts of us that operate out of fear and distrust, having little faith in the creative power of the universe.

[4]The "great man" or "superior man" in the *I Ching* is a term referring to our innate wisdom, which operates in accord with the Creative.

Renunciation and Daring

Chögyam Trungpa

The situations of fear that exist in our lives provide us with stepping stones to step over our fear. On the other side of cowardice is bravery. If we step over properly, we can cross the boundary from being cowardly to being brave. We may not discover bravery right away. Instead, we may find a shaky tenderness beyond our fear. We are still quivering and shaking, but there is tenderness, rather than bewilderment.

Tenderness contains an element of sadness. It is not the sadness of feeling sorry for yourself or feeling deprived, but it is a natural situation of fullness. You feel so full and rich, as if you were about to shed tears. Your eyes are full of tears, and the moment you blink, the tears will spill out of your eyes and roll down your cheeks. In order to be a good warrior, one has to feel this sad and tender heart. If a person does not feel alone and sad, he cannot be a warrior at all. The warrior is sensitive to every aspect of phenomena—sight, smell, sound, feelings. He appreciates everything that goes on in his world as an artist does. His experience is full and extremely vivid. The rustling of leaves and the sounds of raindrops on his coat are very loud. Occasional butterflies fluttering around him may be almost unbearable because he is so sensitive. Because of his sensitivity, the warrior can then go further in developing his discipline. He begins to learn the meaning of renunciation.

In the ordinary sense, renunciation is often connected with asceticism. You give up the sense pleasures of the world and embrace an austere spiritual life in order to understand the higher meaning of existence. In the Shambhala context,* renunciation is quite different. What the warrior renounces is anything in his experience that is a barrier between himself and others. In other words, renunciation is making yourself more available, more gentle and open to others. Any hesitation about opening yourself to others is removed. For the sake of others, you renounce your privacy.

The positive aspect of renunciation, what is cultivated, is caring for others. But in order to care for others, it is necessary to reject caring only for yourself, or the attitude of selfishness. A selfish person is like a turtle carrying its home on its back wherever it goes. At some point you have to leave home and embrace a larger world. That is the absolute prerequisite for being able to care for others.

In order to overcome selfishness, it is necessary to be daring. It is as though you were dressed in your swimsuit, standing on the diving board with a pool in front of you, and you ask yourself: "Now what?" The obvious answer is: "Jump." That is daring. You might wonder if you will sink or hurt yourself if you jump. We are so accustomed to accepting what is bad for us and rejecting what is good for us. We are attracted to our cocoons, our selfishness, and we are afraid of selflessness, stepping beyond ourselves. So in order to overcome our hesitation about giving up our privacy, and in order to commit ourselves to others' welfare, some kind of leap is necessary.

But then, once you have made a leap of daring, you might become arrogant. You might say to yourself: "Look, I have jumped! I am so great, so fantastic!" But arrogant warriorship does not work. It does nothing to benefit others. So the discipline of renunciation also involves cultivating further gentleness, so that you remain very soft and open and allow tenderness to come into your heart. The warrior who has accomplished true renunciation is completely naked and raw, without even skin or tissue. He has renounced putting on a new suit of armor or growing a thick skin, so his bone and marrow are exposed to the world. He has no room and no desire to manipulate situations. He is able to be, quite fearlessly, what he is.

At this point, having completely renounced his own comfort and privacy, paradoxically, the warrior finds himself more alone. He is like an island sitting alone in the middle of a lake. Occasional ferry boats and commuters go back and forth between the shore and the island, but all that activity only expresses the further loneliness, or the aloneness, of the island. Although the warrior's life is dedicated to helping others, he

*The Shambhala tradition from Central Asia represents secular teachings about the path of the warrior, or living fearlessly (Ed.).

realizes that he will never be able to completely share his experience with others. The fullness of his experience is his own, and he must live with his own truth. Yet he is more and more in love with the world. That combination of love affair and loneliness is what enables the warrior to constantly reach out to help others. By renouncing his private world, the warrior discovers a greater universe and a fuller and fuller broken heart. This is not something to feel bad about: it is a cause for rejoicing. It is entering the warrior's world.

Dancing on the Razor's Edge

John Welwood

Relationship is a powerful, often dizzying dance of polarities—sometimes delightful and seductive, sometimes fierce and combative, sometimes energizing, sometimes exhausting.

The dance begins as soon as we find ourselves attracted to another person. On the one hand, we long to go out to that person, break out of the shell of separateness, expand our boundaries, and meet this being who moves and touches us in ways that we can hardly begin to understand. On the other hand, we also experience fear—going outside ourselves involves giving up something, and we find that we are hanging on for dear life to the very separateness we long to overcome.

The dance of relationship always involves such alternations—between coming together and moving apart, taking hold and letting go, yielding and taking the lead, giving ourselves and maintaining our integrity. It is not an easy dance to learn. Many couples soon lose the rhythm and wind up deadlocked in opposing positions, knowing only how to attack or withdraw. Teachers of this art are few, and as the years go by the conventional dance steps we have been taught seem increasingly stiff, outmoded, and constricting. Where, we may wonder, can we learn to dance with grace and power?

Meditation can teach us a great deal about this dance because it is designed to help us overcome the split between self and other. I am specifically referring here to mindfulness meditation, a formless style of meditation in which one simply follows the breath, allowing thoughts and feelings to arise and pass away. Since this practice provides no fixed object of attention, it allows us to simply be with ourselves and to discover the obstacles we create to avoid being present—such as identifying ourselves with thoughts and feelings we like, while trying to get rid of thoughts and feelings we don't like. However, if we can come back to the breath and unhook ourselves from identifying with any side in this struggle, we can glimpse a larger, underlying awareness that is free of struggle. These glimpses of our larger nature are like a refreshing breeze. They allow us to relax, to just be here as we are, and to make friends with ourselves.

This style of meditation is a way of working with the basic polarities of being human—polarities that all relationships intensify. On the one hand, it involves settling down on one spot, rooting ourselves to this piece of earth. Coming down to earth, we find that we cannot escape this form, this body, these needs and feelings, this karma, these personal characteristics and traits, this history. Sitting makes a connection with the earth through a balanced, grounded posture—a straight back, neither too tight nor too loose, with upright head and shoulders. On the other hand, following the breath and returning again and again to the present moment allows us to experience a greater sense of openness and space. In this openness we can glimpse a way out of imprisonment in our karma.

In Chinese philosophy these two sides of human nature are called heaven and earth. The heaven principle involves expansiveness and openness. The earth principle involves solidity and groundedness. Maintaining a grounded, upright posture opens up the soft, vulnerable front of the body, through which we let the world and other people in.

We learn from meditation that keeping our seat—not getting entirely carried away by the wild horse of the mind and the emotions—allows us to let go and open out to the world and to others. In a relationship, keeping our seat might mean not letting others manipulate or dominate us, but rather maintaining our own vital integrity and power. At the same. time, letting go and dissolving back into the breath corresponds in a relationship to not making our personal identity a solid fortress, but being willing to open our heart, let down our guard, and risk ourselves in love. The Buddha likened meditation practice to tuning a musical instrument—the strings must be neither too tight nor too loose. If we hold on too tight, or if we let ourselves go too much, we lose our balance.

In relationship this same kind of balancing act takes place. Somehow we have to respect our own needs and wants (the earth principle) yet also be able to step back from being overly identified with them (the heaven principle). We have to dissolve our boundaries in order to unite with another person, yet if we simply merge with the other, we may lose ourselves in the relationship—which usually spells disaster. Relationship is full of these contradictions. We want to be free, yet we also want some stability and commitment. How can we have both? We want to be loving, yet a lot of anger and critical feelings arise. How do we deal with that? How can we surrender in a relationship without losing our power and being controlled by the other person? How can we move closer and really get to know the other while continuing to see him or her with fresh eyes? If we could just maintain a safe distance and a clear set of boundaries to protect us from risking too much. . . . Or if we could simply merge with the other person and lose ourselves in the relationship. . . . But neither way alone is satisfactory. In learning to balance between too tight and too loose, our movements become more fluid, and the dance develops grace and vigor.

The path of working with the polarities and contradictions of being human—called in classical Buddhist terms "the middle way"—involves learning not to identify with anything: neither pleasure nor depression, neither separateness nor togetherness, neither attachment nor detachment. In the practice of the middle way, we find balance by bringing awareness to the act of *losing* our balance. In losing our seat, the very act of falling wakes us up; and in waking up, we regain our seat again. Continually coming back to the present, we let go of identifying with this or that position and take a fresh look at what is, what needs to be done right now. Not that we should never take a stand—right now the situation with my partner may require me to take a stand, assert what I want, even fight for it if I have to. But tomorrow circumstances may call on me to let go of this stand, give in, and let her needs take precedence.

Hardening into a position, no matter how just it may seem, dulls our sensitivity to what is needed right now and therefore makes us less available to the call of love, less attuned to the rhythm of the dance. The paradox of relationship is that it calls on us to be ourselves fully, to express who we are without hesitation, to take a stand on this earth, and also to let go of our fixed positions and not get solidly identified with them. Nonattachment in relationship doesn't mean that we should have no needs or that we should pay no attention to them. If we don't respect and acknowledge our real needs, we are not being ourselves, and therefore we have less to offer our partner. Nonattachment in the best sense means that we are not completely identified with our needs, our likes and dislikes. We recognize our needs, yet we can also tap into a larger way of being, a larger awareness inside us where those needs do not have a hold over us. Then we can either assert our desire or let it go, according to the dictates of the moment. When two people become too identified with their positions, they become polarized (for example, "I want more closeness" versus "I want more space"), and the dance grinds to a halt.

In Tantric Buddhism the middle way is experienced as "the razor's edge." If we slip and fall into freezing and identifying with any position—wanting more closeness or space, separateness or togetherness, freedom or commitment—we can actually cut and hurt ourselves because we lose touch with the whole of what we are, in favor of one isolated part. We have to keep coming back again and again to the present moment, which is sharp and thin as a razor's edge.

This dynamic balance—continually coming back to now—involves a slight jolt which wakes us up from our fantasies and daydreams. These little moments of waking up to the present—what Suzuki Roshi calls "beginner's mind"—are pulsing with uncertainty. In the split second of nowness I realize that I really don't know what's going on. How could I? I just got here! When I return from the fantasy of the relationship I'm in and look into my partner's eyes, I suddenly realize, "I don't know who you are." And further, I don't know who I am, I don't know what this relationship is. In this moment we have the freedom to start fresh again. We don't have to get stuck in our hopes or images about who we are or where this relationship is going. Nor can we make not knowing into a solid position, never making up our minds whether or not to commit ourselves to this partnership—for that too would throw the relationship out of balance.

Dancing on the razor's edge means including and embracing all of what we are as human beings. After a fight with my partner, part of me wants to nurse my anger, and another part of me wants to drop it and express my love instead. This uncertainty brings me back again to the knife-edge of the present. Feeling all that I feel at this moment—I am very angry, and I also love you intensely—is quite painful. Yet we can taste in such moments what it means to be human: we have these emotions, yet we are not trying to deny or transcend them. Nor are we getting stuck in our angry thoughts, making them into a solid story with which to justify ourselves and attack the other person. Here on this edge of uncertainty, where we cannot settle into this or that position, we have to simply be here and respond to what is happening. The pain of feeling all that we are, stretching to include it all, and not settling into a secure position actually awakens the heart and allows a larger love to flow, free of attachment to any viewpoint.

Personally I have found meditation to be the most effective practice for learning how to face the difficulties of relationship—practice for the further practice of loving another.

I don't know which practice is harder.

Learning to Love

Rainer Maria Rilke

You are so young, so before all beginning, and I want to beg you, as much as I can, to be patient toward all that is unsolved in your heart and to try to love the *questions themselves* like locked rooms and like books that are written in a very foreign tongue. Do not now seek the answers, which cannot be given you because you would not be able to live them. And the point is, to live eveything. *Live* the questions now. Perhaps you will then gradually, without noticing it, live along some distant day into the answer.

Resolve to be always beginning—to be a beginner!

I hold this to be the highest task of a bond between two people: that each should stand guard over the solitude of the other. For, if it lies in the nature of indifference and of the crowd to recognize no solitude, then love and friendship are there for the purpose of continually providing the opportunity for solitude. And only those are the true sharings which rhythmically interrupt periods of deep isolation. . . .

I am of the opinion that "marriage" as such does not deserve as much emphasis as it has acquired through the conventional development of its nature. It does not occur to anyone to expect a single person to be "happy"—but if he marries, people are much surprised if he *isn't*! (And for that matter it really isn't at all important to be happy, whether single or married.) Marriage is, in many respects, a simplification of one's way of life, and the union naturally combines the forces and wills of two young people so that, together, they seem to reach farther into the future than before. Above all, marriage is a new task and a new seriousness—a new challenge to and questioning of the strength and generosity of each partner and a great new danger for both.

It is a question in marriage, to my feeling, not of creating a quick community of spirit by tearing down and detroying all boundaries, but rather a good marriage is that in which each appoints the other guardian of his solitude, and shows him this confidence, the greatest in his power to bestow. A *togetherness* between two people is an impossibility, and where it seems, nevertheless, to exist, it is a narrowing, a reciprocal agreement which robs either one party or both of his fullest freedom and development. But, once the realization is accepted that even between the *closest* human beings infinite distances continue to exist, a wonderful living side by side can grow up, if they succeed in loving the distance between them which makes it possible for each to see the other whole and against a wide sky!

Therefore this too must be the standard for rejection or choice: whether one is willing to stand guard over the solitude of a person and whether one is inclined to set this same person at the gate of one's own solitude, of which he learns only through that which steps, festively clothed, out of the great darkness.

At bottom no one in life can help anyone else in life; this one experiences over and over in every conflict and every perplexity: that one is alone.

All companionship can consist only in the strengthening of two neighboring solitudes, whereas everything that one is wont to call giving oneself is by nature harmful to companionship: for when a person abandons himself, he is no longer anything, and when two people both give themselves up in order to come close to each other, there is no longer any ground beneath them and their being together is a continual falling.

There is scarcely anything more difficult than to love one another. That it is work, day labor, day labor, God knows there is no other word for it. And look, added to this is fact that young people are not prepared for such difficult loving; for convention has tried to make this most complicated and ultimate relationship into something easy and frivolous, has given it the appearance of everyone's being able to do it. It is not so. Love is something difficult and it is more difficult than other things because in other conflicts nature herself enjoins men to collect themselves, to take themselves firmly in hand with all their strength, while in the heightening of love the impulse is to give oneself wholly away. But just think, can that be anything beautiful, to give oneself away not as something whole and ordered, but haphazard rather, bit by bit, as it comes? Can such giving away, that looks so like a throwing away and dismemberment, be anything good, can it be happiness, joy, progress? No, it cannot. . . . When you give someone flowers, you arrange them beforehand, don't you? But young people who love each other fling themselves to each other in the impatience and haste of their passion, and they don't notice at all what a lack of mutual esteem lies in this disordered giving of themselves; they notice it with astonishment and indignation only from the dissension that arises between them out of all this disorder. And once there is disunity between them, the confusion grows with every day; neither of the two has anything unbroken, pure, and unspoiled about him any longer, and amid the disconsolateness of a break they try to hold fast to the semblance of their happiness. Alas, they are scarcely able to recall any more what they meant by happiness. In his uncertainty each becomes more and more unjust toward the other; they who wanted to do each other good are now handling one another in an imperious and intolerant manner, and in the struggle somehow to get out of their untenable and unbearable state of confusion, they commit the greatest fault that can happen to human relationships: they become impatient. They hurry to a conclusion; to come, as they believe, to a final decision, they try once and for all to establish their relationship, whose surprising changes have frightened them, in order to remain the same now and *forever* (as they say). That is only the last error in this long chain of errings linked fast to one another. What is dead cannot even be clung to (for it crumbles and changes its character); how much less can what is living and alive be treated definitively, once and for all.

Self-transformation is precisely what life is, and human relationships, which are an extract of life, are the most changeable of all, rising and falling from minute to minute, and lovers are those in whose relationship and contact no one moment resembles another. People between whom nothing accustomed, nothing that has already been present before ever takes place, but many new, unexpected, unprecedented things. There are such relationships which must be a very great, almost unbearable happiness, but they can occur only between very rich natures and between those who, each for himself, are richly ordered and composed; they can unite only two wide, deep, individual worlds. Young people—it is obvious—cannot achieve such a relationship, but they can, if they understand their life properly, grow up slowly to such happiness and prepare themselves for it. They must not forget, when they love, that they are beginners, bunglers of life, apprentices in love—must *learn* love, and that (like *all* learning) wants peace, patience, and composure!

To take love seriously and to bear and to learn it like a task, this it is that young people need. Like so much else, people have also misunderstood the place of love in life, they have made it into play and pleasure because they thought that play and pleasure were more blissful than work; but there is nothing happier than work, and love, just because it is the extreme happiness, can be nothing but work. So whoever loves must try to act as if he had a great work: he must be much alone and go into himself and collect himself and hold fast to himself; he must work; he must become something!

For believe me, the more one is, the richer is all that one experiences. And whoever wants to have a deep love in his life must collect and save for it and gather honey.

To speak of solitude again, it becomes always clearer that this is at bottom not something that one can take or leave. We *are* solitary. We may delude ourselves and act as though this were not so. That is all. But how much better it is to realize that we are so, yes, even to begin by assuming it. We shall indeed turn dizzy then; for all points upon which our eye has been accustomed to rest are taken from us, there is nothing near any more and everything far is infinitely far. A person removed from his own room, almost without preparation and transition, and set upon the height of a great mountain range, would feel something of the sort: an unparalleled insecurity, an abandonment to something inexpressible would almost annihilate him. He would think himself falling or hurled out into space, or exploded into a thousand pieces: what a monstrous lie his brain would have to invent to catch up with and explain the state of his senses!

So for him who becomes solitary all distances, all measures change; of these changes many take place suddenly, and then, as with the man on the mountaintop, extraordinary imaginings and singular sensations arise that seem to grow out beyond all bearing. But it is necessary for us to experience *that* too. We must assume our existence as *broadly* as we in any way can; everything, even the unheard-of, must be possible in it. That is at bottom the only courage that is demanded of us: to have courage for the most strange, the most singular, and the most inexplicable that we may encounter. That mankind has in this sense been cowardly has done life endless harm; the experiences that are called "visions," the whole so-called "spirit-world," death, all those things that are so closely akin to us, have by daily parrying been so crowded out of life that the senses with which we would have grasped them are atrophied. To say nothing of God.

But fear of the inexplicable has not alone impoverished the existence of the individual; the relationship between one human being and another has also been cramped by it, as though it had been lifted out of the river-bed of endless possibilities and set down in a fallow spot on the bank, to which nothing happens. For it is not inertia alone that is responsible for human relationships repeating themselves from case to case, inde-scribably monotonous and unrenewed; it is shyness before any sort of new, unforeseeable experience with which one does not think oneself able to cope. But only someone who is ready for everything, who excludes nothing, not even the most enigmatical, will live the relation to another as something alive and will himself draw exhaustively from his own exis-tence. For if we think of this existence of the individual as a larger or smaller room it appears evident that most people learn to know only a corner of their room, a place by the window, a strip of floor on which they walk up and down. Thus they have a certain security. And yet that dangerous insecurity is so much more human which drives the prisoners of Poe's stories to feel out the shapes of their horrible dungeons and not be strangers to the unspeakable terror of their abode.

We, however, are not prisoners. No traps or snares are set about us, and there is nothing which should intimidate or worry us. We are set down in life as in the element to which we best correspond, and over and above this we have through thousands of years of accommodation become so like this life, that when we hold still we are, through a happy mimicry, scarcely to be distinguished from all that surrounds us. We have no reason to mistrust our world, for it is not against us. Has it terrors, they are *our* terrors; has it abysses, those abysses belong to us; are dangers at hand, we must try to love them. And if only we arrange our life according to that principle which counsels us that we must always hold to the difficult, then that which now still seems to us the most alien will become what we most trust and find most faithful. How should we be able to forget those ancient myths that are at the beginning of all peoples, the myths about dragons that at the last moment turn into princesses; perhaps all the dragons of our lives are princesses who are only waiting to see us once beautiful and brave. Perhaps everything terrible is in its deepest being something helpless that wants help from us.

To love is good, too: love being difficult. For one human being to love another: that is perhaps the most difficult of all our tasks, the ulti-mate, the last test and proof, the work for which all other work is but preparation. For this reason young people, who are beginners in every-thing, cannot yet know love: they have to learn it. With their whole being, with all their forces, gathered close about their lonely, timid, up-ward-beating heart, they must learn to love. But learning-time is always a long, secluded time, and so loving, for a long while ahead and far on into life, is—solitude, intensified and deepened aloneness for him who loves. Love is at first not anything that means merging, giving over, and uniting with another (for what would a union be of something unclarified and unfinished, still subordinate—?); it is a high inducement to the individual to ripen, to become something in himself, to become world, to become world for himself for another's sake; it is a great exacting claim upon him, something that chooses him out and calls him to vast things. Only in this sense, as the task of working at themselves, might young people use the love that is given them. Merging and surrendering and every kind of communion is not for them (who must save and gather for a long, long time still), is the ultimate, is perhaps that for which human lives as yet scarcely suffice.

But young people err so often and so grievously in this: that they (in whose nature it lies to have no patience) fling themselves at each other, when love takes possession of them, scatter themselves, just as they are, in all their untidiness, disorder, confusion. . . . And then what? What is life to do to this heap of half-battered existence which they call their communion and which they would gladly call their happiness, if it were possible, and their future? Thus each loses himself for the sake of the other and loses the other and many others that wanted still to come. And loses the expanses and the possibilities, exchanges the approach and flight of gentle, divining things for an unfruitful perplexity out of which nothing can come any more, nothing save a little disgust, disillusionment and poverty, and rescue in one of the many conventions that have been put up in great number like public refuges along this most dangerous road. No realm of human experience is so well provided with conventions as this: life-preservers of most varied invention, boats and swimming bladders are here; the social conception has managed to supply shelters of every sort, for, as it was disposed to take love-life as pleasure, it had also to give it an easy form, cheap, safe and sure, as public pleasures are.

Whoever looks seriously at it finds that neither for death, which is difficult, nor for difficult love has any explanation, any solution, any hint or way yet been discerned; and for these two problems that we carry wrapped up and hand on without opening, it will not be possible to discover any general rule resting in agreement. But in the same measure in which we begin as individuals to put life to the test, we shall, being individuals, meet these great things at closer range. The demands which the difficult work of love makes upon our development are more than life-size, and as beginners we are not up to them. But if we nevertheless hold out and take this love upon us as burden and apprenticeship, instead of losing ourselves in all the light and frivolous play, behind which people have hidden from the most earnest earnestness of their existence—then a little progress and an alleviation will perhaps be perceptible to those who come long after us; that would be much.

Sex is difficult; yes. But they are difficult things with which we have been charged; almost everything serious is difficult, and everything is serious. If you only recognize this and manage, out of yourself, out of your *own* nature and ways, out of your *own* experience and childhood and strength to achieve a relation to sex wholly your own (*not* influenced by convention and custom), then you need no longer be afraid of losing yourself and becoming unworthy of your best possession.

Physical pleasure is a sensual experience no different from pure seeing or the pure sensation with which a fine fruit fills the tongue; it is a great unending experience, which is given us, a knowing of the world, the fullness and the glory of all knowing. And not our acceptance of it is bad; the bad thing is that most people misuse and squander this experience and apply it as a stimulant at the tired spots of their lives and as distraction instead of a rallying toward exalted moments. Men have made even eating into something else: want on the one hand, superfluity upon the other, have dimmed the distinctness of this need, and all the deep, simple necessities in which life renews itself have become similarly dulled. But the individual can clarify them for himself and live them clearly (and if not the individual, who is too dependent, then at least the solitary man). He can remember that all beauty in animals and plants is a quiet enduring form of love and longing, and he can see animals, as he sees plants, patiently and willingly uniting and increasing and growing, not out of physical delight, not out of physical suffering, but bowing to necessities that are greater than pleasure and pain and more powerful than will and withstanding. O that man might take this secret, of which the world is full even to its littlest things, more humbly to himself and bear it, endure it, more seriously and feel how terribly difficult it is, instead of taking it lightly. That he might be more reverent toward his fruitfulness, which is but *one*, whether it seems mental or physical; for intellectual creation too springs from the physical, is of one nature with it and only like a gentler, more ecstatic and more everlasting repetition of physical delight. "The thought of being creator, of procreating, of making" is nothing without its continuous great confirmation and realization in the world, nothing without the thousandfold concordance from things and animals—and enjoyment of it is so indescribably beautiful and rich only because it is full of inherited memories of the begetting and the bearing of millions. In one creative thought a thousand forgotten nights of love revive, filling it with sublimity and exaltation. And those who come together in the night and are entwined in rocking delight do an earnest work and gather sweet-

nesses, gather depth and strength for the song of some coming poet,
who will arise to speak of ecstasies beyond telling. And they call up the
future; and though they err and embrace blindly, the future comes all the
same, a new human being rises up, and on the ground of that chance
which here seems consummated, awakes the law by which a resistant
vigorous seed forces its way through to the egg-cell that moves open
toward it. Do not be bewildered by the surfaces; in the depths all becomes
law. And those who live the secret wrong and badly (and they are very
many), lose it only for themselves and still hand it on, like a sealed letter,
without knowing it. And do not be confused by the multiplicity of names
and the complexity of cases. Perhaps over all there is a great motherhood,
a common longing. The beauty of the virgin, a being that "has not yet
achieved anything," is motherhood that begins to sense itself and to prepare, anxious and yearning. And the mother's beauty is ministering
motherhood, and in the old woman there is a great remembering. And
even in the man there is motherhood, it seems to me, physical and spiritual; his procreating is also a kind of giving birth, and giving birth it is
when he creates out of inmost fullness. And perhaps the sexes are more
related than we think, and the great renewal of the world will perhaps
consist in this, that man and maid, freed of all false feelings and reluc-
tances, will seek each other not as opposites but as brother and sister, as
neighbors, and will come together *as human beings*, in order simply,
seriously and patiently to bear in common the difficult sex that has been
laid upon them.

The girl and the woman, in their new, their own unfolding, will but
in passing be imitators of masculine ways, good and bad, and repeaters of
masculine professions. After the uncertainty of transitions it will become
apparent that women were only going through the profusion and the
vicissitude of those (often ridiculous) disguises in order to cleanse their
own characteristic nature of the distorting influences of the other sex.
Women, in whom life lingers and dwells more immediately, more fruit-
fully and more confidently, must surely have become fundamentally riper
people, more human people, than easygoing man, who is not pulled
down below the surface of life by the weight of any fruit of his body, and
who, presumptuous and hasty, undervalues what he thinks he loves.
This humanity of woman, borne its full time in suffering and humiliation,
will come to light when she will have stripped off the conventions of
mere femininity in the mutations of her outward status, and those men
who do not yet feel it approaching today will be surprised and struck by
it. Some day, some day there will be girls and women whose name will no
longer signify merely an opposite of the masculine, but something in

itself, something that makes one think, not of any complement and limit, but only of life and existence: the feminine human being.

This advance will (at first much against the will of the outstripped men) change the love-experience, which is now full of error, will alter it from the ground up, reshape it into a relation that is meant to be of one human being to another, no longer of man to woman. And this more human love (that will fulfill itself, infinitely considerate and gentle, and kind and clear in binding and releasing) will resemble that which we are preparing with struggle and toil, the love that consists in this, that two solitudes protect and border and salute each other.

Notes on Contributors

FRANCESCO ALBERONI is one of Italy's eminent sociologists. He is the author of *Movement and Institution* and *Falling in Love*.

CAROL ANTHONY is an *I Ching* consultant and author of *A Guide to the I Ching* and *The Philosophy of the I Ching*.

J. G. BENNETT was a teacher of the Gurdjieff work whose books include *The Masters of Wisdom, Intimations*, and *Sex*.

WENDELL BERRY is a writer and poet whose books include *The Unsettling of America, The Gift of Good Land*, and *Standing by Words*.

ELEANOR BERTINE was a close student of Jung, one of the first to bring Jungian methods to America, a founder of the New York Analytical Society, and author of *Human Relationships*.

ROBERT BLY is a poet and translator who has been a force in American poetry for more than two decades. His books include *The Light Around the Body, News of the Universe*, and *The Man in the Black Coat Turns*.

DENNIS BRISSETT is Professor of Behavioral Science and Sociology at the University of Minnesota–Duluth School of Medicine, author of numerous articles on the sociology of sex, and co-editor of *Life as Theater*.

ELIZABETH BUGENTAL is a California licensed marriage, family, and child counselor with a background in theater arts.

SUKIE COLEGRAVE has a background in Chinese language and history and is author of *The Spirit of the Valley: The Masculine and Feminine in Human Conciousness*.

JULIUS EVOLA is an Italian philosopher and author of *The Metaphysics of Sex*.

ADOLF GUGGENBÜHL-CRAIG is a Jungian analyst and author of *Power in the Helping Professions* and *Marriage Dead or Alive*.

ARIEL RUTH HOEBEL, artist, writer, psychic, and ritualist, is engaged in extensive research and exploration of shamanism, psychic phenomena, and Goddess lore.

BERND JAGER is Professor of Psychology at Sonoma State University and a California licensed clinical psychologist who has authored numerous articles on phenomenological psychology.

ROBERT JOHNSON is a Jungian analyst and author of *He: Understanding Masculine Psychology*, *She: Understanding Feminine Psychology*, and *We: Understanding the Psychology of Romantic Love*.

D. H. LAWRENCE, who once referred to himself as a "priest of love," devoted most of his literary output to the study of the man/woman relationship. His works include *Sons and Lovers*, *Women in Love*, *Lady Chatterley's Lover*, and *The Rainbow*. Most of his essays on love are included in two posthumous volumes, *Phoenix* and *Phoenix II*.

LIONEL LEWIS is Professor of Sociology at the State University of New York at Buffalo. He is author of *Scaling the Ivory Tower* and numerous articles on the sociology of sex.

ANNE MORROW LINDBERGH is the author of *North to the Orient*, *Listen! The Wind*, and *Gift from the Sea*. She was the first woman in America to obtain a glider pilot's license, and she accompanied her husband, Charles, as a radio operator on many of his flights.

A. R. ORAGE was a literary critic, journalist, and editor of the original journal entitled *The New Age* in London around the turn of the century. He was a teacher of the Gurdjieff work and worked closely with Gurdjieff on his writings.

JOSÉ ORTEGA Y GASSET was a Spanish philospher whose works include *The Revolt of the Masses*, *The Modern Theme*, and *On Love*.

M. SCOTT PECK is a psychiatrist and author of *The Road Less Traveled: A New Psychology of Love, Traditional Values, and Spiritual Growth*.

STANTON PEELE is a social psychologist who has taught at Harvard for many years. He is author of *Love and Addiction*.

RAINER MARIA RILKE is my favorite poet. Although he lived most of his life alone as a wandering poet, he was quite sensitive to the existential issues facing men and women in their connection. Much more significant in his life than his brief marriage was his friendship with Lou Andreas Salome, whose writing and thought influenced him greatly. His major books include *The Book of the Hours*, *The Duino Elegies*, and *Sonnets to Orpheus*.

BETTY ROSZAK is a feminist writer, journalist, and critic, and co-editor of *Masculine/Feminine: Readings in Sexual Mythology and the Liberation of Women*.

THEODORE ROSZAK is Professor of History and Chairman of the Religious Studies Program at California State University, Hayward. His books include *The Making of a Counter Culture*, *Where the Wasteland Ends*, and *Person/Planet*.

LILLIAN RUBIN is a psychotherapist as well as Senior Research Associate at the Institute for the Study of Social Change at the University of California at Berkeley. Her books include *Women of a Certain Age: The Midlife Search for Self* and *Intimate Strangers: Men and Women Together*.

JOHN SANFORD is a Jungian analyst and Episcopal priest. His books include *Healing and Wholeness* and *The Invisible Partners*.

VLADIMIR SOLOVYOV was a Russian theologian, philosopher, and poet of the last century. Among his books was *The Meaning of Love*.

ROBERT STEIN is a Jungian analyst and author of *Incest and Human Love: The Betrayal of the Soul in Psychotherapy*.

KEITH THOMPSON is a northern California writer who is presently collaborating with Robert Bly on a book, *Conversations on the Wild Man*.

CHÖGYAM TRUNGPA is the founder and president of Naropa Institute in Boulder, Colorado, and a scholar and meditation master trained in the Kagyü and Nyingma traditions of Tibetan Buddhism. His books include *Cutting Through Spiritual Materialism*, *The Myth of Freedom*, and *Shambhala: The Sacred Path of the Warrior*.

ALAN WATTS, who held a doctorate of divinity, was a witty and original thinker whose seminal work in bringing together East and West influenced a generation. His major works include *The Joyous Cosmology*; *Nature, Man and Woman*; *The Way of Zen*; and *Beyond Theology*.

JOHN WELWOOD is a clinical psychologist and psychotherapist in San Francisco who teaches extensively on the issues facing modern couples. His books include *The Meeting of the Ways: Explorations in East/West Psychology* and *Awakening the Heart: East/West Approaches to Psychotherapy and the Healing Relationship*. He is presently completing a book on intimate relationships as a path of transformation.

Acknowledgments

I would like to extend my deep appreciation to the authors and publishers who granted permission to excerpt and reprint copyrighted material in this volume, especially those who went out of their way to help me meet a rather compressed time deadline. I would also like to thank Ken Wilber, Emily Hilburn Sell, and Judith Osgood for their help and support with various aspects of this undertaking. I am grateful to Robert Bly for waking me up to certain key concerns in being a man, and to Tiziana De Rovere for helping me go further in fully embracing and making friends with the feminine.

Finally, special thanks and appreciation are due Barbara Green and Stephan Bodian for going through the whole manuscript and giving me detailed feedback and evaluation, and to Barbara Green for her tireless efforts as my editorial consultant in all phases of this project.

Chapter 1 is comprised of excerpts from *On Love* by José Ortega y Gassett, translated by Toby Talbot. Copyright © 1957, 1985 by Toby Talbot. Reprinted by arrangement with New American Library, New York, New York.

Chapter 2 is comprised of excerpts from *The Road Less Traveled* by M. Scott Peck. Copyright © 1978 by M. Scott Peck. Reprinted by permission of Simon and Schuster, Inc.

Chapter 3 is an excerpt from *We: Understanding the Psychology of*

Romantic Love by Robert A. Johnson. Copyright © 1983 by Robert A. Johnson. Reprinted by permission of Harper & Row, Publishers, Inc.

Chapter 4 is comprised of excerpts from *Play to Live* by Alan Watts, edited by Mark Watts. Copyright © 1982 by Mark Watts. Reprinted by permission of And Books, South Bend, Indiana, The Alan Watts Institute, P. O. Box 361, Mill Valley, CA 94942.

Chapter 5 is comprised of excerpts from *Love and Addiction* by Stanton Peele and Archie Brodsky. Copyright © 1975 by Stanton Peele and Archie Brodsky. Published by Taplinger Publishing Co., Inc. Reprinted by permission.

Chapter 6 is comprised of excerpts from *Falling in Love* by Francesco Alberoni, translated by Lawrence Venuti. Translation copyright © 1983 by Laurence Venuti. Reprinted by permission of Random House, Inc.

Chapter 7 is comprised of excerpts from *A Solovyov Anthology*, translated by Natalie Duddington. Reprinted by permission of SCM Press Ltd., London.

Chapter 8 is comprised of excerpts from "Love Was Once a Little Boy," in *Phoenix II: Uncollected, Unpublished, and Other Prose Works* by D. H. Lawrence. Copyright © 1959, 1963, 1968 by the Estate of Frieda Lawrence Ravagli. Reprinted by permission of Viking Penguin Inc. All rights reserved.

Chapter 9 is an excerpt from *The Myth of Freedom* by Chögyam Trungpa. Copyright © 1976 by Chögyam Trungpa. Reprinted by permission of Shambhala Publications.

Chapter 11 is an excerpt from Foreword to *Masculine/Feminine: Readings in Sexual Mythology and the Liberation of Women*, edited by Betty Roszak and Theodore Roszak. Copyright © 1969 by Betty Roszak and Theodore Roszak. Reprinted by permission of Harper & Row, Publishers, Inc.

Chapter 12 is comprised of excerpts from *The Invisible Partners* by John A. Sanford. Copyright © 1980 by John Sanford. Used by permission of Paulist Press.

Chapter 13 is comprised of excerpts from *The Spirit of the Valley* by Sukie Colegrave. Copyright © 1979 by Sukie Colegrave. Reprinted by permission of J. P. Tarcher, Inc., and Houghton Mifflin Company.

Chapter 14 contains material that appeared in *New Age Journal* and *Dromenon*. Copyright © 1982 by Keith Thompson. Reprinted by permission.

Chapter 15 is comprised of excerpts from "On Being a Man," in *Phoenix II: Uncollected, Unpublished, and Other Prose Works* by D. H. Lawrence. Copyright © 1959, 1963, 1968 by the Estate of Frieda Lawrence Ravagli. Reprinted by permission of Viking Penguin Inc. All rights reserved.

Chapter 16 is an excerpt from *Incest and Human Love* by Robert Stein. Copyright © 1973 by Robert Stein. Reprinted by permission of Spring Publications, Inc.

Chapter 17 is comprised of excerpts from *Intimate Strangers: Men and Women Together* by Lillian B. Rubin. Copyright © 1983 by Lillian B. Rubin. Reprinted by permission of Harper & Row, Publishers, Inc.

Chapter 18 is comprised of excerpts from "An Essay for Women" by Ruth Hoebel, in *Maitreya 4: Woman*. Copyright © 1973 by Shambhala Publications. Reprinted by permission of Shambhala Publications.

Chapter 19 is comprised of excerpts, reprinted by permission, from *Human Relationships* by Eleanor Bertine. Copyright © 1958 by Eleanor Bertine. Published by David McKay Company, Inc.

Chapter 20 is comprised of excerpts from *Gift from the Sea* by Anne Morrow Lindbergh. Copyright © 1955 by Anne Morrow Lindbergh. Reprinted by permission of Pantheon Books, a Division of Random House, Inc.

Chapter 21 is comprised of excerpts from *Marriage Dead or Alive* by Adolf Guggenbühl-Craig. Copyright © 1977 by Adolf Guggenbühl-Craig. Reprinted by permission of Spring Publications, Inc.

Chapter 22 is comprised of excerpts from "A Propos of Lady Chatterley's Lover," in *Phoenix II: Uncollected, Unpublished, and Other Prose Works* by D. H. Lawrence. Copyright © 1959, 1963, 1968 by the Estate of Frieda Lawrence Ravagli. Reprinted by permission of Viking Penguin Inc. All rights reserved.

Chapter 23 is comprised of excerpts from "Poetry and Marriage," one of the essays in *Standing by Words: Essays by Wendell Berry*, copyright © 1983 by Wendell Berry. Published by North Point Press and reprinted by permission.

Chapter 24 is comprised of excerpts from "Coupling/Uncoupling" by Robert Stein in *Spring*, 1981. Reprinted by permission of Spring Publications, Inc.

Chapter 25 is comprised of excerpts from *Sex* by J. G. Bennett. Copyright © 1982 by Elizabeth Bennett. Reprinted by permission of Samuel Weiser, Inc., York Beach, Maine.

Chapter 26 is comprised of excerpts from "On Intimacy and Death" by Elizabeth K. Bugental, in *Experiences in Being*, edited by Bernice Marshal, 1971. Reprinted by permission of the author.

Chapter 27 is comprised of excerpts from "Sex as Work" by Lionel S. Lewis and Dennis Brissett. Reprinted from *Social Problems*, volume 15,

1967, pp. 9–17, with the permission of the Society for the Study of Social Problems and the authors.

Chapter 28 is comprised of excerpts from *Nature, Man, and Woman* by Alan W. Watts. Copyright © 1958 by Pantheon Books, Inc. Reprinted by permission of Pantheon Books, a Division of Random House, Inc.

Chapter 29 is comprised of excerpts from chapter one of *The Metaphysics of Sex* by Julius Evola, published by Inner Traditions International, Ltd., New York. Copyright © 1983 by Inner Traditions. Reprinted by permission of the publisher.

Chapter 30 is comprised of excerpts from "Toward a Phenomenology of the Passions" by Bernd Jager in *Existential-Phenomenological Alternatives for Psychology*, edited by Ronald S. Valle and Mark King. Copyright © 1978 by Oxford University Press, Inc. Reprinted by permission.

Chapter 31 is comprised of excerpts from *Aspects of Love in Western Society* by Suzanne Lilar, translated by Jonathan Griffin. Copyright © 1965 by Thames and Hudson, London. Reprinted by permission of the publisher.

Chapter 32 is comprised of excerpts from *On Love* by A. R. Orage. Copyright © 1974 by Janus Press. Reprinted by permission of Samuel Weiser, Inc., York Beach, Maine.

Chapter 33 is comprised of excerpts from *The Philosophy of the I Ching* by Carol K. Anthony. Copyright © 1981 by Carol K. Anthony. Reprinted by permission of Anthony Publishing Company, Stow, Massachusetts.

Chapter 34 is comprised of excerpts from *Shambhala: The Sacred Path of the Warrior* by Chögyam Trungpa. Copyright © 1984 by Chögyam Trungpa. Reprinted by permission of Shambhala Publications.

Chapter 35 was originally published in *Yoga Journal*, September 1984.

Chapter 36 is comprised of excerpts from *Rilke on Love and Other Difficulties: Translations and Considerations of Rainer Maria Rilke* by John J. L. Mood, by permission of John J. L. Mood and W. W. Norton & Company, Inc. Copyright © 1975 by W. W. Norton & Company, Inc. Selections reprinted here are from *Letters to a Young Poet* by Rainer Maria Rilke, translated by M. D. Herter Norton (W. W. Norton & Company, Inc., 1954), *Letters of Rainer Maria Rilke*, translated by Jane Bannard Greene and M. D. Herter Norton (W. W. Norton & Company, Inc., 1954, 1948), and *The Notebooks of Malte Laurids Brigge*, translated by M. D. Herter Norton (W. W. Norton & Company, Inc., 1949).

Bibliography

Helpful books on relationships are relatively rare. The following bibliography includes: (1) works cited in this book and (2) other volumes that I have found to contain useful material bearing on male/female issues.

Alberoni, F. *Falling in Love*. Translated by Lawrence Venuti. New York: Random House, 1983.

Allione, T. *Women of Wisdom*. London: Routledge and Kegan Paul, 1984.

Andreas (Andreas Capellanus). *The Art of Courtly Love*. Translated by John J. Parry. New York: Columbia University Press, 1941.

Bennett, J. G. *Sex*. York Beach, Maine: Weiser, 1981.

Colegrave, S. *The Spirit of the Valley: The Masculine and Feminine in Human Consciousness*. Los Angeles: Tarcher, 1979.

de Castillejo, I. C. *Knowing Woman*. New York: Harper & Row, 1974.

de Rougemont, D. *Love in the Western World*. Translated by Montgomery Belgion. New York: Pantheon, 1956.

Eliade, M. *The Two and the One*. New York: Harper & Row, 1969.

Evola, J. *The Metaphysics of Sex*. New York: Inner Traditions, 1983.

Freud, S. "Being in Love and Hypnosis." In *Group Psychology and the Analysis of the Ego*. New York: Bantam Books, 1965.

Fromm, E. *The Art of Loving*. New York: Harper & Row, 1956.

Greer, G. *The Female Eunuch*. New York: McGraw-Hill, 1971.

Guggenbühl-Craig, A. *Marriage Dead or Alive*. Zurich: Spring, 1977.

Harding, M. E. *The Way of All Women*. New York: Putnam's, 1970.

Henry, J. *Culture Against Man*. New York: Random House, 1963.

Jacobi, J. *The Psychology of C. G. Jung*. New Haven, Conn.: Yale University Press, 1973.

Johnson, R. *We: Understanding the Psychology of Romantic Love*. New York: Harper & Row, 1983.

Jung, C. G. "Marriage as a Psychological Relationship." In *The Development of Personality*. Translated by R. F. C. Hull. *Collected Works*. Vol. 17. New York: Pantheon, 1954.

Jung, C. G. *Letters*. Vol. 1. Princeton, N.J.: Princeton University Press, 1973.

Khan, H. *The Sufi Message of Hazrat Inayat Khan*. Vol. 5. London: Barrie and Rockliff, 1962.

Krishnamurti, J. *Freedom from the Known*. London: Gollancz, 1969.

Lawrence, D. H. "Study of Thomas Hardy." In *Phoenix: The Posthumous Papers of D. H. Lawrence*. Edited by Edward McDonald. London: Heinemann, 1936.

Lawrence, D. H. *Psychoanalysis and the Unconscious*. New York: Viking, 1960a.

Lawrence, D. H. *Fantasia of the Unconscious*. New York: Viking, 1960b.

Lawrence, D. H. *Women in Love*. London: Penguin Books, 1960c.

Lawrence, D. H. *A Propos of Lady Chatterley's Lover*. Middlesex, England: 1961.

Lawrence, D. H. "On Being a Man." In *Phoenix II: Uncollected, Unpublished, and Other Prose Works by D. H. Lawrence*. Edited by Warren Roberts and Harry T. Moore. New York: Viking, 1970.

Lawrence, D. H. "We Need One Another." In *Phoenix: The Posthumous Papers of D. H. Lawrence*. Edited by Edward McDonald. London: Heinemann, 1936.

Mead, M. *Male and Female*. New York: Morrow, 1949.

Miners, S. (Ed.). *A Spiritual Approach to Male/Female Relations*. Wheaton, Ill.: Quest Books, 1984.

Ortega y Gasset, J. *On Love*. Translated by Tony Talbot. New York: Meridian Books, 1957.

Peck, M. S. *The Road Less Traveled*. New York: Simon & Schuster, 1978.

Plato. *Symposium*. In I. Edman (Ed.), *The Philosophy of Plato*. Translated by Irwin Edman. New York: Modern Library, 1928.

Rilke, R. M. *Letters to a Young Poet*. Translated by Stephen Mitchell. New York: Random House, 1984.

Rubin, L. *Intimate Strangers*. New York: Harper & Row, 1983.

Solovyov, V. *The Meaning of Love*. London: Geoffrey Bles, 1945.

Steiner, R. *The Gospel of St. John*. New York: Anthroposophic Press, 1973.

Stendhal. *On Love*. New York: Doubleday, 1957.

Storm, H. *Seven Arrows*. New York: Harper & Row, 1962.

Trungpa, C. *Shambhala: The Sacred Path of the Warrior*. Boston: Shambhala, 1984.

Ulanov, A. B. *The Feminine in Jungian Psychology and Christian Theology*. Evanston, Ill.: Northwestern University Press, 1971.

van Gennep, A. *The Rites of Passage*. Chicago: University of Chicago Press, 1969.

Watts, A. *Nature, Man and Woman*. New York: Pantheon, 1958.

Welwood, J. (Ed.). *The Meeting of the Ways: Explorations in East/West Psychology*. New York: Schocken, 1979.

Welwood, J. (Ed.). *Awakening the Heart: East/West Approaches to Psychotherapy and the Healing Relationship*. Boston: Shambhala, 1983.

Wilhelm, R. *The Secret of the Golden Flower*. New York: Harcourt Brace Jovanovich, 1970.

Wilhelm, R. Translation of the *I Ching* rendered into English by C. F. Baynes. Princeton, N.J.: Princeton University Press, 1950.
Wolfenstein, M. "The Emergence of Fun Morality." In. E. Larrabee and R. Meyerson (Eds.), *Mass Leisure*. Glencoe, Ill.: Free Press, 1958.

Index

AG5T